STUDENT-GENERATED DIGITAL MEDIA IN SCIENCE EDUCATION

Student-generated Digital Media in Science Education supports secondary school teachers, lecturers in universities and teacher educators in improving engagement and understanding in science by helping students unleash their enthusiasm for creating media within the science classroom.

Written by pioneers who have been developing their ideas in students' media making over the last 10 years, it provides a theoretical background, case studies and a wide range of assignments and assessment tasks designed to address the vital issue of disengagement amongst science learners. It showcases opportunities for learners to use the tools that they already own to design, make and explain science content with five digital media forms that build upon each other – podcasts, digital stories, slowmation, video and blended media. Each chapter provides advice for implementation and evidence of engagement as learners use digital tools to learn science content, develop communication skills and create science explanations. A student team's music video animation of the Krebs cycle, a podcast on chemical reactions presented as commentary on a boxing match, a wiki page on an entry in the periodic table of elements and an animation on vitamin D deficiency among hijab-wearing Muslim women are just some of the imaginative assignments demonstrated.

Student-generated Digital Media in Science Education illuminates innovative ways to engage science learners with science content using contemporary digital technologies. It is a must-read text for all educators keen to effectively convey the excitement and wonder of science in the twenty-first century.

Garry Hoban is Professor in the Faculty of Social Science at the University of Wollongong, Australia.

Wendy Nielsen is Senior Lecturer in the Faculty of Social Science at the University of Wollongong, Australia.

Alyce Shepherd is a PhD candidate in the Faculty of Social Science at the University of Wollongong, Australia.

'This timely and innovative book encourages us to "flip the classroom" and empower our students to become content creators. Through creating digital media, they will not only improve their communication skills, but also gain a deeper understanding of core scientific concepts. This book will inspire science academics and science teacher educators to design learning experiences that allow students to take control of their own learning, to generate media that will stimulate them to engage with, learn about and become effective communicators of science.'

Susan Jones and Brian F. Yates, Australian Learning and Teaching Council Discipline Scholars for Science

'Represents a giant leap forward in our understanding of how digital media can enrich not only the learning of science but also the professional learning of science teachers.'

Tom Russell, Queen's University, Ontario, Canada

'This excellent edited collection brings together authors at the forefront of promoting media creation in science by children and young people. New media of all kinds are the most culturally significant forms in the lives of learners and the work in this book shows how they can move between home and school and provide new contexts for learning as well as an understanding of key concepts.'

John Potter, London Knowledge Lab, Department of Culture, Communication and Media, University College London, UK

STUDENT-GENERATED DIGITAL MEDIA IN SCIENCE EDUCATION

Learning, explaining and communicating content

Edited by Garry Hoban, Wendy Nielsen and Alyce Shepherd

Routledge
Taylor & Francis Group

LONDON AND NEW YORK

First published 2016
by Routledge
2 Park Square, Milton Park, Abingdon, Oxon OX14 4RN

and by Routledge
711 Third Avenue, New York, NY 10017

Routledge is an imprint of the Taylor & Francis Group, an informa business

British Library Cataloguing in Publication Data
A catalogue record for this book is available from the British Library

Library of Congress Cataloging in Publication Data
Student-generated digital media in science education : learning,
explaining and communicating content / edited by Garry Hoban,
Wendy Nielsen and Alyce Shepherd.
pages cm
1. Science—Study and teaching. 2. Creative thinking—Study and
teaching. 3. Media programs (Education) 4. Digital media. I. Hoban,
Garry F. (Garry Francis), 1953- editor. II. Nielsen, Wendy (Wendy S.),
editor. III. Shepherd, Alyce, editor.
Q181.S8284 2015
502.85′67—dc23
2015004294

ISBN: 978-1-138-83382-1 (hbk)
ISBN: 978-1-138-83383-8 (pbk)
ISBN: 978-1-315-73519-1 (ebk)

Typeset in Bembo
by Swales & Willis Ltd, Exeter, Devon, UK

Every new academic needs a Garry, I raise my JS to you!

CONTENTS

FIGURES

TABLES

CONTRIBUTORS

Ruth Amos is a lecturer in science education at the Institute of Education, University of London. Her research interests include the use of new technologies in science education. She taught in London schools and is studying for a PhD looking at authentic science learning experiences.

Emma Bartle was a lecturer in the School of Biological, Biomedical and Chemical Sciences at the University of Western Australia, where she coordinated and taught the large first-year units across multiple campuses. She was responsible for the implementation and evaluation of several eLearning teaching innovations, and her work in this area was recognised with a 2010 UWA Teaching Excellence (Early Career) Award. She now works as an academic developer in the School of Medicine at the University of Queensland, and her current research focuses on work-integrated learning, students' development of scientific and clinical reasoning, and mobile technologies and digital literacies.

Iouri Belski (PhD) is a Professor of Engineering Problem Solving with the School of Electrical and Computer Engineering at the Royal Melbourne Institute of Technology. His research interests include engineering creativity and transformation from novices to experts in engineering. Iouri is a recipient of the 2009 Australian Award for Teaching Excellence.

Regina Belski (PhD) is a senior lecturer and researcher in the Department of Dietetics and Human Nutrition at La Trobe University. She is also an accredited practising clinical and sports dietitian. In 2014 she was awarded the Australian Office of Learning and Teaching Citation for outstanding contribution to student learning.

Sandra Campbell was, until recently, a lecturer in science education at the Institute of Education, University of London. Her main research interest is in teacher development. She taught in London schools before working in teacher development at the London Science Museum and Science Learning Centre London. She is studying for a PhD centred on reflective practice.

Julian M. Cox is the former Associate Dean (Education) in Science and incoming Associate Dean (International) in Engineering at UNSW, Australia. His background is in food microbiology, though his teaching spans from discipline areas to graduate capabilities, first-year transition and professional acculturation. His teaching marries longstanding interest in graduate capabilities and use of peer review as teaching strategy with use of technology for teaching and learning. He uses Moodle activities extensively, particularly the Workshop activity to facilitate peer review and assessment, and he has been using student-generated video for over 15 years to support professional identity development.

Amelia Hine is a PhD student at the University of Queensland investigating aesthetic design of post-mining landscapes. She has a Master's degree in museum studies from the University of Queensland and a Bachelor of Interior Design (Honours) from the Queensland University of Technology. She has worked as a research assistant for projects ranging from science communication to mine rehabilitation.

Garry Hoban is a Professor of Science Education and Teacher Education at the University of Wollongong, Australia. He has been teaching and researching the value of student-generated digital media for the last 10 years. He is the creator of both 'slowmation' and 'blended media' and is interested in understanding how and why students learn science by creating various forms of digital media. In 2013 he was awarded an Australian Office of Learning and Teaching National Senior Teaching Fellowship to support science academics and science teacher educators to implement assignments using student-generated digital media. He has designed two websites to support student-generated digital media: www.slowmation.com and www.digiexplanations.com.

Dennis Jablonski is an Associate Professor in the School of Education at Southern Oregon University. His primary areas of teaching are in educational technology and action research, and his faculty duties include field supervision and coordination of graduate programs. With over 20 years' experience using technology in the classroom, Dr Jablonski's research interest is studying the benefits of technology integration, including examining teachers' pedagogical beliefs about technology, using mp3s with audiobooks to improve reading fluency and comprehension, and incorporating multimedia to increase learning and engagement.

Matthew Kearney, Kimberley Pressick-Kilborn and Peter Aubusson are core members of the Centre for Research in Learning & Change at the University of Technology, Sydney (UTS). Associate Professor Matthew Kearney's main research interests are in the area of technology-enhanced learning in K–12 and teacher education contexts. Dr Kimberley Pressick-Kilborn has a focus on innovative science and technology education in her research and teaching. Professor Peter Aubusson is Head of the School of Education at UTS and conducts research in science education and teacher learning and development.

Stephen Keast and **Rebecca Cooper** team-teach the General Science Method in the Faculty of Education, Monash University and they have done this for many years. This experience has led to many research opportunities including an investigation of team teaching, self-studies of their development as science teacher educators along with exploration of the use of slowmation to assist pre-service teachers to develop pedagogical knowledge. Stephen and Rebecca both previously worked as secondary school science and mathematics teachers prior to completing PhDs and transitioning to teacher education. They work with pre-service and in-service science teachers and their research interests include the development of pedagogical knowledge, improving the quality of science teaching to increase student engagement and working with teachers to promote values in science and develop scientifically literate students.

Gillian Kidman has research and teaching interests in science, mathematics and ICT education. She is particularly interested in inquiry forms of teaching and learning and the potential inquiry has for the integration of science and mathematics via ICT. She is currently working on the interpretation of the Inquiry strands of the Australian Curriculum in Science, History and Geography, and the overlap with problem solving in mathematics. Her work in the area of slowmation with pre-service teachers is providing a fertile ground for the exploration of inquiry-based learning, teaching and skill acquisition.

Gwen Lawrie is a teaching-focused academic who has transitioned from chemistry laboratory research into chemistry education research and the scholarship of teaching and learning. Her research explores strategies to address student diversity and engagement in very large classes through collaborative inquiry tasks, the implementation of undergraduate research experiences and mechanisms for provision of formative feedback to support self-regulated learning. Through innovative approaches to technology-enhanced learning environments, Gwen has demonstrated assessment strategies that evidence learning gains in student-created products, such as vlogs and wiki-lab notebooks. The core theme of her research and teaching practice is to increase students' awareness of their own thinking.

Wendy Nielsen is a senior lecturer at the University of Wollongong in Australia. Her current research interests include use of technology tools for teaching and learning in science; complexity thinking in education; pre-service teacher education; supervising teacher knowledge; metacognition in the service of group learning activity and environmental education.

Karma Pearce has research interests in food science, nutrition, health communication and education. She is particularly interested in capstone projects and blended inquiry-based teaching and learning. She is currently working on embedding small-group, inquiry-based 'discovery' tasks into her food product development classes to facilitate problem solving and critical thinking, as well as to aid in applying complex theory to real-world situations. Extemporary communication skills are critical for all health professionals. Her work with blended media and slowmation animation is providing a medium for students to both understand the complex issues underpinning individuals with low health literacy while helping the students to reduce complex scientific theory to lay language so that they can effectively communicate with all members of the community.

Emily Purser teaches and researches in the field of academic language and learning development at the University of Wollongong. She works across disciplines to understand specific learning needs related to students' knowledge and understanding of English, and to apply research-based English-language education to mainstream teaching and learning. She is particularly interested in creating sustainable opportunities for students' ongoing linguistic growth within the University's Faculty of Science, Medicine and Health, through collaborative curriculum-development projects, and the design of classroom and technology-enhanced learning environments.

Gerry M. Rayner is an education-focused academic with 15 years of tertiary teaching experience. He has innovated in pedagogical areas including curriculum development and renewal, enhancement of student generic skills and peer-assisted learning (PAL), with an overall aim to enhance student engagement and achievement in science. In the area of information and communication technologies, Gerry has initiated and evaluated student use of digital media for group research projects, designed a virtual field trip and developed instructional videos to enhance student preparedness for practicals. Together with science colleagues, Gerry developed interdisciplinary inquiry-oriented learning in science and conducted professional development for tutors to enhance their capability with respect to these pedagogies.

Will Rifkin is Chair of Social Performance in the University of Queensland's Sustainable Minerals Institute and has an honorary position at the University of Sydney co-facilitating the Science and Mathematics Network of University Science Educators (SaMnet). Rifkin once developed engines to run off concentrated solar heat, helped to launch a postgraduate program combining economics, information technology and organisational behaviour, and pioneered methods for student-generated web content. An engineer-turned-sociologist, he has degrees from MIT, the University of California-Berkeley and Stanford University. His specialty is communication between technical and non-technical people.

Pauline Ross is known for being a creative and innovative biology academic. She has held a number of senior educational leadership positions at Australian universities, including Co-ordinator of the Science Teacher Education program at Macquarie University and Assistant Associate Dean Academic at University of Western Sydney. She has won multiple excellence in teaching awards, including an Australian Award for University Teaching (AAUT). Pauline's research on the impact of climate change on marine organisms is internationally recognised and funded by the Australian Research Council. In 2014–2015 Pauline was made a National Teaching Fellow by the Australian Office for Learning and Teaching.

Alyce Shepherd is a qualified primary school teacher and works as an Educational Designer at the University of Wollongong. In this roles, Alyce collaborates with academics to enrich teaching and learning practices and supports the use of innovative assessment and curriculum design in addressing pedagogical goals. She also provides assistance regarding the purposeful use of new technologies in teaching and assessment and draws on her research and teaching experiences in student-created digital and blended media, multimodal learning and digital literacies. Alyce was awarded first-class honours and the university medal for her Bachelor of Primary Education (Honours) at the University of Wollongong in 2011, and is currently completing her PhD in the field of student-generated digital media for multimodal literacy and social skill development in special education.

Jessica Vanderlelie has a PhD in biochemistry and a commitment to the development and implementation of practice-based curriculum for teaching undergraduate biochemistry courses within Griffith University's School of Medical Science and School of Medicine. Through her approach, Jessica creates an engaging learning environment, inspiring students to master the complexities of biochemistry. Jessica's research focuses on effective curriculum and assessment design for biochemistry teaching and the role of oxidative stress and micronutrition in pregnancy. Jessica received a national citation for her work in biochemistry assessment design and the Australian Award for Excellence in Teaching (early career) in 2012.

PREFACE

This book took 24 months to write a proposal, sign a contract, collect chapters and edit, but in actuality it has been in production for 10 years. That is how long some of the chapter authors have been experimenting with student-generated media in their teaching. I started playing around with students doing stop-motion animations in 2004 and kept simplifying it until I created *slowmation* (abbreviated from 'slow animation') in 2005. Other chapter authors, such as Gerry Rayner and Julian Cox, were experimenting with student-generated videos over 5 years ago. In fact most of the chapter authors have been encouraging students to make different media forms for several years, refining it each time they have a new cohort. Jessica Vanderlelie has been encouraging her students to put the words describing complex biochemical pathways to the music of popular songs since 2012 and telling them that she does not know anything about technology, hence, her students have developed some of the most creative media representations! It seems ironic, therefore, that the 2014 *Horizon Report for Higher Education* predicts that students will be creating content via media making in 3–5 years. It is clearly already happening and many of the chapter authors are pioneers in their fields. The purpose of this book, therefore, is to help any academic (and school teacher as many of the media making ideas can be used in schools) who wants to implement student-generated media in their student assignments.

Several key organisations and people have enabled this book to happen. First of all, Will Rifkin was instrumental in establishing the 'New Media' network of science discipline academics several years ago and was generous in allowing me to infiltrate his group and hopefully extend their ideas. Many of the chapter authors are from this group of media making pioneers. Second, the University of Wollongong has always been supportive of my media making ideas although I originally got a bit of flak for using so much Play-doh in my science lessons. Finally, my National Senior Teaching Fellowship, funded by the Australian Government Office for Learning and Teaching (OLT), supported my vision to publish this book with Routledge. The OLT promotes and supports excellence and innovation in higher education learning and teaching in Australia. The OLT's fellows are leading academics and educators in Australia. OLT fellowships afford such leaders the opportunity to create lasting improvements and positive impacts to higher education practice in Australia.

The three endorsements on the back cover are also from key people. Susan Jones and Brian Yates are the authors of the new Australian Learning and Teaching Academic Standards that specify five Threshold Learning Outcomes for Science. In particular, media making will help students to achieve Threshold Learning Outcome 1, *Understanding Science* and Threshold Learning Outcome 4, *Communication*, which states that "graduates will be effective communicators of science by communicating scientific results, information, or arguments, to a range of audiences, for a range of purposes, using a variety of modes" (2011, p. 11). Professor Tom Russell from Queen's University is a long term collaborator and enthusiastic user of technology in science education. Dr John Potter is a senior lecturer of media studies at the London Knowledge Lab at the University College of London and provided several key insights about media making when I visited the lab in December 2013.

It is also important that you get some background on the editorial team who are all based at the University of Wollongong, which is 100 km south of Sydney, Australia. I commenced work there as a lecturer in science education in 1998. When a vacancy came up for a science educator in 2009, I wanted to work with someone who had a passion for both teaching and research. The job was advertised nationally but we did not appoint from the applicants who applied. It was on a chance trip to the University of British Columbia in Canada to teach pre-service teachers about slowmation that I met up with Wendy Nielsen. Both Wendy and I were graduates of the Centre for the Study of Teacher Education within the Faculty of Education at the University of British Columbia. It was fortuitous that Wendy was looking for a job when I was looking for a science educator. When I met Wendy I said something like, "Are you feeling adventurous and possibly interested in coming to work in Wollongong?". "Where's Wollongong?" she replied. The rest is history: Wendy applied, got interviewed, was successful and arrived in Wollongong in June, 2009. She had never been to Wollongong and had to believe my stories, thus began a great teaching and research collaboration. We have different styles but they complement each other so well. My interpretation is that I have 'big picture' ideas and Wendy has an incredible mind for detail. The best part of the collaboration is that we negotiate our ideas for both teaching and research, often at our staff meetings whilst sharing a jug of JS. For example, whilst I created slowmation, it was Wendy who was able to upscale the quality of academic writing so that we have now published about it in the world's top science education journals – *Journal of Research in Science Teaching, International Journal of Science Education* and *Research in Science Education.*

The formation of this book was another fine example of our collaboration. I had the contacts to invite both the science discipline academics and science teacher educators and I wrote the submission to Routledge, but Wendy has been meticulous in reading the chapter submissions and organizing the feedback to the chapter authors. We were further supported by our third editor, Alyce Shepherd, who is my

PhD student. She was a 'guinea pig' in some of our initial research studies and trialled some ideas in her media making such as blended media. She has progressed to implementing some of the media making ideas in her own PhD with autistic high school students. We predict that Alyce will have an outstanding career in academia and will carry the 'student media making' torch, so to speak, when we are long gone. Hence I feel privileged to have had such a productive collaboration with both Wendy and Alyce within my own institution.

It is no accident that this book has been designed to focus on five forms of student-generated media – podcast, digital story, video, slowmation and blended media. Although there are other forms of student-generated media, such as a screencast, the five forms we have featured can all be made on students' own technology using free movie making software such as iMovie or Windows Movie Maker. All five link students' own technology with their creativity in representing science content and each media form has unique affordances for communicating meaning and build upon each other. For example, a podcast is the simplest to create using one mode of communication, which is voice, and is in fact the key mode as all the media forms are narrated. A digital story uses the modes of still images and voice; a video uses the modes of fast moving images and voice; a slowmation uses the modes of slow moving images, still images and voice; and a blended media can use all modes of communication – voice, still images, slow moving images, fast moving images, writing – hence the term 'multimodal'. In short, the five media forms increase in modal complexity and an understanding of the affordances of each mode is important in order for students to make informed decisions about their media making. Hence, this book has been designed in three parts. Part I provides the context for science learning in the twenty-first century, Part II provides a section on each of the five media forms with exemplars within each chapter, and Part III outlines what we believe is the future of student-created media for science learning in the twenty-first century. The chapter contributors are either science discipline academics or science teacher educators as the ideas have applicability in both university contexts.

We are genuinely excited about the prospects of student-generated media. In 2015 we will attempt to write some research publications about 'blended media' and we predict that this media form will have a major influence on the higher education sector in the years to come. What excites us is the creativity fostered when students create blended media because the process collides the ease of student media making with infinite visual resources on YouTube and students' imagination. Finally, good luck to my academic colleagues who wish to try student-generated media in their teaching. We hope that the ideas in this book are useful. Our passion for teaching is fuelled by our students' creativity, so we hope you get the same 'buzz' out of it.

Garry Hoban

Professor, University of Wollongong, December 2014

PART I

Twenty-first-century science education

1

PROMOTING ENGAGEMENT IN SCIENCE EDUCATION

Wendy Nielsen

The leaky pipeline

Over the past 20 years, there has been a disturbing trend in science in many different countries; declining enrolments in science courses at both high school and university levels (Adamuti-Trache, Bluman & Tiedje, 2013; Goodrum, Druham & Apps, 2012; Rice, Thomas & O'Toole, 2009). This is despite the 'Science for All' mantra from 20 years ago (Mutegi, 2011). The 'leaky pipeline' means that up to 50% fewer students now undertake senior science subjects in undergraduate and high school science relative to 20 years ago. For example, in Australia, high school participation rates are at their lowest point in 20 years (Office of the Chief Scientist, 2014). The leaky pipeline trend continues into post-doctoral research and tenure-track academic positions (US National Research Council, 2009), which are the main pathways to developing the next generation of researchers, technicians, science discipline academics and, of course, science teachers. The reasons for the trend are many, including length of qualification period, perceived difficulty of science and gender bias, at least in some cultural contexts (Händel, Duan, Sutherland & Ziegler, 2014). Davis, Petish and Smithey (2006) blame the commonly used 'stand-and-deliver' science teaching methods; most students find the traditional lecture format to be boring and tedious and they become disengaged when asked to memorise and regurgitate vast quantities of information. There is very little excitement and 'real science' in this way of learning. Becoming disinterested in high school science leads to lack of engagement with the advanced levels (where, arguably, the more interesting science is encountered), resulting in progressively declining science enrolments. At the university level, in the discipline of science, Nobel Laureate Carl Wieman (2010) noted that while science knowledge continues to grow expansively, university science education has often not utilised contemporary learning or information technologies to become relevant or effective for the twenty-first century. In a similar vein, Professor John Gilbert (2010), in a recorded interview as editor of the *International Journal of Science Education*, argued that science needs to be made more relevant in order to reflect the inherent interests and curiosities of both learners and the wider population. Thus, science education needs to imagine new ways to teach science and side-step the conservative forces of prescriptive curriculum that maintains 'how we were taught'.

Science educators in pre-service teacher education, science for non-science majors and the science disciplines all argue that science learning (and teaching) needs to be re-imagined (Feinstein, Allen & Jenkins, 2013; Tytler, 2007; Wieman, 2012). To re-imagine science education means developing new ways to help students engage with science content. These new ways should use contemporary teaching approaches and draw on educational technologies and learning theory to inspire students to learn deeply and develop a genuine interest in science (Swarat, Ortony & Revelle, 2012). They also propose that students engage in authentic science learning through personal research rather than just being consumers of content. Thus, new approaches to teaching and assessing science may help to mitigate the problem of the leaky pipeline in the longer term.

In the shorter term, curriculum reform in many jurisdictions has led to the development of Science, Technology and Society, with Science as a Human Endeavour and scientific literacy as core aims in science education at both the school level (American Association for the Advancement of Science, 2013; Australian Curriculum Assessment and Reporting Authority, 2013; National Governors Association Center, 2010; Roberts, 2007; US National Research Council, 2013) and the post-secondary level (Talanquer, 2014). There are also more wide-reaching policy shifts, such as the Common Core Standards or Next Generation Science that include aims for science literacy (e.g. US National Research Council, 2013), the UK subject benchmark statements (e.g. Quality Assurance Agency for Higher Education, 2007) or the Tuning Project (2008) in the EU. All of these documents make specific reference to digital literacies and/or communication skills for undergraduate science degree programs.

Science literacy matters for personal decision making, participation in civic and cultural affairs and economic productivity (US National Research Council, 1996). Thus, the goals and aims for science education also require attention at primary and junior school levels. At the level of schooling, there is a well-documented problem of teachers with weak science knowledge and who lack confidence to teach science (Appleton, 2006; Scamp, 2012). The point is not to blame primary school teachers; much of the school curriculum is driven by a compulsory focus on literacy and numeracy outcomes at school levels. A predictable result is that science is now among the least-taught subjects in primary classrooms (New South Wales Board of Studies, 2014). In Australia, the state of New South Wales recommends 6–10% of instructional time in years K–6 be devoted to Science and Technology, which is the same for Creative Arts and Physical Education. As a point of comparison, Mathematics and English are allocated 20–35% of classroom time. To be fair, the allocations become more equal as students advance through the year levels, achieving parity for English, Mathematics and Science at years 9 and 10. In the earlier years, attention to literacy and numeracy outcomes is important, however, the low amount of curricular attention to science (at least in terms of time allocated to its teaching) may offer some explanation for why science as a school subject does not capture and maintain interest more broadly. It is also reasonable to ask where the next generation of scientists and technicians will come from if these trends continue. We can also wonder who will become the next generation of science teachers.

Engaging those who will become school teachers is one facet of the bigger problem. Disinterest in science means low motivation generally to develop scientific (or other) literacies that could enable public engagement with society's big ideas. This is the scientific literacy argument in policy documents and government reports (Office of the Chief Scientist, 2014; US National Research Council, 1996) consistent with Roberts' (2007) definitions of science literacy; students should graduate from high school with basic levels of science knowledge (Vision I) and scientific literacy to enable this public engagement and participation (Vision II). Quality school science is also needed to keep students engaged and to generate a population of students ready and willing to study sciences at the university level. However, traditional didactic teaching approaches still predominate in high school and university, and hence the leaky pipeline represents widespread diminishing engagement with science as a subject area in many countries.

New approaches to science teaching and learning

Aims for teaching and learning in science have shifted over time, often in response to a perceived challenge to national interests, diminishing results on international assessments or as positioning to drive technological or economic innovation. The particular responses vary around the world and, arguably, there is a global agenda for changes to how science is taught. Curriculum projects based in the US have historically permeated science teaching agendas around the world and many were introduced to create a new pool of scientists and technicians (e.g. Bruner, 1960; Bybee, 1977; DeBoer, 2000; Rutherford, 1988).

Beyond a somewhat instrumentalist aim for a strong and relevant science curriculum to drive nationalistic goals or a knowledge economy, more broadly, arguments are compelling in the 'Science for All' policy agenda that science education needs to generate a scientifically literate and well-educated populace (Rutherford & Ahlgren, 1990). More recently, new waves of curricular reform have reacted to sliding standing in international assessments (PISA, TIMSS), particularly in Western democracies (Voogt & Roblin, 2012). Recent national and international reports suggest that science and mathematics teaching and learning need to change, particularly where national rankings have fallen or remain stagnant. Curriculum reform is often introduced to improve student results, national standing and enhance economic outlook.

A perception of degraded economic opportunity drives political rhetoric for reforms, with curricular goals aiming toward supporting the culture of innovation that underpins high-technology industries. The rhetoric calls into question education and, more particularly, science curriculum and teaching as failing to support the agenda. In Australia, as in the US and UK, advanced technologies drive innovation across the spectrum of national industries, including health care, logistics, energy production and distribution, communication, transportation, response to climate change, agriculture and defence. Basic research in many sectors as well as innovation in high technology requires a stream of new scientists and technicians with qualifications and knowledge to turn the science into products and new knowledge. These sectors depend on a science and technology-based workforce and the products generated from them. The high-technology industry has created new ways for people around the world to engage with each other, generate new forms of knowledge and enhance economic activity. Sectors such as ICT lead investment, growth and innovation, including new possibilities for teaching and learning.

Introducing the use of more technology in science classrooms is one way to improve student engagement. Web 2.0 technologies now pervade all aspects of modern life and educators around the world are using contemporary technology tools to engage learners and help them learn content knowledge in new ways. The diffusion of cell phones, computer gaming devices and Internet access (e.g. Brown, 2000; Ito *et al.*, 2010; Oblinger & Oblinger, 2005; Pedró, 2012; Watkins, 2009) means that learners expect to use these sorts of tools to engage with their own learning (Clark, Logan, Luckin, Mee & Oliver, 2009; Kennedy, Judd, Dalgarno & Waycott, 2010), and these expectations drive a changing context for learning across the lifespan. Hand-held mobile personal technologies represent the new frontier for engaging science learners, and science educators must embrace these in meaningful and creative ways. This is the contemporary context for science learning and is one way to address the challenge of declining enrolments.

Engagement and student-generated media

The notion of 'engagement' seems straightforward: it is the entry point for learners to learn new things. This assumes that learners will be motivated to engage with learning activity when it is interesting or when the information is presented in interesting and relevant ways. Learners, of course, are likely to have their own reasons or motivations to engage, reasons that may or may not be consistent with science educators' expectations for such engagement or students' perceptions of the effort required to develop deep understandings. The level of cognitive challenge is relevant here, as is the need to balance novelty and autonomy in terms of task complexity. While engagement may be seen as an indicator of high-quality learning and an expected outcome of classroom or university science content delivery, learners may not be willing to put in the effort to either engage or sustain the types of learning activity that produce the needed depth of understanding (White & Gunstone, 1992).

From a learning sciences perspective, engagement is entangled with motivation and reflects "student willingness to invest and exert effort in learning, while employing the necessary cognitive, metacognitive, and volitional strategies that promote learning" (Blumenfeld, Kempler & Krajcik, 2006, p. 475). Learners must be willing to develop and use such strategies and, as instructors, we can consider how to engage learners to use learning strategies at each of the three levels.

The three levels of strategies to which Blumenfeld *et al.* (2006) refer are how learners engage with content knowledge and the processes of their own learning. Learners use cognitive strategies when they elaborate and organise content information to learn something new. Metacognitive strategies involve goal setting, planning and monitoring, as well as evaluating progress toward learning goals (Flavell, 1979). These strategies underlie learners' thinking about their own learning and managing the processes accordingly. According to Ann Brown (1987), a learner also needs something to be metacognitive about, which is a role for the instructor in task design. Blumenfeld *et al.* (2006) argue that volitional strategies are responsible for regulating attention, affect and effort and, when a learner uses these, decision making about the learning activity is focused, productive, responsive and effective. Strategies at these three levels – cognitive, metacognitive and volitional – involve complex learning behaviour, which we argue can be promoted when students use various technologies to create digital media to explain or re-represent content or skills.

Keeping in mind these aspects of learner engagement, digital media explanations created by students can be analysed for their potential for promoting student engagement. In designing and making a digital explanation, learners are meaningfully engaged on many levels because digital tools enable interaction with content knowledge in multiple ways. When learners conduct background research and search for information, as in the first step in producing a digital explanation, they engage cognitively with the content. A well-designed task creates a 'need to know' as part of the task and, ideally, such searches let learners encounter new material and consider what they already know about the topic. This goes beyond memorising or simply reproducing content information (Hoban & Nielsen, 2013) because the learners must re-represent the content to produce a multimodal digital creation. The creations are multimodal because they use a range of modes, such as image, sound, graphics, movement, text and symbols to convey meaning. Deciding which media and mode to use in one's own creation involves volitional strategies to consider how best to represent and communicate the information to a particular audience, which includes decisions about how to ensure that the modes complement each other.

The decision making also engages learners on a metacognitive level since learners must understand the content well enough to represent it – thus, recognising their own level of understanding is a prerequisite. The learner must constantly monitor the current state of understanding during the task of creating a digital explanation, which provides a context for metacognitive monitoring. For example, there are many decisions to be made about which modes to use in the product. Learners typically generate a wide range of displays, graphs and simulations as part of a digital explanation, which becomes a 'multiple representation' of aspects of a concept (Ainsworth, 1999). Even traditional learning processes require learners to interpret information from expert-created displays of various sorts and make meaning through their interpretation (Prain & Waldrip, 2010; Tytler, Prain & Hubber, 2013). However, personal digital technology tools and software enable even novice users to generate their own digital representations. As learners construct their own representations digitally and combine modes, they add layers of meaning to the representations (Hoban & Nielsen, 2011; Jamani, 2011; Prain & Tytler, 2013), which is different in significant ways from when learners were limited to interpreting representations made by others (or simply copying them). In traditional learning activities, learners must interpret information and build meaning as conveyed through the modes presented, usually as text and diagrams in textbooks or voice and diagrams during lectures. However, digital technologies create opportunities for learners to generate a range of new representational forms and engage cognitively, metacognitively and volitionally. Additionally, they can use tools that they already have in their personal collections – laptops, smartphones, digital cameras and tablets. Further, pedagogies that are carefully designed and implemented using digital technologies can specifically encourage students' cognitive, metacognitive and volitional strategies and, thereby, increase engagement.

Our aim in this book is to share a range of examples and a theory whereby contemporary technology tools, especially media-making tools embodied in personal technologies, are being used to meaningfully engage learners. Importantly, the examples of students using technology in this book are not about 'passive media spectatorship' (Jenkins, 2006, p. 6) or learners as mere recipients of content, but rather provide clear evidence of students engaging with science content as media creators.

The book presents a wide range of assessment tasks/assignments to engage learners with science content and skills, whereby students use their own technologies to create science explanations. The process of creating science explanations as multimodal representations gives the science learner an authentic reason for developing the sequence of representations and, thus, serves a motivational purpose to achieve accuracy in the representation, which reflects the learner's content knowledge (Hoban & Nielsen, 2013). In attending to the audience, the creator of a digital representation makes many, many decisions about which content information will be conveyed, which modes to use to convey the information effectively and how to best present it at a level suitable for the intended audience. Alongside the wide range of available digital tools, the incredible range of different contexts for science learning also creates rich opportunities to engage learners with their own learning, while using their own technologies.

However, there is a key role for science educators in promoting student engagement. In designing their courses, science educators make the decisions about how technology is used and the types of assessment tasks that students complete. Students have the disposition and technology in their pockets for making media – they are doing it daily in their social media interactions with peers. As science educators, we need to channel students into how to use the technology and ideas for science learning and communication. We encourage instructors to consider their own 'pedagogical orientations' (Law, 2009) towards teaching with technology and ask whether using technology is about how the instructor presents content using slides and videos in lectures, positioning students as consumers of content, or if technology enables students to creatively engage with content? How instructors use technology should not be seen as a dichotomy; technology is useful in searching for and displaying science content, but students need to do something with it beyond copying or memorising. This represents an exciting challenge for the pedagogies and technologies that science educators use in the twenty-first century. We now invite you to consider the wide range of media forms and technologies used by students as demonstrated in this book. Furthermore, the chapter authors are all pioneers who have been developing their ideas around students' media making over the last 10 years, so you have the privilege of accessing their extended experiences.

This book, therefore, provides a range of assessment strategies focusing on students' media making for engaging tertiary-level science learners in discipline-based science and pre-service teacher education courses. Each chapter provides advice for implementation and evidence of engagement as learners use digital tools to learn science content and develop communication skills in creating explanations. The collected edition provides innovative ways to engage science learners with contemporary digital technologies and foster meaningful learning activity by virtue of rich tasks that invite creativity and provocative decision making while utilising affordances for interpersonal communication. Your challenge, should you wish to accept it (cue *Mission Impossible* theme), is to design the assignments in your course so that students use the cognitive, metacognitive and volitional strategies that contribute to student engagement with science. It is our hope that the innovative assessment tasks in this book will both guide and inspire you as you enact your own decision making in ways that engage your students to learn science in new and creative ways. By the way, instructors do not have to be media-making experts. Most of the students are ahead of you anyway in terms of technology use and they are always using technology such as YouTube to find out how to do things, and the same goes for their media making. As science educators, we can begin to stem the flow of the leaky pipeline of student disengagement – using the increasingly available media tools has the potential to take the hope beyond just imagining new ways to engage future students with science, but to actually use the tools in meaningful ways to engage students in learning content and at the same time develop communication skills that are essential for twenty-first-century employment.

References

Adamuti-Trache, M., Bluman, G. & Tiedje, T. (2013). Student success in first-year university physics and mathematics courses: Does the high-school attended make a difference? *International Journal of Science Education, 35*(17), 2905–2927.

Ainsworth, S. (1999). The functions of multiple representations. *Computers and Education, 33*, 131–152.

American Association for the Advancement of Science (2013). *Benchmarks for scientific literacy.* New York: Oxford University Press.

Appleton, K. (2006). Science pedagogical content knowledge and elementary school teachers. In K. Appleton (Ed.), *Elementary science teacher education: International perspectives on contemporary issues and practice* (pp. 31–54). Mahwah, NJ: Lawrence Erlbaum.

Australian Curriculum Assessment and Reporting Authority (2013). *The Australian National Curriculum.* Retrieved from: www.acara.edu.au (accessed 17 March, 2015).

Blumenfeld, P. C., Kempler, T. M. & Krajcik, J. S. (2006). Motivation and cognitive engagement in learning environments. In R. K. Sawyer (Ed.), *The Cambridge handbook of the learning sciences* (pp. 475–488). New York: Cambridge University Press.

Brown, A. (1987). Metacognition, executive control, self-regulation and other more mysterious mechanisms. In F. E. Weinert & R. H. Kluwe (Eds.), *Metacognition, motivation and understanding* (pp. 65–116). Hillsdale, NJ: Lawrence Erlbaum.

Brown, J. S. (2000). Growing up digital: How the Web changes work, education, and the ways people learn. *Change, 32*(2), 11–20.

Bruner, J. (1960). *The process of education.* Cambridge, MA: Harvard University Press.

Bybee, R. W. (1977). The new transformation of science education. *Science Education, 61*(1), 85–97.

Clark, W., Logan, K., Luckin, R., Mee, A. & Oliver, M. (2009). Beyond Web 2.0: Mapping the technology landscapes of young learners. *Journal of Computer Assisted Learning, 25*(1), 56–69. doi: 10.1111/j.1365-2729.2008.00305.x

Davis, E. A., Petish, D. & Smithey, J. (2006). Challenges new science teachers face. *Review of Educational Research, 76*(4), 607–651.

DeBoer, G. E. (2000). Scientific literacy: Another look at its historical and contemporary meanings and its relationship to science education reform. *Journal of Research in Science Teaching, 37*(6), 582–601.

Feinstein, N. W., Allen, S. & Jenkins, E. (2013). Outside the pipeline: Reimagining science education for nonscientists. *Science, 340*(6130), 314–317.

Flavell, J. H. (1979). Metacognition and cognition monitoring: A new area of cognitive-development inquiry. *American Psychologist, 34*(10), 906–911.

Gilbert, J. (2010). Interview with Professor John Gilbert. Audio recording. Retrieved from: http://www.educationarena.com/expertInterviews/interviewcategory11/tsed.asp (accessed 21 March, 2015).

Goodrum, D., Druham, A. & Apps, J. (2012). *The status and quality of year 11 and 12 science in Australian schools.* Canberra: Australian Academy of Science.

Händel, M., Duan, Z., Sutherland, M. & Ziegler, A. (2014). Successful in science education and still popular: A pattern that is possible in China rather than Germany or Russia. *International Journal of Science Education, 36*(6), 897–907. doi: 10.1080/09500693.2013.830232.

Hoban, G. & Nielsen, W. (2011). Engaging preservice primary teachers in creating multiple modal representations of science concepts with 'slowmation'. *Research in Science Education, 35*(1), 119–146. doi: 10.1007/s11165-011-9236-3.

Hoban, G. & Nielsen, W. (2013). Learning science through designing and making a narrated stop-motion animation: A case study of preservice teachers' conceptual change with slowmation. *International Journal of Science Education, 35*(1), 119–146. doi: 10.1080/09500693.2012.670286

Ito, M., Baumer, S., Bittanti, M., Boyd, D., Cody, R., Herr-Stephenson, B., et al. (2010). *Hanging out, messing around, and geeking out.* Cambridge, MA: MIT Press.

Jamani, K. J. (2011). A semiotics discourse analysis framework: Understanding meaning making in science education contexts. In S. C. Hamel (Ed.), *Semiotics theory and applications* (pp. 192–208). Hauppauge, NY: Nova Science.

Jenkins, H. (2006). *Convergence culture: Where old and new media collide.* New York: New York University Press.

Kennedy, G., Judd, T., Dalgarno, B. & Waycott, J. (2010). Beyond natives and immigrants: Exploring types of net generation students. *Journal of Computer Assisted Learning, 26*(5), 332–343. doi:10.1111/j.1365-2729.2010.00371.x

Law, N. (2009). Mathematics and science teachers' pedagogical orientations and their use of ICT in teaching. *Education and Information Technologies, 14,* 309–323.

Mutegi, J. W. (2011). The inadequacies of 'Science for All' and the necessity and nature of a socially transformative curriculum approach for African American science education. *Journal of Research in Science Teaching, 48*(3), 301–316.

National Governors Association Center and Council of Chief State School Officers (2010). *Standards for literacy in history/social studies, science, and technical subjects.* Retrieved from http://www.corestandards.org/ (accessed 17 March, 2015).

New South Wales Board of Studies (2014). *Parent's guide to the NSW primary syllabus.* Retrieved from www.k6.boardofstudies.nsw.edu.au (accessed 17 March, 2015).

Oblinger, D. & Oblinger, J. (2005). *Educating the net generation.* EDUCAUSE. Retrieved from https://net.educause.edu/ir/library/pdf/pub7101.pdf (accessed 17 March, 2015).

Office of the Chief Scientist (2014). *Australia's future: Science technology engineering and mathematics.* Canberra: Author.

Pedró, F. (2012). *Connected minds: Technology and today's learners.* Paris: Centre for Educational Research and Innovation, OECD. doi:10.1787/9789264111011-en

Prain, V. & Tytler, R. (2013). Representing and learning science. In R. Tytler, V. Prain & P. Hubber (Eds), *Constructing representations in science* (pp. 1–14). Amsterdam: Sense.

Prain, V. & Waldrip, B. (2010). Representing science literacies: An introduction. *Research in Science Education, 40,* 1–3. doi: 10.1007/s11165-009-9153-x

Quality Assurance Agency for Higher Education (2007). *Subject benchmark statement: Earth sciences, environmental sciences and environmental studies* (2nd ed). Gloucester, UK: Author.

Rice, J. W., Thomas, S. M. & O'Toole, P. (2009). *Tertiary science education in the 21st century.* Sydney: Australian Learning and Teaching Council.

Roberts, D. A. (2007). Scientific literacy/science literacy. In S. K. Abell & N. G. Lederman (Eds), *Handbook of research on science education* (pp. 729–780). London: Routledge.

Rutherford, F. & Ahlgren, A. (1990). *Science for all Americans.* New York: Oxford University Press.

Rutherford, F. J. (1988). Sputnik and science education. Symposium paper for the Center for Science, Mathematics and Engineering Education. Retrieved from http://www.nas.edu/sputnik/ruther1.htm (accessed 17 March, 2015).

Scamp, K. (2012). *Teaching primary science.* Report prepared for the Australian Government Department of Education, Employment and Workplace Relations. Canberra: Australian Academy of Science.

Swarat, S., Ortony, A. & Revelle, W. (2012). Activity matters: Understanding student interest in school science. *Journal of Research in Science Teaching, 49*(4), 515–537.

Talanquer, V. (2014). DBER and STEM education reform: Are we up to the challenge? *Journal of Research in Science Teaching, 51*(6), 809–819.

Tuning Project (2008). *Reference points for the design and delivery of degree programmes in physics.* Bilbao, Spain: Publicationes de la Universidad de Deusto. Retrieved from http://unideusto.org/tuningeu (accessed 17 March, 2015).

Tytler, R. (2007). *Re-imagining science education: Engaging students in science for Australia's future.* Retrieved from http://research.acer.edu.au/aer/3 (accessed 17 March, 2015).

Tytler, R., Prain, V. & Hubber, P. (Eds) (2013). *Constructing representations to learn science.* Amsterdam: Sense.

US National Research Council (1996). *National science education standards.* Washington, DC: National Academies Press.

US National Research Council (2009). *Gender differences at critical transitions in the careers of science, engineering and mathematics faculty.* Washington, DC: National Academies Press.

US National Research Council (2013). *A framework for K–12 science education: Practices, crosscutting concepts, and core ideas.* Retrieved from http://www.nextgenscience.org/ (accessed 17 March, 2015).

Voogt, J. & Roblin, N. P. (2012). A comparative analysis of international frameworks for 21st century competences: Implications for national curriculum policies. *Journal of Curriculum Studies, 44*(3), 299–321.

Watkins, S. C. (2009). *The young and the digital: What the migration to social-network sites, games, and anytime, anywhere media means for our future.* Boston, MA: Beacon.

White, R. T. & Gunstone, R. F. (1992). *Probing understanding.* London: Falmer.

Wieman, C. E. (2010). Science education for the 21st century: Using the insights of science to teach/learn science. *Proceedings of the 41st ACM Technical Symposium on Computer Science Education.* doi: 10.1145/1734263.1734333

Wieman, C. E. (2012). Applying new research to improve science education. *Issues in Science and Technology, 29*(1), 25–32.

2

THE CASE FOR STUDENT-GENERATED DIGITAL MEDIA ASSIGNMENTS IN SCIENCE COURSES

Will Rifkin and Amelia Hine

Introduction

A student team's music video animation of the Krebs cycle, a podcast on chemical reactions presented as commentary on a boxing match, a wiki page on an entry in the periodic table of elements and an animation on vitamin D deficiency among hijab-wearing Muslim women are examples of assessment tasks in this book. These examples illustrate new ways in which students can engage with, create and represent scientific content. Yet such assignments, where students must identify, comprehend and select traditionally presented scientific knowledge to script and produce their own digital media representation for an audience in another medium are not that common in science education. Why not?

Academics who wish to change their practice and implement new media assignments face a challenge – they need to rethink the pedagogies that underpin their teaching and consider how they are presenting scientific content to students. Many of those who are most intrigued by new media assignments perceive the nature of 'new media' and lessons that new media assignments can impart about communication, teamwork, critical thinking and so on, as 'non-essential' or an 'add on'. For many there is a common disassociation between the acquisition of scientific knowledge – a high priority in the university science teaching community – and the use of new media assignments. This disassociation suggests that some methods employed by advocates to promote the uptake of new media assignments have been counter-productive. These methods highlight the use of specific technology (e.g. student creation of videos) to foster the acquisition of graduate attributes, such as abilities in writing, oral presentation, teamwork, critical thinking and ethics. These arguments are based on findings that students assigned to create multimedia have developed generic employability skills (e.g. Hager & Holland, 2006).

There has been a growing emphasis on the need to build these student graduate capabilities, as highlighted in a number of studies both in Australia and internationally (e.g. Australian Council of Deans of Science, 2001; Lowden, Hall, Elliott & Lewin, 2011). A majority of Australian academics appear to agree with this importance, such as the 73% of academics surveyed by de la Harpe *et al.* (2009). However, de la Harpe *et al.* also found that these academics report being more confident in teaching traditional abilities – critical thinking, problem solving and written communication – and less confident in teaching teamwork, information literacy and use of information and communication technologies, the latter areas being the hallmark of new media assignments. So, adoption of new media assignments is commonly hindered by both low priority and low confidence among potential adopters because it conflicts with their existing ways of teaching and assessment.

While the need for students to develop graduate attributes has repeatedly been identified as important, justifying the introduction of new media assignments primarily in terms of their potential to bolster these skills undersells its potential. The advantages of new media assignments for improving the learning of scientific content have remained a secondary consideration. Instead, academics who champion the use of new media assignments can be seen to be prioritising generic skills over acquisition of scientific knowledge. This bias is underlined in the learning objectives given to the students for an assignment where first-year biology students create videos: "The assignment will concentrate on the themes of (i) communication of science, (ii) working with other scientists in a team, and (iii) researching the science behind an issue" (Kuchel & Wilson, 2010, p. 6).

Proponents of new media assignments appear to be seeking to overturn not only traditional methods of teaching and assessing in university science, but also traditional values that emphasise scientific content. As a result, a new media assignment is in danger of being relegated to a string of teaching innovations in science that have not been widely adopted (Fairweather, 2008). Such problematic attitudes and practices within the broader university science teaching community can mask the genuine learning advantages of the new media output in terms of development of graduate attributes and knowledge of course content (see Hoban, Loughran & Nielsen, 2011).

This chapter draws on insights and interviews from a two-year project – New Media to Develop Graduate Attributes of Science Students – which was supported by the Australian Learning and Teaching Council (ALTC). The research investigators engaged with pioneers and potential early adopters of new media assignments to find out if and how they were using student-generated media in their courses. They facilitated workshops involving a total of 200 academics and fostered collaboration and sharing of insights among a core group of 40 academics. In addition, the project team completed in-depth interviews with 20 academics among the pioneers and potential early adopters. The insights gleaned from these interviews augment our analysis of recent literature in the scholarship of learning and teaching in articulating the arguments offered in this chapter.

We will begin by introducing a debate about what counts as 'new media' within the framework of university science teaching. The chapter then briefly touches on key values in university science – research and content – which can be seen as salient in inhibiting adoption of new media assignments. This leads into a discussion of the opportunities for learning offered by visualisation, and new media's attraction as an avenue to develop graduate attributes. Insights from science educators who either employed or were interested in potentially employing new media assignments follows. Our assessment of their statements suggests that the most visible arguments in support of new media assignments need to be stronger in the minds of proponents, in the dialogue with early adopters and in print if wider adoption is to be stimulated. A need to rethink the pedagogical arguments around the introduction of new media assignments is supported by evidence – the slow growth in their number across Australia. Our findings should guide steps to highlight the pedagogical value and potential reach of new media assignments, such as those described in this book.

What counts as new media?

New media occur in a broad variety of forms, as evidenced in this volume. Information technology can be a medium for distribution of materials, but new media also encompass material created through the use of digital technologies (Manovich, 2007). Some definitions refer to the use of the Internet as a platform for collaboration and group work (Hew & Cheung, 2013) and it can, to some degree, be considered synonymous with the term 'Web 2.0'. This domain also includes social media such as YouTube and Facebook. Forms of new media that students have been assigned to create within university science assignments include podcasts, video productions (both stop motion and documentary), wikis, blogs and web pages (Rifkin, Longnecker, Leach & Davis, 2012b; Wilson, Niehaus, White, Rasmussen & Kuchel, 2009).

Despite its rapid evolution, new media consistently connotes accessibility and public discourse. This connotation of public access aligns with the domain of science communication within university science teaching and refers to communication about science with audiences of non-scientists. The science communication agenda is salient when assigning students to communicate with outside audiences in accessible and easily digestible formats. Students who produce such media can not only enhance their learning but also tackle the need for better communication between the scientific community and public audiences (Pacurar, 2011). Anyanwu (2003) makes a vital distinction between the role of new media as a medium for instruction (e.g. provision of content) and new media as a subject for instruction (e.g. enhancement of students' insights on communication). Academics considering new media assignments thus need to ask what balance they should strike among: (1) providing their students with instructional materials employing new media; (2) having their students create new media; and (3) teaching their students to critique what they find on the web about science, as all three domains appear to count as new media.

University science, graduate attributes and authentic assessment

University context, science context

Any innovation, such as a new media assignment, must prove its worth as an effective educational tool so that it does not require an increased input of time or energy from academic staff. That is because there exists an incentive structure in which "professors still get evaluated almost exclusively on their achievements in research" (Feixas & Zellweger, 2010, p. 88). This structure discourages innovative teaching, as the time and effort that staff invest in teaching development is seen to detract from their ability to succeed in academic research. It can be argued that any new approach in teaching should ideally demonstrate a time saving for the academic as well as increased learning by students in terms of both course content and graduate attributes. Traditional science academics would emphasise the former (content), while advocates of a more 'rounded' science curriculum would emphasise the latter (graduate attributes).

To achieve these aims – time saving, content learning and development of graduate attributes – the hyperbole that often surrounds the use of information technology in education must be restrained, overcoming "the tendency of educators and scholars ... to focus specifically on kinds of technology and ignore how technology is actually used or can be harnessed in the classroom" (Wilkin, Rubino, Zell & Shelton, 2013, p. 82). Advantages of new media assignments must be articulated in a way that is compatible with the pedagogical context (Mishra, Koehler & Kereluik, 2009) and the political context within university science, that is, *a research and content orientation*.

Learning capabilities and visualisation

New media assignments can improve student learning of science content. According to Ainsworth, Prain and Tytler (2011), increased understanding results from the creation of new forms of representation through personal reflection on a scientific topic, non-passive engagement, forced clarification and specificity for effective communication and the development of visual literacy skills – what Gilbert (2005) terms 'metavisual capability'. Similarly, Hoban, Nielsen and Carceller (2010) suggest that media making results in students creating a sequence of representations that tap into each element of Peirce's notion of a semiotic triad. A semiotic triad essentially involves, in this case, a scientific concept, an interpretation by the student and the student's representation of that interpretation for an audience. Ainsworth *et al.* (2011) underline the importance of development of visualisations, as they draw on or refer to abstracted mental models (as suggested by Peirce's semiotic triad) that are constructed by the student throughout the learning process. Williamson (2011) states that visualisations are essential for effective understanding.

Studies suggest that mental models can be formed through exposure to and creation of a range of models in various media, from physical models through to diagrams, images, writing and computer modelling (Akaygun & Jones, 2013; Hoban *et al.*, 2011; Williamson & José, 2008). Employing a variety of media for visualisation within the classroom environment can, therefore, enable the formation of more-complete mental models. New media offer avenues for such visualisation via video, stop-motion animation, still images, pictures painted with words via podcasts or links to image-rich media via wikis, blogs and websites, generally.

Graduate attributes

An important advantage of new media assignments is the development of a student's graduate attributes or capabilities. This aspect of new media usage has been emphasised by Australia's new media community of practice (Herok, Chuck & Millar, 2013), even though it has not been extensively documented (Tatalovic, 2008). Employability skills for science graduates remain conceptually entangled with the current technology 'revolution', which masks the pedagogical advantages of new media (Mishra *et al.*, 2009), that is, students are seen to learn to use new technology rather than to learn by using new technology. The essential nature of graduate attribute acquisition in university courses and programs was outlined by the Australian Government's recently formed Tertiary Education Quality Standards Agency (Herok *et al.*, 2013). In response to this ongoing need, assignments oriented toward boosting students' graduate attributes have emerged, including the World-Wide Day of Science interview exercise (Rifkin, 2012), first-year reflective chemistry blogs (Lawrie & Bartle, 2013) and video explanations of scientific concepts (Rifkin, Longnecker, Leach & Davis, 2012a).

Such assignments represent forms of authentic assessment, whereby the student is given a taste of relevance to, and engagement with, the field of professional science and the wider community (Guertin, 2014). This engagement occurs when students assemble a video and present their composition on a public platform. Activities that demand active participation and display of a composition outside the classroom, as new media assignments are able to do, cultivate development of graduate attributes in much the same manner that work-integrated learning has proven successful (see Crebert, Bates, Bell, Patrick & Cragnolini, 2004), introducing a sense of professionalism alongside inquiry-based learning. These assessment tasks can enable science graduates to satisfy the selection criteria of entry-level roles that increasingly call for technical knowledge, interpersonal skills and the ability needed to deal with complex and varied work environments (West, 2012).

Thus, new media assignments promise to be pedagogically sound on a number of fronts. They engage students in constructing a sequence of representations, employ the strengths of visualisation, involve development of graduate attributes and have aspects of authentic assessment practices. This promise is not embraced by many science academics, though, as we found in developing and attempting to disseminate new media assignments in Australia through the ALTC New Media for Science project.

Perceptions of new media pioneers and early adopters

ALTC New Media for Science project

The New Media for Science project was formulated with the intention of promoting the use of new media in assessment tasks. The four project leaders had been developing such assignments in their classes for up to a decade. The project had three main objectives: (1) establish and identify teaching strategies and materials; (2) select web platforms for publishing student work in new media; and (3) form a network of science academics who are employing new media assignments (Rifkin et al., 2012a).

The project team, in the course of its two years of effort, identified more than 30 science academics across Australia who were actively developing or using new media assignments. An additional 150 academics expressed interest in new media assignments but proved hesitant to implement one during the two years of the project. Another 200 academics attended workshops or conference presentations in various forms; they could be seen on the periphery of the nascent community of practice. These figures add up to 10% of an estimated 4000 full-time science academics in Australia. Twenty academics were interviewed in depth to explore their attitudes toward and practices with information technology/digital media in relation to teaching, research and administration. Statements about new media ranged from the outright sceptical to the highly receptive. The variation in responses was striking given that most of those interviewed belonged near the core of the emerging new media for science community of practice.

New media conflicts with traditional teaching values

Whilst new media is popular with students, assigning it to students in assessment tasks is relatively rare. One striking reason given for hesitance in adoption of new media assignments was the apparent conceptual separation – and suggestion of incompatibility – between traditional teaching and the use of new media technology. This contrast emerged particularly in relation to first-year teaching. The academics interviewed emphasised a need to build engagement in a subject among students who seemed reluctant to engage fully, for example, first-year students in a service subject. The argument here is that the traditional didactic approach of much content-focused science teaching tends to alienate first-year students in service subjects, whereas new media assignments had proven to engage them. A second emphasis among these academics was the need to address students' different learning styles. Again, a traditional lecturing style of teaching and individual, paper-based assignments were cast as insufficient. Both of these rationales frame the new media assignment in opposition to traditional methods of teaching.

Interviewees noted that new media presented a varied, information-rich learning environment, where far more information can be conveyed – within the student's attention span – through certain technological platforms than through a text. Interestingly, the notion of media richness in the academics' explanations remained separated from the idea of engagement. Furthermore, these responses seem to focus on new media as an alternative means for delivering information to students rather than as an alternative means for students to create their own representations of scientific concepts. In other words, the critique of traditional university science teaching presented new media approaches as a contrast, not as a complement, and as an alternative with quite limited aims.

Deep learning or distraction?

Comments about student engagement seemed to be associated with interviewees' views of deep learning. Some saw it as being enhanced through the use of new media, while others did not share this view. 'Deep learning' refers to a process of learning that builds on existing knowledge and enables creation of more long-lasting conceptual understanding. It is seen in opposition to more passive 'surface learning', which is often epitomised as rote memorisation (Hulme *et al.*, 2009).

Some interviewees were still to be convinced of the advantages of new media assignments in cultivating deep learning, when compared to traditional techniques (e.g. problem sets or research reports). This disagreement about the merits for learning using new media assignments comes across from two perspectives. One perspective is that the volume of course content to be covered in undergraduate years does not allow for such luxurious teaching methods:

> I remain to be convinced that [new media] will ever replace practicals and lectures in terms of what we do . . . For us in the biomedical world, we have such a bulk of information that needs to go across to the students, I'm not really sure how else we could get all that information across in a time-efficient manner. (Academic A)

This point is expressed in an exaggerated way, hinting at the impossibility that most or all science practicals and lectures could be replaced by new media. Notably, this is not what has been promoted. Additionally, there is no differentiation here between employing new media for delivery of content versus having students create new media in assignments. Nonetheless, the basic sentiment reflects the hesitance of many lecturers to replace existing assignments with new media alternatives.

Lecturers also questioned the opportunities for deep learning through new media assignments, by arguing that attention to gaining suitable technical skills to produce a blog or podcast will distract a student from the process of engaging with and learning content. This concern also underlines the priority given to learning of content over development of a graduate attribute, such as capability with information technology.

A number of lecturers noted that new media assignments might support only surface learning. They referred to the fleeting way in which they felt that students obtain relevant information online, for example, 'quick answers, superficial seven-second sound grab[s]', which was particularly concerning for lecturers in light of the increased time they noted would be involved in preparation when they incorporate new media. However, such comments on increased preparation time seem to attend to the teacher creating the new media, not the students creating new media as part of an assignment. The notion of academic as content provider is evidenced in comments such as:

> You can spend hours and hours making a two-minute video and that may or may not be effective. (Academic B)

and

> I think we also do have to/need to think about the effort that we are going to put into something to think it is going to be worthwhile, not 100 hours of work that might please one student, research the most efficient ways to use the technology. (Academic C)

This concern is amplified when considering the numbers of interview responses that cited a belief that new media can actively interfere with learning. These responses pointed to the novelty and accessibility of technology acting as a distraction to students by focusing on the use of technology for the sake of it rather than using it as a way to understand content.

Teacher-generated content versus student-generated content

The forms of technology most commonly used by the science academics interviewed are usually a means for using technology to present content from lecturers to students rather than students using technology to interpret and represent content. They encompass passive tools or direct replacements for offline equipment. These formats include online lecture recordings, document cameras, electronic assessment feedback, wiki articles, YouTube depictions of experiments, podcasts of lecture material, online quizzes and Google Docs for document sharing.

Aligned with these views, creative possibilities for engagement seem to be overlooked in favour of more traditional approaches to cultivating content knowledge. The features of new media are played down: "whether you write it in words or whether you write it online on a wiki, it is six of one a half dozen of the other to some degree . . . you are still writing" (Academic F). Little evidence emerged in the interviews of active engagement by students or collaboration or inquiry-based learning, even though these activities are hallmarks of the Web 2.0 world. It is clear academics are not differentiating technology-for-content-delivery from technology-enabling-student-creativity.

Hurdles and contradictions

The academic staff we interviewed expressed concern about the investment of time and energy when new media-based communication just provides another avenue for traditional, face-to-face dialogue. Importantly, they failed to distinguish between new media employed by the academic to deliver content, or to provide a quiz for students, and the opportunity for students to employ new media creatively in responding in an assessment task.

Thus, one can see a number of contradictions within the emerging community of practice in new media for science assignments as well as conflicts with the mainstream community. For the latter, new media assignments may conflict with traditional teaching values that have a focus on the presentation of content. They can be seen as a distraction from the 'core business' of content learning. What is done online is seen – even by the early adopters interviewed – not as a novel means to learn science but merely as another avenue for conveying the scientist's content. One might conclude that this nascent community of practice among Australian academics does not have a coherent, internally consistent and convincing argument for use of new media assignments.

Conclusions

It should not come as a surprise that the new media community of practice among Australia's science academics seems to have grown slowly over the past decade, despite the uses and capacity of Web 2.0 technology having expanded by leaps and bounds. There has been minimal growth in the evidence of the impact on the learning of scientific content from the innovative teaching examples and methodologies that have emerged. Regardless of the evidence, the interviews quoted in this chapter suggest that no strong argument for such assignments has emerged.

Our analysis suggests, in addition, that a discourse gap exists between advocates of new media and the wider university science teaching community. Arguments for the introduction of new media assignments are at odds with the predominant pedagogical concerns of university science lecturers, rather than supporting them. This latter community has been characterised as a conservative one, hesitant to adopt new teaching strategies without a direct connection to the familiar pedagogies to which they currently adhere. These pedagogies centre on imparting extensive content knowledge to students within a short space of time. The advocates of new media assignments are not emphasising the ability of the assignments to enhance the students' learning of scientific content. Perhaps more research is needed to substantiate the claim that student media making in science has the potential to result in higher-quality learning. This research should monitor short-term learning within a course and long-term retention beyond the course. Without such evidence, it is not hard to understand how the mainstream community in university science courses could perceive the use of new media assignments as an unnecessary distraction unrelated to their number one pedagogical aim – the presentation and delivery of content.

Despite a dissonance between promotion of, and resistance to, adoption of new media assignments, the assignments' advantages actually do encompass shared pedagogical objectives, as discussed throughout this book. Rather than focusing on how new media creation enhances students' understanding of scientific content, however, the promoters of new media assignments have emphasised the acquisition of graduate attributes as the primary pedagogical advantage. This argument is understandably responding to successive studies calling attention to this dimension of the university science curriculum.

The introduction of graduate attributes into university science teaching undeniably needs attention. A new national policy in Australia on science standards identifies 'communication' as one of the five Threshold Learning Outcomes, specifically stating that "graduates will be effective communicators of science by communicating scientific results, information or arguments, to a range of audiences, for a range of purposes, and using a variety of modes" (Jones & Yates, 2011, p. 11). However, attempts to introduce two new teaching elements – graduate attributes and new media – simultaneously, would seem ill-advised given the known conservatism of the university science teaching community. Arguments about how they enhance the learning of content knowledge can make new media assignments more readily a part of mainstream discourse and practice. Some might argue that there is no need to forefront the acquisition of graduate attributes so long as their development is still inherent in the forms of assessment promoted. Acquisition of graduate attributes via new media assessments seems likely given the fundamental principles involved (e.g. authenticity) and strategies employed, as well as data from the assignments developed and documented to date.

There is an increasing opportunity to expand the use of new media assignments in the university science curriculum, but we must experiment with a range of ways to demonstrate their efficacy for engagement and quality learning to increase their introduction and use in the curriculum. A frame of reference, that is, a focus on graduate attribute development, which fails to be inclusive of the wider university science teaching community, is detrimental in the long run. While there has been some success in building the kernel of a community of practice, this community encompasses an all-too-small percentage of the total number of science academics, not just in Australia but globally. Growth of this community requires accommodation of a disinterested majority, sceptical that a new technology might just be a distraction. They could well be swayed by evidence of student learning – in the short term and long term – for an economy of effort, such as offered in the examples in this book.

Acknowledgements

The New Media for Science project was led by Associate Professor Will Rifkin (Queensland), Professor Nancy Longnecker (Otago), Associate Professor Joan Leach (Queensland) and Professor Lloyd Davis (Otago) and supported by funding from the Australian Learning and Teaching Council (2009–2011), an organisation funded by the Australian Government. The views expressed in this chapter are not necessarily the views of the Australian Learning and Teaching Council (now called the Office of Learning and Teaching). Interviews referred to in this chapter were completed with human research ethics clearance from the University of Western Australia.

References

Ainsworth, S., Prain, V. & Tytler, R. (2011). Drawing to learn in science. *Science*, *333*(6046), 1096–1097.

Akaygun, S. & Jones, L. (2013). Dynamic visualizations: Tools for understanding the particulate nature of matter. In G. Tsaparlis & H. Sevian (Eds.), *Concepts of matter in science education* (pp. 281–300). Dordrecht, The Netherlands: Springer.

Anyanwu, C. (2003). Myth and realities of new media technology: Virtual classroom education premise. *Television & New Media*, *4*, 389–409.

Australian Council of Deans of Science (2001). *What did you do with your science degree? A national study of employment outcomes for science degree holders 1990–2000*. Melbourne, Australia: Centre for the Study of Higher Education, University of Melbourne.

Crebert, G., Bates, M., Bell, B., Patrick, C. J. & Cragnolini, V. (2004). Developing generic skills at university, during work placement and in employment: Graduates' perceptions. *Higher Education Research & Development*, *23*, 147–165.

de la Harpe, B., David, C., Dalton, H., Thomas, J., Girardi, A., Radloff, A. & Lawson, A. (2009). *The B Factor Project: Understanding academic staff beliefs about graduate attributes, final report*. Sydney: Australian Learning and Teaching Council.

Fairweather, J. (2008). *Linking evidence and promising practices in science, technology, engineering, and mathematics (STEM) undergraduate education: A status report*. Washington, DC: National Academies National Research Council Board of Science Education.

Feixas, M. & Zellweger, F. (2010). Faculty development in context: Changing learning cultures in higher education. In U.-D. Ehlers & D. Schneckenberg (Eds.), *Changing cultures in higher education* (pp. 85–102). Berlin: Springer.

Gilbert, J. (2005). Visualization: A metacognitive skill in science and science education. In J. Gilbert (Ed.), *Visualization in science education* (pp. 9–27). Dordrecht, The Netherlands: Springer.

Guertin, L. (2014). Introducing university students to authentic, hands-on undergraduate geoscience research in entry-level coursework. In V. Tong (Ed.), *Geoscience research and education* (pp. 215–221). Dordrecht, The Netherlands: Springer.

Hager, P. & Holland, S. (2006). Introduction. In P. Hager & S. Holland (Eds), *Graduate attributes, learning and employability* (pp. 17–47). Dordrecht, The Netherlands: Springer.

Herok, G., Chuck, J. & Millar, T. (2013). Teaching and evaluating graduate attributes in science based disciplines. *Creative Education*, *4*, 42–49.

Hew, K. F. & Cheung, W. S. (2013). Use of Web 2.0 technologies in K–12 and higher education: The search for evidence-based practice. *Educational Research Review*, *9*, 47–64.

Hoban, G., Loughran, J. & Nielsen, W. (2011). Slowmation: Preservice elementary teachers representing science knowledge through creating multimodal digital animations. *Journal of Research in Science Teaching*, *48*, 985–1009.

Hoban, G., Nielsen, W. & Carceller, C. (2010). Articulating constructionism: Learning science through designing and making 'slowmations' (student-generated animations). *Proceedings of the ASCILITE 2010 Conference* (pp. 433–443). Sydney: University of Sydney.

Hulme, E., Nakamura, J., Lowe, P. A., Raad, J. M., Wells, K. J., Biswas-Diener, R. & Ackerman, C. A. (2009). Deep learning. In S. J. Lopez (Ed.), *The Encyclopedia of Positive Psychology* (pp. 275–290). Blackwell Reference Online. Retrieved from http://onlinelibrary.wiley.com/book/10.1002/9781444306002 (accessed 23 March, 2015).

Jones, S. & Yates, B. (2011). *Learning and Teaching Academic Standards Project*. Sydney: Australian Learning and Teaching Council.

Kuchel, L. & Wilson, R. (2010). Student instructions: University of Queensland – BIOL1030 biodiversity and our environment. In J. Righetti, W. Rifkin, N. Longnecker, J. Leach & L. Davis (Eds.), *New Media for Science Wiki*. Retrieved from http://newmediaforsciencere-search.wikispaces.com/Project+information (accessed 1 June, 2014).

Lawrie, G. & Bartle, E. (2013). Chemistry vlogs: A vehicle for student-generated representations and explanations to scaffold their understanding of structure–property relationships. *International Journal of Innovation in Science and Mathematics Education, 21*(4), 27–45.

Lowden, K., Hall, S., Elliot, D. & Lewin, J. (2011). *Employers' perceptions of the employability skills of new graduates*. Edge Foundation, University of Glasgow, SCRE Center. Retrieved from http://www.kent.ac.uk/careers/docs/Graduate_employability_skills%202011.pdf (accessed 17 March, 2015).

Manovich, L. (2007). What is new media? In R. Hassan & J. Thomas (Eds.), *The new media theory reader* (pp. 5–10). New York: McGraw-Hill Education.

Mishra, P., Koehler, M. & Kereluik, K. (2009). The song remains the same: Looking back to the future of educational technology. *TechTrends, 53,* 48–53.

Pacurar, A. (2011). Science communication, science journalism and the new media. *Revista Româna de Jurnalism si Comunicare, 6,* 22–28.

Rifkin, W. (2012). World-wide what? Assigning students to publish on the Web. In J. Peterson, O. Lee, T. Islam & M. Piscioneri (Eds.), *Effectively implementing information communication technology in higher education in the Asia–Pacific region* (pp. 346–366). New York: Nova.

Rifkin, W., Longnecker, N., Leach, J. & Davis, L. (2012a). Assigning students to publish on the web: Examples, hurdles, and needs. *Journal of the NUS Teaching Academy, 2,* 79–94.

Rifkin, W., Longnecker, N., Leach, J. & Davis, L. (2012b). *New media to develop graduate attributes of science students*. Sydney: Australian Learning & Teaching Council.

Tatalovic, M. (2008). Student science publishing: An exploratory study of undergraduate science research journals and popular science magazines in the US and Europe. *Journal of Science Communication, 7*(3). Retrieved from http://www.reu.pdx.edu/Participant%20 Information/Science%20Communication.pdf (accessed 17 March, 2015).

West, M. (2012). *STEM education and the workplace*. Office of the Chief Scientist, Occasional Paper Series, Issue 4. Canberra: Australian Government.

Wilkin, C. L., Rubino, C., Zell, D. & Shelton, L. M. (2013). Where technologies collide: A technology integration model. In C. Wankel & P. Blessinger (Eds.), *Increasing student engagement and retention using classroom technologies: Classroom response systems and mediated discourse technologies. Cutting-edge technologies in higher education,* Vol. 6, Part E (pp. 81–106). Bingley, UK: Emerald Group.

Williamson, V. M. (2011). Teaching chemistry with visualizations: What's the research evidence? In D. M. Bunce (Ed.), *Investigating classroom myths through research on teaching and learning* (pp. 65–81). Washington, DC: American Chemical Society.

Williamson, V. M. & José, T. J. (2008). The effects of a two-year molecular visualization experience on teachers' attitudes, content knowledge and spatial ability. *Journal of Chemical Education, 85*(5), 718–723.

Wilson, R., Niehaus, A., White, J., Rasmussen, A. & Kuchel, L. (2009). Using video documentary-making to enhance learning in large first year biology classes. *Integrative and Comparative Biology, 49,* e325.

3

RESEARCHING SCIENCE LEARNING THROUGH STUDENT-GENERATED DIGITAL MEDIA

Garry Hoban

Background

This chapter provides a theoretical background to the notion of researching learning when students create assignments in science and in science teacher education courses using digital media. Surprisingly, the number of research articles on students learning science through creating media is less than 50 worldwide. Students are increasingly making media for their social media sites; the notion of them creating media as assignments in science is under-utilised and under researched, as explained in Chapter 2. The combination of the students' accessibility to technology, ease of use and the possibilities for engagement in learning should make the implementation of media making in student assignments very attractive to academics. It is, we think, a rich landscape for research in teaching and is applicable to students in both science teacher education and science discipline courses, hence the need for this chapter.

As explained in Chapter 1, engaging students in quality science learning has never been more important and more challenging. From national reports in both science discipline and science teacher education courses, falling enrolments should be a concern for all science educators and this indicates a desperate need for new ways to engage students in learning science. Moreover, many students still claim that didactic teaching approaches are commonly used in universities. But this is not the fault of the academics, as they are caught on the horns of a dilemma. Science knowledge is developing exponentially and course content depends on large amounts of content being delivered in preparation for subsequent courses to complete a degree. So science academics are pressured to cover a large volume of content. But perhaps 'less is more' in terms of promoting quality student learning, thus the dilemma for educators, especially in the science disciplines.

A significant challenge, therefore, for all science educators is to find new ways to re-imagine and energise teaching approaches that encourage students to engage with learning science beyond the common methods of copying and memorising facts (Tytler, 2008). As explained in Chapter 2, one approach to engage students with content is to get them to undertake assessment tasks that involve the creation of digital media to explain science. Nearly all students have access to media-making devices, such as mobile phones, and free movie-making software on their computers to create various forms of digital media to explain science. A wide range of media products can be easily made by students, such as podcasts, videos, digital stories, animations, screencasts and combinations or blends (collectively called 'digital explanations').

Personal technologies will continue to evolve rapidly in the twenty-first century, making it increasingly easier for students to be media creators of content. It is no wonder, therefore, that one of the six trends predicted in the *NMC Horizon Report: 2014 Higher Education Edition* (Johnson, Adams Becker, Estrada & Freeman, 2014) is a "shift from students as consumers to students as creators" (p. 14). This report predicts trends in technology use and states that "students across a wide variety of disciplines are learning by making and creating rather than from the simple consumption of content. Creativity, as illustrated by the growth of user-generated videos ... is increasingly the means for active, hands-on learning" (Johnson *et al.*, 2014, p. 14). The report predicts that this shift will drive changes in higher education within three to five years. They are wrong, the shift is happening now.

Why get students to create digital media explanations in university assignments?

There are four main reasons why academics should consider using student-generated digital media as assignments in their subjects. First, students find it engaging to create media using their own technology, because that is what they are familiar with in their own social media. The accessibility of cheaper and easy to use media-making devices accompanied by multiple options to disseminate digital products has generated a *"participatory culture* that contrasts with older notions of passive media spectatorship" (Jenkins, 2006, p. 6). Researchers in media studies use the term 'convergence' to describe the ubiquity and capabilities involved in student media making. In this digital age, nearly all university students have access to digital still and video cameras, media devices for playing and recording sound tracks and computers preloaded with free movie-making software.

In particular, the expanding capacities of mobile devices like smartphones allow students to create digital media any time and any place (Cochrane, 2010). The rapid evolution of technology as linked to internet advancements is clear: Web 1.0 emphasised read-only content and student access to information; Web 2.0 emphasised user-generated content blurring the line between students as consumers and producers of content and Web 3.0, which is evolving, emphasises personal digital spaces and unlimited personal creativity. It is, therefore, not surprising that the most popular websites in the world – Facebook, Wikipedia, Twitter, Instagram and YouTube – depend upon user-generated content. We are now seeing a rapid increase in the different forms of digital media – animation, video, podcast, digital story and combinations or blends – being generated by science discipline and teacher education students as new opportunities for learning in university classrooms.

Second, as citizens of the twenty-first century, it is critical that students develop digital literacies and communication skills. Change in the way scientists communicate within their disciplines is a prime example. Twenty years ago, the principal mean of communicating new knowledge was in print journals such as *Nature* and *Science* using the modes of writing, diagrams, charts and static images. The journals now have an online presence with explanations of new knowledge being demonstrated in hypertext linking to a range of digital representations using a variety of modes in weblinks, animations, audio segments, virtual reality and simulations (Gilbert, 2007). Furthermore, a growing number of science journals are moving away from print versions to a strictly digital format. Thus, developing digital literacies is a growing need, which means students developing multimodal literacies in order to understand and compose multimodal representations of science. According to Gilbert (2007), "all expert scientists – chemists, physicists, biologists, earth scientists – must be readily able to visualise a model when it is met in any one of the modes, or submode, of representation and at any level of representation" (p. 14). This involves both spectatorship and participation, and students as communicators of science in different media forms is now a key part of national standards for tertiary science in Australia, as students graduating with undergraduate degrees should "be effective communicators of science by communicating scientific results, information, or arguments, to a range of audiences, for a range of purposes, and using a variety of modes" (Australian Learning and Teaching Council, 2011, p. 11). Thus, 'communication' is one of the five Threshold Learning Outcomes for undergraduate science students in the new Australian Learning and Teaching Academic Standards Statement for discipline science (Australian Learning and Teaching Council, 2011). In teaching science communication, degree programs can help students to develop digital literacies and communication skills and we believe that creating digital media serves the dual purpose of building quality content knowledge and communicative skills with multimodal texts. Indeed, the evolving US Common Core for schools uses the term 'digital literacies' 98 times in the documents (US National Research Council, 2013).

Third, getting students to create digital explanations as assessment tasks has been shown to be effective for student learning (Hoban & Nielsen, 2013). We draw from research in the cognitive sciences to show how the creation of a digital media task to explain science can result in quality learning. The educational principle of learners constructing explanations has been called the 'self-explanation effect', whereby the process of making an explanation helps understanding (Chi, Bassok, Lewis, Reimann & Glaser, 1989; Chi, de Leeuw, Chiu & LaVancher, 1994). In experimental studies by Chi and colleagues, a group of participants was asked to explain mathematics problems to themselves and others whilst being compared to other groups who did not do this self-explaining. Results showed that self-explainers outperformed non-explainers in various forms of tests to assess understanding and demonstrate transfer of the knowledge. Lombrozo (2012) recently summarised this field in her chapter in *The Oxford Handbook of Thinking and Reasoning*, identifying three ways in which making an explanation can promote understanding: (1) a personal motivation to understand content; (2) processes involved in the evaluation of explanations; and (3) the very process of generating explanations. Lombrozo notes that:

> there has been much more research into how explanations are evaluated rather than into how they are generated. This is in part because explanation generation confronts many of the most difficult questions in cognitive science concerning the content and structure of general beliefs . . . how can the study of explanation generation be informed by research on representation? (Lombrozo, 2012, p. 272)

A more recent study also points to the value of students preparing assessment tasks as teaching resources to explain science to a particular audience. Nestojko, Bui, Kornell and Bjork (2014), in the journal *Memory and Cognition*, conducted a series of reading-and-recall experiments in which one group of students was told to expect a test on a particular topic while a second group was duped into believing that they would have to teach the passage to other students. The participants expecting to teach a passage produced more complete and better organised free recall and answered more questions correctly. The researchers claimed that "expecting to teach appears to encourage effective learning strategies such as seeking out key points and organizing information into a coherent structure" (p. 1047). This research complements the well-known phrase that one of the best ways to learn something is to teach it. Any teacher in a school or university will tell you that in preparing a new lesson, lab, tutorial or lecture, the instructor needs to first understand the content, design a sequence of content to suit the audience, think of resources to support the learning and consider the type of language that is suitable for the audience. In short, getting students to create a digital explanation as an assessment task is a good way for them to learn the content. It is also important for the student to consider not only the purpose but also the audience, so that the language used in the explanation is suitable for other students, the community or children. You will notice in the examples of implementation provided in this collection that most of the teacher education digital explanations are for school children, whereas most of the science discipline explanations are for peers or community members.

A fourth reason for getting students to create digital media about science is that students can be creative with content. How often do we hear students complaining that science is boring? Most science students are familiar with the traditional assessment tasks of writing lab reports, answering multiple-choice questions and doing PowerPoint presentations. Hence, creating digital media as an assessment task gives students a new challenge and allows them to creatively combine different modes of communication to represent their science ideas. Science information is usually expressed in books and on internet sites in writing, still images and video on

YouTube (fast-moving images). When students make a digital media representation they have to change the science content into other modes, such as slow moving images (animation) or speech (narration), which allows them to think in different ways about how to represent the science ideas.

Theoretical framework for science learning through media making

If academics wish to substantiate the claims about the quality of the student learning involved when students create a digital media assessment task, they will want to use a theoretical framework that can help to examine student learning, but it also must match the process of multimedia construction. There are two theoretical frameworks that were commonly used in the 1980s and 1990s to explain learning using technology. The first was Seymour Papert's notion of constructionism, which focused on the social influence of creating an artefact to share. Seymour Papert introduced the term in his 1987 National Science Foundation grant application entitled, *A New Opportunity for Elementary Science Education*. He defined the term in the grant abstract:

> The word constructionism is a mnemonic for two aspects of the theory of science education underlying this project. From constructivist theories of psychology we take a view of learning as reconstruction rather than as a transmission of knowledge. Then we extend the idea of manipulative materials to the idea that learning is most effective when part of an activity the learner experiences is constructing a meaningful artifact. (Papert, 1987, p. 2)

In essence, he argued that learning was related to reconstructing personal meaning but that it was strongly connected to an artefact that is made, which also has a strong social influence.

A second framework was von Glaserfeld's (1989) notion of constructivism, which focused the reconstruction of personal knowledge and its strong relationship to prior knowledge. This theory of learning was based on two principles:

1. Knowledge is not passively received but actively built up by the cognizing subject.
2. The function of cognition is adaptive and serves the organisation of the experiential world, not the discovery of ontological reality.

Whilst these cognitive and social learning influences are useful because they draw attention to the personal and social nature of learning and to the value of students manipulating physical objects in the learning process, the frameworks were theorised some time ago and hence do not take into account the enormous shift in capacity, accessibility and usability of technologies, particularly mobile devices. We believe that these general learning theories do not adequately focus on the key processes of media construction in terms of how different modes are designed and integrated in digital multimodal representations and how they influence student learning in the short and longer term. Also, such theories tend to focus on students' motivation and cognitive processes but neglect the semiotic factors at play in the planning and construction of representations and how these influence learning (Tytler & Prain, 2010).

Because making a media product must involve learners planning to use a sequence of representations (e.g. summary notes, storyboard, models, images, video), our research uses semiotic theory (Peirce, 1931/1955). Semiotics is the study of signs or symbols and, according to Peirce, when students make a 'sign' as a representation of content, which he called the 'referent', it makes students think about the content and thus meaning is generated, which Peirce called the 'interpretant'. We are crossing over into the world of literacy when trying to understand learning through media making. But why not? A media product is a digital literacy representation and that is why we have chosen to seek new theoretical reasoning in that field. A particularly important term in our theoretical framework is the word 'mode'. According to Kress (2010):

> *Mode* is a socially shaped and culturally given semiotic resource for making meaning. *Image, writing, layout, music, gesture, speech, moving image, soundtrack and 3D objects* are examples of modes used in representation communication . . . different modes offer different potentials for making meaning . . . in a social-semiotic approach to mode, equal emphasis is placed on the *affordances* of the material 'stuff' on the mode. (pp. 79–80)

In summary, most media products are multimodal (except perhaps a monomodal podcast having the one mode of 'speech'), incorporating multiple modes of communication including speech as narration, still images, moving images, layout or writing. Hence, in this edited book, we have chosen to use 'multimodality' as the theoretical framework of the book and so, in each of the example chapters, there is reference to the multimodality of the digital assessment task created by students to specify not only the particular modes of communication used but also the relationships between them. Therefore, a key digital literacy is that in designing a digital explanation, students should pay attention to which modes of communication they have selected to provide the best possible digital representation.

In regard to learning when students design a digital explanation, science education researchers claim that meaning-making is enhanced when students 're-represent' concepts using different modes of communication: "multiple representations refers to the practice of re-representing the same concept through different forms, including verbal, graphic and numerical modes, as well as repeated student exposures to the same concept" (Prain & Waldrip, 2006, p. 1844). This process of re-representing content using different modes is central to the literature on multimodal learning (Bezemer & Kress, 2008; Hand & Choi, 2010; Kress, 2010; Kress, Jewitt, Ogborn & Tsatsarelis, 2001; Waldrip, Prain & Carolan, 2010), whereby making decisions about changing content from one mode into another (e.g., changing a monomodal writing-based explanation of a science concept into a multimodal combination of models, images and speech) promotes thinking in multiple ways and, further, could be a context for generating discussions (Hoban & Nielsen, 2014).

The theoretical framework of multimodality is closely related to two key constructs in multimodal learning. First, when students interpret knowledge of a discipline and re-represent information in a new way, there can be a modal shift from interpreting writing into image to the final narrated animation. This is one aspect of a more general 'register shift' (Jones, 2010; Macken-Horarik, Devereux, Trimingham-Jack & Wilson, 2006) and is similar to the notion of 'transduction' (Bezemer & Kress, 2008; Kress, 2010). Most research conducted when students create digital explanations has been in science teacher education but no doubt there will be more examples in science discipline courses as a result of this book. By analysing group discussions during the creation of the slowmation to explain the concept of 'life cycle of a ladybird beetle', Hoban, Loughran and Nielsen (2011) found that the key to pre-service teacher learning was the process of re-representing content through a sequence of representations that involved decision making around which modes to use, and how, when and why to use them. Further, social interaction and creativity in explaining the science were also influential for learning (Hoban & Nielsen, 2013). In particular, each of the representations offered affordances that influenced the students' thinking in particular ways (Hoban & Nielsen, 2010). The pre-service teachers did not learn science the first time they engaged with the content as summarised in their notes but, rather, revisited the content many times as they translated and built their ideas from one representation to the next in a "cumulative semiotic progression" (Hoban & Nielsen, 2013): Rep 1: writing research notes ⇒ Rep 2: designing a storyboard ⇒ Rep 3: making models ⇒ Rep 4: taking still photographs of the manual movements ⇒ Rep 5: using technology to integrate the different modes to make a digital explanation. Writing research notes developed the students' background knowledge; designing a storyboard encouraged students to break down the concept into 'chunks'; making models focused the students' thinking on physical features of the phenomenon; and so on.

Second, the resulting animation combined modes as the pre-service teachers made many decisions about which still images to use, how to make moving images and writing (labels) complementary to the voice-over narration (Painter, Martin & Unsworth, 2013; Unsworth, 2006). Hence, the students' learning was also related to their decision making to achieve what we call 'modal coherence'. This means that students have to make the modes complementary in terms of how they fit together to provide a coherent explanation.

In summary, we hypothesise that there are many affordances for learning when students create digital explanations, consistent with Jonassen, Myers and McKillop's (1996) claim that, "the people who learn the most from instructional materials are the designers . . . we have all stated at one time or another that the quickest way to learn about subject matter is to have to teach (design) it" (p. 95). The field of student-created digital explanations is still in its infancy and needs additional research, especially with university students who have both a disposition and

TABLE 3.1 Projects researching student-generated media

Purpose	Research Questions	Methodology	Example Articles
1. The organisation and implementation of the assessment task incorporating student-generated digital media	1. How and why do students create digital explanations of science concepts?	Explanation with interviews with several students.	Hoban, 2005; Hoban and Nielsen, 2010
2. Students' decision making in constructing a digital explanation	1. What are students' perceptions of making a digital explanation? 2. How did the students represent the concept in the digital explanation?	Get students to keep a journal on their decision making in regard to media design and engagement with content. Interview students after they have created their explanation about how and why they created the digital explanation they did. Get them to justify the design. This is the simplest research study.	Hoban and Nielsen, 2012
3. Quality of the students' learning during construction. Research students' learning in constructing a digital explanation	1. How do the pre-service teachers create a slowmation? 2. How does this process of construction influence their science learning?	Case study of a group of students using a simplified discourse analysis to show process of learning. Show quality of learning of pre-service teachers in constructing a slowmation over several hours.	Hoban and Nielsen (2012) Hoban and Nielsen (2013)
4. The social interaction as students in a small group create a digital explanation	1. What is the type of discussion generated when students create digital media to explain science? 2. What are the affordances of the media created during the construction process that facilitate discussion?	Case study of a group of students using simplified discourse analysis to show type of discussion generated (analysis of the type of interaction).	Hoban and Nielsen (2014)
5. Students' long term learning from creating a digital explanation	1. How resilient is the science knowledge after creating the digital explanation? 2. How did the decision making help to develop the media?	Types of media analysed. Interviews immediately after making and 1 year post.	

personal technology for making their own digital media. It should be noted, however, that theoretical frameworks for this sort of work are also in their infancy and need further research to better understand students' meaning-making when creating a digital explanation of science content.

Possible research projects

Over the last 10 years we have been exploring different research directions for student-created digital media and while most apply for slowmation, they could also be used for different media forms. Table 3.1 outlines five ways to approach research projects and includes references as examples. These projects were conducted with pre-service primary teachers, but projects like these could be conducted across a wide range of other science learning contexts. Many are also relatively simple to implement. In essence, a particular research question, methodology and theoretical framework need to be chosen to suit the type of research. For example a research focus on social interaction in media making needs a question that focuses on student relationships, a methodology that analyses social interaction and a theoretical framework focusing on social dynamics. Conversely a research focus on learning during media making needs a question that focuses on student learning, a methodology that analyses the nature and quality of learning and a theoretical framework that positions the learning.

In summary, we are hoping that the ideas in the remaining chapters of this book will give you some ideas for how to implement an assignment using student-generated digital media. Furthermore, the directions provided in Table 3.1 will give you guidance in how to research the quality of the learning and student decision making when creating digital media assignments. It is undeniable that as the twenty-first century unfolds students will have more creative media-making ideas and, using the devices in their pockets and Internet connectivity, will be able to learn science in ways that are beyond what we can currently imagine. So, as we begin to explore some of these ideas, science learners can begin to experience science learning that helps them to develop digital literacies and communications skills.

References

Australian Learning and Teaching Council (2011). *Learning and teaching academic standards statement*. Sydney: Australian Council of Deans of Science.

Bezemer, J. & Kress, G. (2008). Writing in multimodal texts. *Written Communication, 25*(2), 166–195.

Chi, M. T. H., Bassok, M., Lewis, L., Reimann, P. & Glaser, G. (1989). Self-explanations: How students study and use examples in learning to solve problems. *Cognitive Science, 13*, 145–182.

Chi, M. T. H., de Leeuw, N., Chiu, M. H. & LaVancher, C. (1994). Eliciting self-explanations. *Cognitive Science, 18*, 439–477.

Cochrane, T. D. (2010). Exploring mobile learning success factors. *Research in Learning Technologies, 18*(2), 133–148.

Gilbert, J. (2007). Visualization. In J. Gilbert (Ed.), *Visualisation in science education* (pp. 9–27). Dordrecht, The Netherlands: Springer.

Hand, B. & Choi, A. (2010). Examining the impact of student use of multiple modal representations in constructing arguments in organic chemistry laboratory classes. *Research in Science Education, 40*(1), 29–44.

Hoban, G., Loughran, J. & Nielsen, W. (2011). Slowmation: Preservice primary teachers representing science knowledge through creating multimodal digital animations. *Journal of Research in Science Teaching, 48*(9), 985–1009.

Hoban, G. & Nielsen, W. (2010). The 5 Rs: Student-generated animations of science concepts. *Teaching Science, 56*(3), 33–37.

Hoban, G. & Nielsen, W. (2012). Using 'slowmation' to enable preservice primary teachers to create multimodal representations of science concepts. *Research in Science Education, 42,* 1101–1119.

Hoban, G. & Nielsen, W. (2013). Learning science through creating a 'Slowmation': A case study of preservice primary teachers. *International Journal of Science Education, 35*(1), 119–146.

Hoban, G. & Nielsen, W. (2014). Creating a narrated stop-motion animation to explain science: The affordances of 'Slowmation' for generating discussion. *Teaching and Teacher Education, 42,* 68-78.

Hoban, G. F. (2005). From claymation to slowmation: A teaching procedure to develop students' science understandings. *Teaching Science: Australian Science Teachers' Journal, 51*(2), 26–30.

Jenkins, H. (2006). *Convergence culture: Where old and new media collide.* New York: New York University Press.

Johnson, L., Adams Becker, S., Estrada, V. & Freeman, A. (2014). *NMC Horizon Report: 2014 higher education edition.* Austin, TX: New Media Consortium.

Jonassen, D., Myers, J. M. & McKillop, A. (1996). From constructivism to constructionism: Learning with hypermedia. In B. G. Wilson (Ed.), *Constructivist learning environments* (pp. 93–106). Englewood Cliffs, NJ: Educational Knowledge Publications.

Jones, P. (2010). Teaching, learning and talking: Mapping 'the trail of fire'. *English Teaching: Practice & Critique, 9*(2), 61–80.

Kress, G. (2010). *Multimodality: A social semiotic approach to contemporary communication.* London: Routledge.

Kress, G., Jewitt, C., Ogborn, J. & Tsatsarelis, C. (2001). *Multimodal teaching and learning: The rhetorics of the science classroom.* London: Continuum.

Lombrozo, T. (2012). Explanation and abductive inference. In K. J. Holyoak & G. R. Morrison (Eds.), *Handbook of thinking and reasoning* (pp. 260–276). Oxford: Oxford University Press.

Macken-Horarik, M., Devereux, L., Trimingham-Jack, C. & Wilson. K. (2006). Negotiating the territory of tertiary literacies: A case study of teacher education. *Linguistics and Education, 17,* 240–257.

Nestojko, J. F., Bui, D. C., Kornell, N. & Bjork, E. L. (2014). Expecting to teach enhances learning and organization of knowledge in free recall of text passages. *Memory & Cognition, 42*(7), 1038–1048.

Painter, C., Martin, J. R. & Unsworth, L. (2013). *Reading visual narratives: Image analysis of children's books.* London: Equinox.

Papert, S. (1987). *Constructionism: A new opportunity for elementary science education.* Washington, DC: National Science Foundation.

Peirce, C. (1955). Logic as semiotic: The theory of signs. In B. Justus (Ed.), *The writings of Peirce* (pp. 98–119). New York: Dover (original work published 1931).

Prain, V. & Waldrip, B. (2006). An exploratory study of teachers' and students' use of multi-modal representations of concepts in primary science. *International Journal of Science Education*, *28*(15), 1843–1866.

Tytler, R. (2008). *Re-imagining science education*. Melbourne, Australia: ACER.

Tytler, R. & Prain, V. (2010). A framework for re-thinking learning in science from recent cognitive science perspectives. *International Journal of Science Education*, *32*(15), 2055–2078.

Unsworth, L. (2006). Towards a metalanguage for multiliteracies education: Describing the meaning-making resources of language-image interaction. *English Teaching: Practice and Critique*, *5*(1), 55–76.

US National Research Council (2013). *A framework for K–12 science education: Practices, crosscutting concepts, and core ideas*. Retrieved from http://www.nextgenscience.org/ (accessed 19 March, 2015).

von Glaserfeld, E. (1989). Constructivism in education. In T. Husen & T. Postlethwaite (Eds.). *The international encyclopedia of education, Vol. 1* (pp. 162–163). Oxford and New York: Pergamon Press

Waldrip, B., Prain, V. & Carolan, J. (2010). Using multi-modal representations to improve learning in junior secondary science. *Research in Science Education*, *40*(1), 65–80.

PART II

Implementation in science discipline and science teacher education courses

PODCAST OVERVIEW

A podcast is usually an audio file that is recorded digitally and posted on a website so that it is accessible by others to download. It can, however, also be a video or a combination. If it is just an audio file then it is monomodal, meaning that it has one mode of communication – voice or speech. It is the easiest of the media forms to create since it can be recorded on most digital devices and usually does not involve any visuals. It can, however, be challenging to create. This is because although only including audio, the challenge for the student creator is to design it in a way that supports the listener in conjuring a mental picture of what is being explained. Hence, there is quite an art to devising an appropriate script that can foster a listener's imagination. This is typically done through the use of an analogy, metaphor or in a creative story line. In Chapter 4, Emma Bartle from the University of Queensland explains how a large number of chemistry students in a compulsory first-year course created podcasts as a compulsory assignment to explain chemistry concepts. Interestingly, some students who were not so engaged in the regular teaching of the subject strongly engaged in creating a podcast to explain acid-base interaction using the analogy of a boxing match. A good way to teach students' media making is to start with a podcast to teach them the nuances of a good narration or voiceover. This is important as the other media forms in this book are narrated and hence voice is the key mode in the other media making forms. There are quite a few YouTube clips on how to do a good narration which include ideas such as speaking slowly, pausing after key phrases, using moderation of voice and emphasis of key words. Listening to good moderators on television is also worthwhile and is a key communication skill to develop especially for trainee teachers.

4

CREATIVE PODCASTING IN CHEMISTRY

A case study

Emma Bartle

Context

This chapter describes the development and implementation of a creative podcasting task for a large (n = 350–400) first-year, introductory chemistry class at a university in Australia. The task was developed and implemented in collaboration with Nancy Longnecker, previously the Director of the Science Communication program at The University of Western Australia (UWA), and Mark Pegrum, from UWA's Graduate School of Education.

The introductory chemistry course was designed for students with little or no background in chemistry who needed to gain an understanding of basic chemistry to be able to move forward in their chosen degree program. Emphasis is on the word 'needed', as the majority of students did not enrol into this course by choice, but rather because they had to. From anecdotal evidence we know that most of the students completing this unit deliberately avoided doing chemistry in high school and were disgruntled to learn they were then required to enrol into an introductory chemistry unit at a tertiary level, even when they were not studying toward a chemistry degree. The students enrolled in this unit came from a range of degree programs – engineering, computing, mathematics, life and physical sciences, and natural and agricultural sciences. Many were not intrinsically engaged in chemistry.

The issue of disengaged students is not unique to this course. It is internationally recognised that student disengagement with the physical sciences, particularly chemistry, is increasing (Fensham, 2004). This issue is particularly evident in introductory-level science courses, such as the introductory chemistry course described in this chapter, as students already start the course with a low level of interest and motivation. The obvious solution is to teach the course content in a way that exposes students to the multidisciplinary applications of chemistry and enables them to identify the relevance of chemistry to their specific course of study. However, teaching the material in a context suitable to all students proves very difficult in reality, as the nature of these introductory-level courses means that enrolments are often high, and the interests and backgrounds of the students varies greatly. These factors, combined with the current climate of shrinking budgets and staffing, means that educators often have no choice but to teach the content in the most-efficient manner, that is, through didactic delivery that focuses on transmission of scientific knowledge, rather than interactive learning activities that motivate students (Bartle, Longnecker & Pegrum, 2011; Lawrie, Matthews & Gahan, 2010).

Unfortunately, it is the curricular focus on attainment of scientific knowledge without attention to the motivational aspects of science, such as real-world applications, that Fensham (2004) suggested as one of the main causes for increased student disengagement with chemistry. A curricular shift to focus on scientific literacy and technology has been noted as a way of encouraging interest in science – while technology may be the cause of much of the distraction in lectures, it also presents pedagogical opportunities to enhance the learning experience and, more specifically, student engagement (Terrion & Aceti, 2012).

New media

New media, enabled by digital technologies, can be used in education to facilitate multimodal media making between students and support learner-centred pedagogical approaches, where students learn through active engagement with content and with peers (Bartle et al., 2011; Pegrum, 2009a, 2009b). Research indicates that when students generate their own representations of content, their learning gains are significantly greater than when they engage with content delivered by an instructor (Kozma & Russell, 2005; Wu & Puntambekar, 2012). The increase in new media has emerged as part of the shift from Web 1.0, the informational web, to Web 2.0, the social web, which involves interaction with web content rather than simply the passive reception of it (Pegrum, 2009a, 2009b).

New media have also increased professional relevance and can engage university students in authentic tasks and work-integrated learning, as well as enhance science communication skills (Bartle et al., 2011; Rifkin, Longnecker, Leach & Davis, 2010). The podcasting activity detailed in this chapter is in fact a spin-off of an Australian Learning and Teaching Council (ALTC) grant entitled 'New Media to Develop Graduate Attributes of Science Students', which aimed to identify and develop new media-based teaching strategies and resources suited to large, tertiary-level science classes (Rifkin et al., 2010). The ability to communicate science to a range of audiences using a variety of modes is one of the threshold level achievements expected of an Australian bachelor-level graduate in science according to the Australian Science Learning and Teaching Academic Standards Statements (Jones & Yates, 2011).

Given that many students are already keen users of digital technologies, which are often well integrated into their everyday lives, the use of new media in education can be very motivating. At the same time, while students may be adept at using new technologies for social and entertainment purposes, they may not always know how to use them appropriately for educational purposes (Cluett, 2010;

Pegrum, 2009b) or indeed, professional purposes such as, in this case, an explanation of important scientific concepts. Incorporating new media techniques such as podcasting into a program of science study, therefore, allows educators to capitalise on students' pre-existing enthusiasm and capacity for digital technologies, as well as guiding them in the appropriate educational and professional applications in using those technologies (Bartle *et al.*, 2011).

Podcasting

A podcast is usually a digital audio recording, typically produced using a portable recording device such as a smartphone or digital voice recorder, and uploaded to a specific online location. It is usually monomodal, using only the mode of voice, hence, it is the easiest of the media forms to create, but this does not mean that it is a simple task. A good podcast needs to be creative to conjure up images of the content in the mind of the listener. This may require the creator to use analogies or metaphors to foster the imagination. The requisite hardware is cheap and portable, the software easy to use and online storage straightforward (Shamburg, 2009, 2010). Using such tools to make podcasts in education is becoming increasingly popular, as demonstrated by a proliferation of dedicated podcasting guides for educators at different levels (e.g. Braun, 2007; Fontichiaro, 2008; King & Gura, 2007; Williams, 2007), alongside more general new technology guides containing sections on podcasting (e.g. Bradley, 2007; Green, Brown & Robinson, 2008; Richardson, 2010).

The most common uses of podcasting in education are 'substitutional' podcasting, where audio recordings of lectures and tutorials are made available to students, and 'supplementary' podcasting, where teachers produce podcasts on key topics that students can listen to on a need-to-know basis (McGarr, 2009; Pegrum, Bartle & Longnecker, 2014). In 'creative' podcasting, students are required to create podcasts themselves. This better exploits the potential of Web 2.0 tools, yet there are limited reports of their use in education. Involving students in the active production of knowledge and design of technology-based resources to explain content requires them to reflect on knowledge in new and meaningful ways, leading to enhanced subject-specific understanding (Jonassen, Myers & McKillop, 1996; Pegrum *et al.*, 2014). Additionally, producing podcasts collaboratively can enhance teamwork skills, develop students' skills with new technologies, promote a deep approach to learning and increase motivation (Cane & Cashmore, 2008; Pegrum *et al.*, 2014). These are the kinds of benefits of creative, student-generated podcasting achieved in the creative task discussed in this chapter.

Implementation

Task design

The creative podcasting assessment task was implemented in a first-year, introductory chemistry unit. The unit ran over 13 weeks and covered the key chemical concepts from the years 11 and 12 Australian chemistry syllabi. Students attended three lectures per week, fortnightly three-hour practical laboratory sessions and completed weekly online quizzes as formative assessment. The large amount of material to be covered required a rigid teaching schedule and it was difficult to deviate from the content during class hours. The creative podcasting task was set as a minor assignment, worth 5% of the overall unit mark, which students were required to complete outside of unit contact hours. Students were given four weeks to complete the assignment. Interestingly, a total of 94% of students completed the podcast activity, despite it being worth much less when compared to other assessment tasks.

As described in Bartle *et al.* (2011), students were required to work in groups of three to create a three-minute podcast on one of two set chemical concepts, 'acids and bases' or 'oxidation and reduction'. The podcast was then shared with their peers via the university's online learning platform. The concepts of 'acids and bases' and 'oxidation and reduction' were chosen as past examination performance and anecdotal evidence suggested that these topics are difficult for students and they have common misconceptions. For example, students often have trouble understanding the concept of acid strength as a measure of dissociation rather than concentration. In the area of oxidation and reduction, they frequently confuse the relationships between oxidising agents and reducing agents, and oxidation and reduction processes (Pegrum *et al.*, 2014).

Students were given creative licence with the actual content of their podcasts. They were told that there were no strict guidelines on what they covered in the podcasts as long as it was related to their allocated topic. They could choose to take one aspect of the topic from the lectures and explain it, develop an analogy to explain it, or find an application from their course of study, discuss it and explain how it related to their topic.

Types of podcasts created

Despite encouraging the students to approach the task creatively, only 18% of student-created podcasts presented content in a contextualised manner using a new context that had not been covered in class. About a third (39%) of the students attempted creativity using contextualisation, however, the examples and applications presented were those that had been used during lectures. The remaining 43% of the podcasts were simply passive reproduction of facts that had been presented during unit lectures, with no further elaboration or contextualisation. Examples of the content covered in each level of contextualisation are given in Table 4.1.

Although most of the students' podcasts simply reproduced scientific content that had been presented in lectures, the podcasting task was found to have a positive effect on students' overall learning gains in terms of content understanding and knowledge retention.

As described in Pegrum *et al.* (2014), students' performance on exam questions related to 'acids and bases' and 'oxidation and reduction' was compared for two

TABLE 4.1 Levels of contextualisation in student-produced podcasts, percentages of podcasts exhibiting each level of contextualisation, and examples of contextualisation at each level

Contextualisation Level	Contextualisation Description	Percentage of Podcasts	Examples of Contextualisation
1.	Passive reproduction of facts provided in class, with no contextualisation	43	• Described different theories (e.g. the Bronsted–Lowry theory states that acids are proton donors and bases are proton acceptors) (AB) • Described characteristic reactions (e.g. when an acid reacts with a base, the products are a salt and water; when an acid reacts with a metal, the products are a salt and hydrogen gas) (AB) • Provided fundamental definitions (e.g. oxidation reactions involve the loss of electrons and reduction reactions involve the gain of electrons) (OR) • Explained fundamental processes (e.g. steps to balance redox half-reactions in acidic and basic solutions) (OR)
2.	Contextualisation using examples provided in class	39	• Explained the action of acid-base buffer systems in the human body (AB) • Mentioned that high-profile criminals throughout history have used the properties and reactions of acids and bases to assist with their crimes (AB) • Explained the principles of redox reactions in rusting processes (OR) • Mentioned the use of plane crash wreckage to make a lemon battery and produce electricity (OR)
3.	Contextualisation using a new context not covered in class	18	• Described 24 hours in the life of an 18-year-old, showing acids and bases used in everyday life (AB) • Used a boxing match as an analogy to explain an acid-base titration reaction (AB) • Explained the chemical basis of how bleaching agents work (OR) • Rewrote the lyrics of 'Ice Ice Baby' (Vanilla Ice) as 'Redox Redox Baby', describing everyday applications of redox (OR)

cohorts of introductory chemistry students enrolled in the unit in consecutive years. A comparison across years was used as we felt it was unethical to do a comparison within a cohort and only offer the potential benefits of creative pod-casting to some students. The unit was coordinated and taught by myself in both years, and each cohort received the same lecture content and supporting resources. The only difference between cohorts was the creative podcasting task.

There was a statistically significant increase in average exam marks on 'acids and bases' for students who had created podcasts on this topic compared with those who had not. On the other hand, there was no significant difference in exam marks on questions on 'oxidation and reduction' for students who created podcasts on this topic as compared with students who did not. Thus the process of creating a podcast on this topic did not negatively affect student learning or exam marks and this is encouraging for educators who wish to adopt creative digital media activities like these, which engage students and have a demonstrated positive impact on students' learning.

Interestingly, the podcasting task seemed to motivate some students who were otherwise generally disengaged from the other unit learning activities. For exam-ple, one group developed a creative analogy to describe an acid-base titration as related to the chemicals participating in a boxing match. The group members adopted the role of ringside commentators and their narrative introduced each of the 'boxers' (chemical species):

> Student 1: Welcome people to fight night, here with Bobby Dazz and Johnny J, and boy are we in for a humdinger tonight. An old-fashioned, acid versus base, grab fight. Johnny J, we haven't seen one of these for some time. Take us through our two contestants.

> Student 2: Thanks Bobby. Our two fighters tonight are the undefeated cham-pion from the human stomach, hydrochloric acid, in red, and in neutrals we have an up-and-coming base all the way from the fertiliser factory going by the name of ammonia.

The ringside commentators then offered a comparison of the relative 'fighting abilities' (relative reactivity of strong/weak acids/bases) of the boxers:

> Student 1: Now Johnny, there's been a bit of controversy surrounding this fight. Can you tell us a little bit about that?

> Student 2: Yeah, look Bobby, HCl, he's no regular acid, sure he turns litmus paper red, he produces ammonium ions when dissolved in water, he's a pro-ton donator. He does everything that is typical of an acid. But this guy is something special. This guy is a strong acid, and there's only a handful of guys in the world that can really call themselves a strong acid, and HCl fits that category. When this guy dissociates, we're talking almost completely, and that's the difference between a champion strong acid and a weaker acid.

Student 1: Where you going with this one, John?

Student 2: Well look now Bobby, as much as ammonia is a serious base and has displayed all the characteristics of a base, I just think he's fighting out of his weight division here.

They included commentary on the 'fight' (the reaction between the acid and base) as the match was overseen by a 'referee' (the indicator, phenolphthalein):

Student 1: OK Johnny lets go down to the titration right now. Round 1 is about to kick off! (bells) HCl is out of that corner in a flash . . . jab! . . . jab! . . . uppercut! OMG! Wow, this fight is over! Johnny, take us through it.

Student 2: As predicted, HCl was way too strong for ammonia . . . We see on the replay that after just a small addition of HCl, referee phenolphthalein turned from pink to clear.

The podcast created by this particular group sticks clearly in my mind. The group members did not attend the unit lectures. They were disengaged during the unit's practical laboratory sessions and would sit at their bench in the back corner refusing to do the experiment. I would have to plead with them during the three-hour session to at least do something and write something in their lab notebook so they did not fail completely. They also performed poorly on the end-of-semester examination. Their podcast, however, was by far the standout of the class. It also received a lot of attention in the WebCT discussion boards with students directing their peers to listen to it. For example, one student wrote: "I just stumbled upon the most awesome podcast! Check out the Wed 2-5 lab group, Alum4 AB; it will seriously be worth your 3 minutes!" This post received a reply: "Yeah big respect to this one . . . takes an uppercut!! Lol".

At the opposite end of the spectrum of learner engagement, the creative podcasting task was also positively received by students who were already highly engaged with the unit content, as they welcomed the opportunity to put chemistry into a relevant context. This demonstrates that creative podcasting tasks like these are engaging learning activities for students at all levels of chemistry. For example, one group of engineering majors, who finished the semester near the top of the class overall, used their podcast as an opportunity to research new battery technology that was being developed in Germany, and related this to the underlying principles of oxidation and reduction:

Student 1: Hello and welcome to Berus Chemistry. I'm <Student 1 name>. In this edition we'll be taking a look at a new battery technology that German engineers hope will revolutionise the electric car. <Student 2 name> is here in the studio to demystify the redox reactions that make the new technology possible, and our agent in the field, <Student 3 name>, will be heading out to take a look under the hood.

What do trees, combustion engines, oil fuels, power plants and your stomach all have in common? Well, they all rely on a special kind of chemical reaction call oxidation and reduction, or affectionately known as redox reactions. Here in the studio to explain the ins and outs of redox is <Student 2 name>.

Student 2: Well understanding oxidation and reduction might seem challenging, it becomes a lot simpler when broken down. A redox reaction is simply the transfer of electrons between two species . . .

Student 1: Every industry is working on developing alternatives to using fossil fuels, and nowhere is this more evident than in the burgeoning market of electric vehicles. <Student 3> reports.

Student 3 (speaking over traffic noise): Five minutes out here and it's easy to see the need for cleaner, quieter electric vehicles. But up until now they've had two big problems: the range of the car before you need to recharge the battery and the several hours that recharging can take . . . Researchers at the <Institute name> in Germany are working to change all that using redox flow technology.

Several groups of students also took the opportunity to use modern popular culture references in their podcasts. Although they were not putting the chemistry concepts into a context relevant to their chosen degree, the use of pop culture still afforded an engaging and worthwhile experience for the students. For example, one group of students described the process of oxidation and reduction using the storyline of a popular teenage movie:

Student 1: The following is a tale of two star-crossed elements and their quest for complete valence shells.

Student 2 (as narrator): Once upon a time, there was an element named Potassium. Potassium moved to a small town named Ionic to live with her Dad, Potash. The town of Ionic was surrounded by the Redox Forest, where it was rumoured dangerous creatures like fluorine, chlorine and bromine were lurking in the cold, dark shadows.

During Potassium's first day at school, she had to sit next to an element named Iodine. Iodine behaved very strangely during class and rushed away from Potassium as soon as he could. Potassium was very confused, because she quite liked the look of Iodine and wondered why he didn't like her.

Potassium was friends with a native element named Sodium. Sodium wanted to be more than friends with Potassium, but Potassium was always thinking about Iodine. Sodium warned Potassium that Iodine was dangerous. Potassium did some Googling and thought she had worked out what the problem was.

The next day Potassium went into the Redox Forest and Iodine followed her. Iodine looked longingly at Potassium.

Student 3 (as Potassium): 'We shouldn't be friends.'

Student 2 (narrator): Iodine bit her lip and said,

Student 3 (as Potassium): 'I know what you are, Iodine, and I'm not afraid of you. You are electronegative and you desire my electron. But that's OK, because I want you to have it. I'm only a half-reaction, and you need two half-reactions to make a whole reaction.'

Student 2 (narrator): After a lot of discussion, motorbike riding and cliff diving, Potassium finally gave into temptation and decided to oxidise. Potassium didn't enjoy the redox reaction. She felt like she was burning and about to burst. Suddenly, the single electron from Potassium's valence shell glowed red and with a burst of glowing energy it leapt across the room and reduced Iodine. The transfer was complete. Potassium was seeing the world in a new way, free from the burden of the electron. And even though he was now negatively charged, Iodine felt complete too. And so they lived happily ever after, oxidising and reducing, reacting to produce a family of Potassium Iodide.

A significant body of research acknowledges that popular culture plays an important and enjoyable role in an individuals' out-of-classroom life, and emphasises it would be remiss for educators not to utilise it in pedagogically productive ways (Alvermann & Hagood, 2000; Alvermann, Moon & Hagood, 1999; Manuel & Robinson, 2002; Misson, 1998). Research has shown that use of popular culture is also an effective way of motivating learners, in particular, at-risk learners (Moni & Jobling, 2008), making it ideal for introductory-level courses such as the one described in this chapter, where students' interest in the course content is often low.

Discussion

As mentioned previously in the chapter, introductory first-year level courses pose a number of challenges for educators – enrolments are often high, students come from a range of faculties and hence their interests and backgrounds vary greatly. Most students despise having to do a compulsory chemistry unit and so their motivation and level of interest is low. Further, these courses are often designed to bring students up to the required level of chemistry knowledge for their home degree as quickly as possible. This last factor is particularly important and makes these introductory courses very difficult for students, as the intensive teaching of content means students do not have the opportunity to assimilate information, consolidate knowledge and form a deep understanding. Given that many students are already keen users of digital technologies, mostly for social media, the use of student-generated digital media activities, such as the creative podcasting task described in this chapter, can be used as a vehicle to enhance student understanding of key chemistry concepts in a creative and engaging manner.

The podcasting task was specifically designed to promote collaboration, contextualisation and digital communication of understanding and, through these, deep learning (Pegrum *et al.*, 2014). The process of learning through creating a podcast is related to students having to understand the content in the first place and then synthesising it into a three-to-five-minute script as a resource to teach other students. Hence, students take information expressed in the mode of writing, still images and video and re-represent or change it into the mode of voice, which is consistent with the process of 'transduction' (Kress, 2010). Students, therefore, have to interpret information and develop a script that has coherent sequences or chunks of content.

Using an analogy also promotes creativity with the content. Deep learning approaches have been found to correlate with higher-quality learning outcomes, such as improved understanding and retention of information (Houghton, 2004). An individual's learning approach is not a fixed characteristic, but rather reflects a choice made in a particular context, especially in relation to the nature of an assessment task (Biggs & Tang, 2007; Ramsden, 2003). Designing learning activities that reward students for forging connections between new knowledge and pre-existing knowledge, facilitate contextualisation to real-world contexts and encourage active engagement with learning tasks (e.g. creative production) maximises the likelihood of a student adopting a deep approach to learning (Institute for Interactive Media & Learning, n.d.).

The active engagement in re-representing content is key to this deep learning. Recent research (Hoban, Loughran & Nielsen, 2011; Waldrip & Prain, 2012; Waldrip, Prain & Carolan, 2010) concluded that engaging students in a triadic model of a semiotic system for representations in science (Peirce, 1931/1955) enabled them to construct representational meanings. Hoban *et al.*'s proposed model involves students thinking about three interdependent aspects: the referent (original information); the representation created; and the interpretant (meaning). The extent of students' understanding of the semiotics and underlying concepts then becomes evident in their associated explanations (Hoban *et al.*, 2011). The creative podcasting task required students to progress through this model. They researched their assigned concept (referent), planned the content and sequence of their podcast, including creating analogies (representation) and finally, added a narration (interpretant), demonstrating that they had made meaning of the information.

Requiring students to generate their own explanations is an integral component of learning in this process (Chi, de Leeuw, Chiu & LaVancher, 1994). Students have to translate their internal representations and understanding into a language appropriate for the audience (Prain, 2002; Yore & Treagust, 2006). In doing so, their level of understanding of the concepts behind the explanations quickly becomes evident and can be used by educators to inform the focus of future teaching (Lawrie & Bartle, 2013).

Requiring students to apply the semiotic model in a digital context is significant. Research at the Open University has found a correlation between students adopting a deep learning approach and positive attitudes toward using technology for studying (Haigh, 2011), suggesting it may be productive to foster student engagement with digital media tasks (Pegrum *et al.*, 2014). This aligned with our experiences with the creative podcasting task and the high level of engagement by students at all levels. As previously described through examples, the podcasting task appeared to motivate students who were otherwise generally disengaged with the unit, whereas at the other end of the spectrum, students who were already highly engaged with the unit content welcomed the opportunity to apply it to a context relevant to their home degree.

A creative podcasting task is a relatively easy assignment for educators to implement into their courses. Students completed the activity outside of class contact hours, and their motivation to do it was evident from the quality of podcasts produced, suggesting that many students had devoted a considerable amount of time to the task. There was minimal need for technical tuition from the teaching staff about how to create and upload a podcast. Overall, the creative podcasting task described in this chapter required little input from the unit instructors and can be considered an efficient use of limited teaching resources resulting in an engaging and worthwhile learning experience for students.

References

Alvermann, D. & Hagood, M. (2000). Fandom and critical media literacy. *Journal of Adolescent and Adult Literacy*, *43*(5), 436–446.

Alvermann, D., Moon, J. S. & Hagood, M. (1999). *Popular culture in the classroom*. Newark, DE: International Reading Association.

Bartle, E., Longnecker, N. & Pegrum, M. (2011). Collaboration, contextualisation and communication using new media: Introducing podcasting into an undergraduate chemistry class. *International Journal of Innovation in Science and Mathematics Education*, *19*(1), 16–28.

Biggs, J. & Tang, C. (2007). *Teaching for quality learning at university: What the student does* (3rd ed). Maidenhead, UK: Open University Press.

Bradley, P. (2007). *How to use Web 2.0 in your library*. London: Facet.

Braun, L. W. (2007). *Listen up! Podcasting for schools and libraries*. Medford, NJ: Information Today.

Cane, C. & Cashmore, A. (2008). Students' podcasts as learning tools. In G. Salmon & P. Edirisingha (Eds.), *Podcasting for learning in universities* (pp. 146–152). Maidenhead, UK: Open University Press.

Chi, M. T. H., de Leeuw, N., Chiu, M.-H. & LaVancher, C. (1994). Eliciting self-explanations improves understanding. *Cognitive Science*, *18*, 439–477.

Cluett, L. (2010). *Online social networking for outreach, engagement and community: The UWA students' Facebook page*. Paper presented at the Teaching & Learning Forum, Edith Cowan University, Perth, Australia.

Fensham, P. (2004). *Engagement with science: An international issue that goes beyond knowledge*. Paper presented at SMEC 2004, Dublin. Retrieved from http://www.dcu.ie/smec/plenary/Fensham,%20Peter.pdf (accessed 19 March, 2015).

Fontichiaro, J. (2008). *Podcasting at school*. Westport, CT: Libraries Unlimited.

Green, T. D., Brown, A. & Robinson, L. (2008). *Making the most of the Web in your classroom: A teacher's guide to blogs, podcasts, wikis, pages, and sites*. Thousand Oaks, CA: Corwin Press.

Haigh, G. (2011). Open University research explodes myth of 'digital native'. *MJO Learning Teaching Technology*. Retrieved from http://www.agent4change.net/resources/research/1088 (accessed 19 March, 2015).

Hoban, G., Loughran, J. & Nielsen, W. (2011). Slowmation: Preservice elementary teachers representing science knowledge through creating multimodal digital animations. *Journal of Research in Science Teaching, 48*, 985–1009.

Houghton, W. (2004). *Deep and surface approaches to learning*. Loughborough, UK: HEA Engineering Resource Centre.

Institute for Interactive Media & Learning (n.d.). *Students' approaches to learning*. Sydney, Australia: Institute for Interactive Media & Learning, UTS. Retrieved from http://www.iml.uts.edu.au/learn-teach/approaches.html (accessed 19 March, 2015).

Jonassen, D., Myers, J. & McKillop, A. (1996). From constructivism to constructionism: Learning with hypermedia rather than from it. In B. Wilson (Ed.), *Constructivist learning environments: Case studies in instructional design* (pp. 93–107). Englewood Cliffs, NJ: Educational Technology.

Jones, S. M. & Yates, B. F. (2011). *Science learning and teaching academic standards statement*. Sydney: Australian Learning and Teaching Council. Retrieved from http://www.olt.gov.au/resource-learning-and-teaching-academic-standards-science-2011 (accessed 19 March, 2015).

King, K. P. & Gura, M. (2007). *Podcasting for teachers: Using a new technology to revolutionise teaching and learning*. Charlotte, NC: Information Age.

Kozma, R. & Russell, J. (2005). Students becoming chemists: Developing representational competence. In J. K. Gilbert (Ed.), *Visualisation in science education: Models and modelling in science education* (pp. 121–146). Dordrecht, The Netherlands: Springer.

Kress, G. (2010). *Multimodality: A social semiotic approach to contemporary communication*. London: Routledge.

Lawrie, G. A. & Bartle, E. (2013). Chemistry vlogs: A vehicle for student-generated representations and explanations to scaffold their understanding of structure–property relationships. *International Journal of Innovation in Science and Mathematics Education, 21*(4), 27–45.

Lawrie, G. A., Matthews, K. & Gahan, L. (2010). Forming groups to foster collaborative learning in large enrolment courses. In M. Sharma (Ed.), *Proceedings of the 16th UniServe Science Annual Conference* (pp. 66–71). Sydney, Australia: UniServ Science.

Manuel, J. & Robinson, D. (2002). What are teenagers reading? The findings of a survey of teenagers' reading choices and the implications of these for English teachers' classroom practice. *English in Australia, 135*, 69–78.

McGarr, O. (2009). A review of podcasting in higher education: Its influence on the traditional lecture. *Australasian Journal of Educational Technology, 25*(3), 309–321.

Misson, R. (1998). Theory and spice, and things not nice: Popular culture in the primary classroom. In M. Knobel & A. Healy (Eds.), *Critical literacies in the primary classroom* (pp. 53–62). Newtown, Australia: Primary English Teaching Association.

Moni, K., & Jobling, A. (2008). A case for including popular culture in literacy education for young adults with Down syndrome. *Australian Journal of Language and Literacy, 46*(1), 72–77.

Pegrum, M. (2009a). Communicative networking & linguistic mashups on Web 2.0. In M. Thomas (Ed.), *Handbook of research on Web 2.0 and second language learning* (pp. 20–41). Hershey, PA: Information Science Reference.

Pegrum, M. (2009b). *From blogs to bombs: The future of digital technologies in education*. Crawley, Australia: University of Western Australia.

Pegrum, M., Bartle, E. & Longnecker, N. (2014). Can creative podcasting promote deep learning? The use of podcasting for learning content in an undergraduate science unit.

British Journal of Educational Technology, Published online 8 January, 2014. doi: 10.1111/ bjet.12133.

Peirce, C. (1931/1955). Logic as semiotic: The theory of signs. In B. Justus (Ed.), *Philosophical writings of Peirce (1893–1910)*. New York, NY: Dover. (Original work published 1931)

Prain, V. (2002). *Learning from writing in secondary science: Some theoretical implications.* Paper presented at Ontological, Epistemological, Linguistic and Pedagogical Considerations of Language and Science Literacy: Empowering Research and Informing Instruction, Victoria, BC, Canada.

Ramsden, P. (2003). *Learning to teach in higher education* (2nd ed). London: Routledge Falmer.

Richardson, W. (2010). *Blogs, wikis, podcasts, and other powerful Web tools for classrooms.* Thousand Oaks, CA: Corwin Press.

Rifkin, W., Longnecker, N., Leach, J. & Davis, L. S. (2010). Students publishing in new media: Eight hypotheses – A house of cards? *International Journal of Innovation in Science and Mathematics Education*, *18*(1), 43–54.

Shamburg, C. (2009). *Student-powered podcasting: Teaching for 21st century literacy.* Eugene, OR: International Society for Technology in Education.

Shamburg, C. (2010). DIY podcasting in education. In M. Knobel & C. Lankshear (Eds.), *DIY media: Creating, sharing and learning with new technologies* (pp. 51–75). New York, NY: Peter Lang.

Terrion, J. L. & Aceti, V. (2012). Perceptions of the effects of clicker technology on student learning and engagement: A study of freshmen chemistry students. *Research in Learning Technology*, *20*(2), 1–11.

Waldrip, B. & Prain, V. (2012). Learning from and through representations in science. In B. Fraser, K. Tobin & J. McRobbie (Eds.), *Second International Handbook of Science Education* (pp. 145–155). Dordrecht, The Netherlands: Springer.

Waldrip, B., Prain, V. & Carolan, J. (2010). Using multi-modal representations to improve learning in junior secondary science. *Research in Science Education*, *40*(1), 65–80.

Williams, B. (2007). *Educator's podcast guide.* Eugene, OR: International Society for Technology in Education.

Wu, H.-K. & Puntambekar, S. (2012). Pedagogical affordances of multiple external representations in scientific processes. *Journal of Science Education and Technology*, *21*, 754–767.

Yore, L. & Treagust, D. (2006). Current realities and future possibilities: Language and science literacy: Empowering research and informing instruction. *International Journal of Science Education*, *28*, 291–314.

DIGITAL STORY OVERVIEW

Digital story is a media form that has mainly evolved through the arts but is now having a stronger presence in the sciences. It is becoming very common in all subject areas because digital stories are relatively easy to create technologically as a media form. A digital story is essentially a narrated slide show (although purists would debate this). Hence, it is a simple form of multimedia usually incorporating two modes of communication – still images accompanied by voice or speech. However, the creation of a good digital story is certainly an 'art form'. A digital story usually involves 10–15 images, a 250-word script and lasts about 2–3 minutes. The key to a powerful digital story is the narration and so that is usually written first. The still images are then added to match the narration but it is often an iterative process in terms of collecting the images and matching the narration so that there is modal coherence. The challenge for the creators is to summarise the content to be represented in a succinct narration and then choose still images to complement the narration to generate meaning.

In Chapter 5, Emily Purser from the University of Wollongong in Australia writes about the importance of students, especially international students, learning communication through creating digital stories. Importantly, she emphasises that communication must be learned in context and so her international students create digital stories about their personal narratives. As such, they learn communication by refining their personal narratives and the skills can be used later when they learn science content knowledge. In Chapter 6, Pauline Ross from the University of Western Sydney poses a very cogent argument that, contrary to the way that science knowledge is portrayed, real science knowledge is not produced in a linear and objective way. The process of producing science knowledge is often subjective, non-linear and value laden. Ross argues for the importance of students engaging with science content in the same personal, subjective way through creating digital stories and, in the process, debunks the myth of science knowledge as objective and impersonal.

5

USING DIGITAL STORIES TO TEACH COMMUNICATION IN THE SCIENCE CURRICULUM

Emily Purser

Context

This chapter takes a slight step back from the volume's main focus, to consider the use of digital stories to teach communication and critical reflection in science disciplines. It describes how using digital media is helping to develop students' communicative repertoire and fluency in a university course, and explains why teaching communication is high on the science education agenda in Australia. While science education may seem mostly about knowing facts, uncommon sense concepts, theoretical principles and how to use laboratory equipment, it is also supposed to be about developing effective communication and good citizenship. When teaching communication becomes official faculty business, serious attention needs to be paid to curriculum design. At an Australian university, students of science are expected to develop not only scientific knowledge and procedures through their degree program, but also the ability to work cooperatively, identify and solve problems, and share their knowledge and understanding of science across various media, for different purposes and with diverse audiences. University curricula also need to respond meaningfully to the fact that their student populations have rapidly and quite radically diversified, and are, at postgraduate level in particular, increasingly international. Before describing and discussing how a digital story can be used in relation to a complex set of learning needs, a bit of background on the need for a better balance in science curricula is presented.

The science curriculum

A carefully balanced curriculum is ideal at all degree levels, according to higher education policy documents such as the *Learning and Teaching Academic Standards Project: Science* (Australian Learning and Teaching Council, 2011), the *Australian Qualifications Framework* (Australian Qualifications Framework Council, 2013) and the general standards-based quality assurance framework (Tertiary Education Quality and Standards Agency, 2012) that regulate teaching and curriculum development. Through governmental statements, strategic planning and institutional policy across the sector, and the scores of educational development projects these inform, it is argued strongly that students, and the nation, are at risk if university degree programs do not provide a good balance of disciplinary knowledge and 'skills'. Whatever the wording, curriculum-framing documents are simply articulating what good educators probably all recognise as basic to the scientific approach, and to humanity – the need to help students experience and understand what it is to work cooperatively on problems, to peer review and to represent what they know and understand of science in various ways, to suit different contexts. In Australian university curricula, achieving balance means organising courses around five learning outcomes to be achieved at or above a 'threshold' or bare minimum level: (1) Understanding science; (2) Scientific knowledge; (3) Inquiry and problem solving; (4) Communication; and (5) Personal and professional responsibility (Australian Learning and Teaching Council, 2011). It is not enough, in other words, to know science in the privacy of the individual mind – universities are tasked to make sure their students participate effectively in collective minds to achieve all five Threshold Learning Outcomes in the program.

Many postgraduate programs have to manage an additional challenge, as institutions attract ever-more students from the expanding, highly mobile and lucrative international 'market'. The need for more, and more-effective, English language education is widely recognised. However, the need to design degree programs and individual courses around the specific language development needs of the students being enrolled by universities (not just let in, but recruited and depended on, financially) is less formally recognised. Students using English as an additional language are obviously not as fluent as those who have been fully immersed in the language since birth, but their need to learn English while learning through English presents something of a 'wicked problem' for institutions. Different stakeholders view the problem as either: (1) having to correct errors – "that should not be occurring at this level of education!"; (2) having to design programs to produce easily measurable outcomes of student learning; or (3) having to convince those who know nothing of the complexities of language learning that language is a process (Halliday, 1993) to which close, careful and theoretically informed attention should be paid through the design of all courses and interactions. However the language education challenge is imagined, some degree of explicit focus on English language development needs to be part of every twenty-first-century science curriculum, which also includes the increasing focus on new media (Johnson, Adams Becker, Estrada & Freeman, 2014) and professional employability.

Communication and language growth by design

The course that is the focus of this chapter uses simple digital story as a media form to address multiple learning needs at one time. It is a Masters-level course at the

University of Wollongong (UOW) in Australia, taught collaboratively by a scientist and an educational linguist. UOW is not unusual in having a very high proportion of international students using English as a second language, or in seeing most of these students in postgraduate programs. Less usual (so far) is the approach this course takes to identifying and meeting their various learning needs simultaneously. The concern has been to design a complete learning environment (tasks, resources, instructional strategies, interaction) around the needs of English language learners within their disciplines, which prompts students to develop proficiency in aspects of English that are key to producing and communicating scientific knowledge. International students in the Master of Science and the Master of Public Health take the class together, as it is a compulsory first course in both degree programs. The students come from a wide range of disciplines, including nutrition and public health, chemistry, biology and earth sciences. They have very different prior experiences in other educational systems, and diverse language backgrounds and many confront the reality of full immersion in Australian academic culture with a degree of shock or trauma. All this informs the design of the course, 'SCIE911: Fundamentals of Science Communication'.

SCIE911 gives students three closely interrelated tasks: to write a literature review, re-present a research publication as an illustrated talk and produce a digital resource of educational value to the '911 community'. The learning processes involved in completing the first two tasks and in doing other courses taken concurrently, provide the immediate institutional context for their digital media task. In planning their digital stories, students are expected to draw on experiences they are having as they proceed through this and other courses at the university. In this course, that includes about 50 hours of instruction and interaction in class and online, students find, analyse, summarise and critically review academic literature from their discipline, choosing topics in consultation with disciplinary educators. They select one of their sources and 'translate' its lexically dense information into a short talk that can be understood by a mixed disciplinary audience, noting key differences between written and spoken English, and the role of images in effective communication of scientific knowledge. At the same time, they consider the new concepts and language that they are being exposed to in other courses. Their task in creating a digital story is to identify a significant concept, difficult procedure or serious problem that they have confronted recently and construct a narrative explanation or conflict-based story. They need to show others an important challenge they have overcome in transitioning into this academic and cultural context in doing academic work in English or in understanding a new concept in public health or science.

Digital stories

Making a digital story is a new experience for students coming into this course, but the medium has instant appeal. Even the most linguistically vulnerable students can communicate a complex and interesting message this way and, compared to academic essays or reports, it feels both an exciting new space and yet deeply familiar territory. Storytelling is a cultural tradition as old as humanity and this is why students from any background can relate to it. Creating a digital story is a relatively simple process to learn using a digital camera, microphone, computer or mobile device, free software and Internet connection. So, anyone can combine voice with images and share the result. As the production technologies become cheaper and easier to use, the more the practice of digital storytelling proliferates online and also because collaborative 'DIY' storytelling projects are great, community-building fun. Sophisticated digital storytelling techniques can be learnt through community workshops run by professional broadcasters in many countries, such as ABC Open (n.d.) in Australia and BBC Wales (2008). A history for such projects can be traced to mobile arts and media-based initiatives for oral history (Meadows, 2003) and the genre and its pedagogy continue to develop around the world, for example, to support community participation (e.g. digistories, 2014), fundraising (e.g. Community Organizer 2.0, 2014), social justice (e.g. Creative Narrations, 2009) and changing the politics of representation of the disempowered (e.g. Australian Centre for the Moving Image, 2014). Such carefully and ethically managed open projects are all influenced by the pioneering work over the past two decades at the Californian Center for Digital Storytelling and are, as they say, a great way to learn how 'to listen to each other'.

Though simple, the digital story has more educational potential than first meets the eye. The genre has been taken up at primary, secondary and tertiary levels (Blocher, 2008), by teachers across all disciplines as a way of framing and encouraging critical reflection, explaining concepts, assessing learning and developing language. It is increasingly recognised as an effective prompt for deep and transformative learning (EDUCAUSE, 2007; Hull & Katz, 2006; Robin & McNeil, 2012) and cultural change (Lambert, 2013). The practice is also becoming a focus for educational research, with countless publications on the topic, and several doctorate-level dissertations completed in recent years on the use of digital storytelling in education (e.g. Robin & McNeil, 2012). In our context, as students use digital storytelling to reflect on their learning in a second language in the Faculty of Science, Medicine and Health, they develop a speaking voice and communicative skill but they are also opening a window to their lived experience that is teaching the teachers and offering the institution an alternative understanding of what it can mean to teach 'communication'.

Implementation

Technically, the digital story as taught in SCIE911 is a 3–5-minute video with voice-over narrative and mainly still images, produced in PowerPoint, PhotoStory, Movie Maker, iMovie or similar software. Students post their work on the class YouTube channel. Student work is showcased semi-privately online via an unlisted YouTube channel (Channel nineoneone, 2014). Three examples illustrate the type of work being created. The first represents a student's view of a concept introduced in another course (Social Determinants of Health), which offered the student a new way of thinking. The second example focuses on writing a literature review, which the student found challenging and worth reflecting on in a way that could help others. The third example presents a social and health issue in the student's home country, of which she became aware while abroad and immersed in a new field of study and wanted to think about and discuss.

Feedback from students about their experiences of doing this task reveals that it is when they actually make the digital story that their understanding of the genre shifts. Initially, all students had a similar understanding of digital story in terms of the production technology involved: 'presenting through multimedia', 'telling a story using electronic multimedia' and 'stories told using images, voice, video, animations'. In a follow-up interview, the author of example one articulated how his appreciation developed slowly. He came to see the assignment as a catalyst to deeper thinking about a topic. Further, he felt that taking a personal stance and putting the spoken voice into the representation was authentic and had more at stake than written communication. He also commented that although the amount of information in his presentation was minimal (and not necessarily accurate), his sense of having learned something seemed stronger than after reading thousands of words on paper. That might seem unlikely, but it is a frequent comment from students doing this activity: the multimodality *per se* seems to add value to the learning experience. There is something powerfully engaging in the act of choosing images to match spoken words and the decision-making process prompts deep reflection as it develops communication.

Improving English is the focus of comments from the author of the second example. She re-recorded her voice-over countless times until she was reasonably satisfied with the pronunciation and even apologetic for any remaining grammatical imperfections in the product. From the teacher's perspective, although the student was still apologetic for any remaining grammatical imperfections in the product, the educational goal was achieved through this autodidactic process, and this was fed back via the class wiki, for all to see:

> The fact that you've done the recording many times is exactly what I would want you to have achieved – you've heard your voice, reread your script, and made improvements as a result of having been able to do that – this kind of development is the point of the exercise, so that's fantastic, don't apologise! . . . It sounds very natural, and I wouldn't change anything, except to add the reference to any music and images that aren't your own . . . The main thing is, I can understand everything you say, what you say is well illustrated, and the exercise has clearly given you opportunity to think carefully about the learning process you're describing.

Measuring the degree to which metalearning occurs and metalinguistic awareness develops are ongoing interests in teaching and researching in this course, but growth in specific areas of linguistic repertoire and proficiency are already apparent.

Educational process

Learning how to make a simple educational resource with digital media can still take some hours for students new to the practice – it is not difficult, but there is much to consider. Informed (or reassured) by the Center for Digital Storytelling (2014), Matthews-DeNatale (2008) and the guidelines from Robin and McNeil (2012), my process now goes something like this:

Step 1. Film Fest: Students see examples – some entertaining, some about famous people in science, some from students past or in other countries, but most on topics of global concern, such as climate change or health (selected from ASPECT, 2011; Banyan Tree Project, 2014; EngenderHealth, 2014). What the showcased stories have in common is their length, relevance to students in this context and a personal perspective.

Step 2. Concept check and mission instructions: The emotional effect and educational value of this form of communication are discussed, along with our purpose in creating educational resources – not to achieve high production values, but to reflect on personal experiences of learning in science or public health. Students choose to either explain a concept, phenomenon or process relevant to their discipline, or create a narrative about a personal learning challenge faced and overcome.

Step 3. Brainstorm: Ideas are developed through open dialogue with peers and teachers. Most students visualise their topic and choose an angle quickly – to help those feeling confused, all ideas are shared on a wiki.

Step 4. Script and critique: Students draft a script and are guided to edit and improve it. Feedback from teacher and peers draws attention to the genre (is it a well-structured story? does it explain?), to wording and to layout (text as a sequence of dot points, to ease storyboarding later). The teaching focus here is on accuracy and on lexico-grammatical differences between written and spoken English, as illustrated by a few excerpts in Table 5.1.

Step 5. Storyboard: With comprehensible and speakable scripts, students gather images to illustrate each of their points, learn about intellectual property issues and where to safely source any images they cannot take themselves. They use storyboard templates or slideshow software to match images to their words.

Step 6. Production: A wide range of tools are linked to the class blog for students to browse and experiment with, and demonstrations are provided in class and through videos on the eLearning and class YouTube sites. Students are encouraged to keep it simple, especially if they are not already familiar with digital media.

Step 7. Reveal and evaluate: Student work is showcased in class and sampled on Channel 911 (the class YouTube channel). Peer review contributes to grading, and the educational process is evaluated through interviews and critical reflection on teaching practice.

TABLE 5.1 Refining the wording of digital story narrations

Before	After
In Nigeria, there is low process in waste management which cause indiscriminate disposal of waste on or around the street as compared to Australia, which has well controllable system of waste disposal and collection.	In Nigeria, there's not much processing of waste, it's just disposed of indiscriminately, on or around the streets . . . but here in Australia, there's a system for collecting and disposing of waste that's well controlled.
I have left the place my home town Nepal, where I was born and lived my almost quarter life, where I was taught everything that has resulted the present me. I am habituated with that environment, with that place, with those people and those traditions. My zone of comfort is mile away and now I am trying to adopt in this new environment	I've left my home in Nepal, where I was born and have spent my life so far, the place that made me the person I am. My comfort zone is miles away now, and I'm struggling to adapt to a new environment . . .
Doing the task together, as it demands, became difficult as we were located about 90 km apart and we met only once a week at university. Thanks to the invention called Internet and applications and programs like WhatsApp, cloud and Google Docs, we were stringed together . . . It was the continuous guidance and comment from our teachers, that showed us the right track whenever we went astray and helped us great deal in accomplishing the task! I express my sincere gratitude to our teacher, our mentor, our *guru*!	The real problem for us was the fact that we were living nearly 100 km apart, and we only saw each other once a week at uni. But we were able to stay connected online, with WhatsApp and Google Docs . . . The constant feedback from teachers kept us on track and helped a lot – thanks!

The central role of scripting in this whole process needs to be made very clear. It seems counter-intuitive to the newcomer, but digital storytelling is as much about writing as speaking. Students tend to assume that if a narration they hear sounds conversational it must have been spoken spontaneously and they need to actually see how effective videos are put together and how draft scripts are developed. In this medium, just as with academic writing, the less effort required comprehending a message, the more effort has probably been expended in the design, drafting and editing. To reinforce the point, it helps to explain scripting through a home-made video as well, which also demonstrates the 'how to' of the video genre, which some students like to emulate in their assignment. Another helpful tip is to openly share the process of script editing. In this course, we use a wiki. Each student has a page, where the script is drafted and feedback is received from teachers and peers, until it is worded effectively. A transparent editorial and peer-review process enables students to observe how academic English differs from conversational English and students come to realise why an essay writing style does not work well in storytelling.

Discussion

There seem to be many educational benefits in digital storytelling and not only for students. But, as with any task and technology the value needs to be questioned and articulated. We want to encourage production of useful resources that are not superficial, pretentious or overly political stories that ignore the complexity of problems (Hug, 2012). In evaluating outcomes, our concern is less the quality of products of student work than effects of the lived process. These are being traced over time, and are only partly realised at the individual level, but students are certainly saying that they enjoy and benefit from making and sharing digital resources, and the benefits happen in multiple ways. There is the refreshing fun of playing with new media in an academic learning environment. Then there is the sense of community that open sharing of students' resources helps build among participants in the course – past, current and future. It helps ease students' transitions into Australian academic life and into critical reflection on learning in this complex, multicultural environment. Within the wider curriculum, the reflective task creates a space where students can pay close attention to language as the process of 'coming to know', stepping aside for a moment from the usual uncritical rush to consume information.

The digital story assignment also helps build students' confidence in speaking English to a diverse and potentially large audience. Unlike a live oral presentation, it allows private rehearsal and self-critique against formal criteria, as well as feedback from peers and teachers before open publication. For the linguistically vulnerable, working with multimodal texts provides a pleasant respite from academic writing, while also forming important bridges between informal and academic writing, between writing and speaking, and between linguistic and visual modes of representation. Working with digital media helps expand students' semiotic 'potential to mean' through both language and multimodal text (Cope & Kalantzis, 2000; Halliday & Matthiessen, 2013), as they learn to match words and images. As revealed through before and after surveys and interviews, the scripting stage, with its copious feedback on drafts and development of wordings that sound natural and fluent in the narration, expands students' linguistic repertoire and raises metalinguistic awareness of how English works in different modes and contexts.

An important marker of quality in digital storytelling practice is, for us, how well students participate in a new digital culture, where the aim is to learn from one another and incrementally improve the collective learning environment by contributing to it. We want graduates to be 'tech savvy' and to know digital and social media can have academic and professional networking purposes, but our greatest concern in using digital media technologies is to engage students in open, intercultural communication and deep personal learning. This kind of collective development of media literacy has transformative potential on both fronts. Learning 'deeply' is a process of creative linguistic 'remixing' where what is read and heard must be interpreted, paraphrased and appropriated, with keen awareness of the source. There is also a strong sense of the voice of each new speaker engaging in these literary practices. For the student group as a whole within the institution, this kind of open talk about what students find challenging, important or compelling in their studies seems to have value both for their reflective practice and for the institution's – we have as much to learn about the nature of the challenges our educational programs present for the students we invite into them as the students have to learn about doing academic work in an English-language research environment. Words of Salman Rushdie, often quoted in discussions of digital storytelling, resonate here, as we create opportunities within the curriculum for students to speak and write in their own voice and be heard:

> . . . power must belong equally to everyone . . . those who do not have power over the story that dominates their lives, power to retell it, rethink it, deconstruct it, joke about it, and change it as times change, truly are powerless, because they cannot think new thoughts. (Rushdie, 1991)

The sharing of personal digital stories has game-changing potential in the power politics of representation (Eades, Simondson, & Thompson, 2011) as it enables those usually marginalised, silenced and invisible to develop voice, tell the world who they are with dignity and be taken seriously. It is from constructing a personal reflection on specific situations and events that important learning emerges as students (and teachers) explore psychological and cultural depths together and develop for the whole academy a more-sophisticated understanding of communication.

The challenges that new media, changing student demographics and policy directives bring to traditional academic practice can be exciting rather than daunting. When educators from different disciplines or institutional positions can freely collaborate, it is not difficult to create a richly resourced eLearning environment that frees teachers to devote more attention to discussion, feedback and peer review that most significantly develops students' language proficiency. It is an interesting story, but not within the scope of this discussion to tell, how academic language, literacy and learning ever came to be conceptualised in terms of extra-curricular 'skills', but the immediate challenge for educators considering the science curriculum is that the language learning needs of students flocking to Australian universities from across the world seeking a good education need to be taken seriously. We hope that encouraging, curating and making student stories visible in the institution will help to increase empathy and interest, as well as provide opportunities to connect and bridge the widely recognised chasm between international and domestic students in higher education. We also want to shift the focus in institutional discussions of 'communication skills' from training and measurement of individual performance in rigidly codified genres toward an understanding of how texts work in context and how proficiency in English language is developed not only through academic reading and writing, but also through meaningful speaking and listening.

Conclusion

In a well-designed course, the digital story assignment does seem more gold than glitter, for its capacity to help achieve several important developments at once. Policies framing higher education expect curricula, including science, to strengthen students' ability to be understood in various contexts. In the postgraduate course described in this chapter, the digital story is proving an interesting and helpful way to explore digital media and the possibilities of multimodal communication in making meaningful connections. It also invites a reconsideration of what is meant by academic literacy and communication. The humble photo-story, telling a personal tale of challenges overcome, provides an engaging task for international students as they simultaneously develop their knowledge of an academic discipline and English language. As a way of assessing understanding of concepts, issues or literate practices in an academic discipline, it can helpfully supplement the traditional essay or report – especially when the students' proficiency in the language of instruction is limited. The digital story enables them to speak in a very personal and authentic voice and in an open environment, this can give us a clearer view of the factors shaping student learning that academic environments normally render invisible. Viewed less in terms of standardised text performance and more in terms of raising the standard of reading, writing, speaking and (above all) listening, the communicative skill that a university curriculum has the potential to develop involves a community of practice, which includes teachers and institutional management as well as students. Digital storytelling is a useful tool in the educator's repertoire. It is a simple and pleasurable yet viable means of pursuing a range of educational goals and practising good intercultural communication. As an assessment task, the digital story stands out as a valuable learning opportunity, representing some of the best things left on our doorsteps by the technological revolution in communication and social connection that is digital culture.

References

ABC Open. (n.d.). *About ABC Open*. Retrieved from https://open.abc.net.au/about (accessed 19 March, 2015).

ASPECT. (2011). *Project background*. Retrieved from http://www.projectaspect.org/about_aspect?page=project_background (accessed 19 March, 2015).

Australian Centre for the Moving Image. (2014). *Indigenous Australian voices*. Retrieved from http://generator.acmi.net.au/education-themes/indigenous-australian-voices-1 (accessed 19 March, 2015).

Australian Learning and Teaching Council. (2011). *Learning and teaching academic standards project: Science learning and teaching academic standards statement*. Sydney: ALTC.

Australian Qualifications Framework Council. (2013). *Australian qualifications framework* (2nd ed). Retrieved from http://www.aqf.edu.au/wp-content/uploads/2013/05/AQF-2nd-Edition-January-2013.pdf (accessed 19 March, 2015).

Banyan Tree Project. (2014). *HIV stories & videos*. Retrieved from http://banyantreeproject.org/wp2014/stories-videos/ (accessed 19 March, 2015)

BBC Wales. (2008). *Capture Wales*. Retrieved from http://www.bbc.co.uk/wales/audiovideo/sites/galleries/pages/capturewales.shtml (accessed 19 March, 2015).

Blocher, M. (2008). Digital storytelling and reflective assessment. In K. McFerrin, R. Weber, R. Carlsen & D. A. Willis (Eds.), *Proceedings of Society for Information Technology & Teacher Education International 2008 Conference* (pp. 892–901). Chesapeake, VA: AACE. Retrieved from http://www.editlib.org/p/27286/ (accessed 19 March, 2015).

Center for Digital Storytelling. (2014). *Homepage*. Retrieved from http://storycenter.org/ (accessed 19 March, 2015).

Channel nineoneone. (2014). *Examples playlist*. Retrieved from http://tinyurl.com/pygj58s (accessed 19 March, 2015).

Community Organizer 2.0. (2014). *Digital storytelling tools*. Presentation at the Mass Non-Profit Network Annual Conference 2013. Retrieved from http://www.slideshare.net/Debask/digital-storytelling-tools-for-nonprofit-organizations?related=2 (accessed 19 March, 2015).

Cope, B. & Kalantzis, M. (2000). *Multiliteracies: Literacy learning and the design of social futures.* South Yarra, VIC: MacMillan.

Creative Narrations. (2009). *Multimedia for community development*. Retrieved from http://www.creativenarrations.net/ (accessed 19 March, 2015).

digistories. (2014). *Your world in digital storytelling*. Retrieved from http://digistories.co.uk/ (accessed 19 March, 2015).

Eades, J., Simondson, H. & Thompson, K. (2011). *Victorian Indigenous communities and digital storytelling: Screening the past*. Retrieved from http://www.screeningthepast.com/2011/08/victorian-indigenous-communities-and-digital-storytelling/ (accessed 19 March, 2015).

EDUCAUSE. (2007). *7 Things you should know about . . . digital storytelling*. Retrieved from http://net.educause.edu/ir/library/pdf/ELI7021.pdf (accessed 19 March, 2015).

EngenderHealth. (2014). *Learn from my story: Women confront fistula in rural Uganda*. Retrieved from http://www.engenderhealth.org/our-work/maternal/digital-stories-uganda-fistula.php (accessed 19 March, 2015).

Halliday, M. A. K. (1993). Towards a language-based theory of learning. *Linguistics and Education, 5*, 93–116.

Halliday, M. A. K. & Matthiessen, C. (2013). *An introduction to functional grammar* (3rd ed). London: Routledge.

Hug, T. (2012). Storytelling – EDU: Educational – digital – unlimited? *Seminar.Net, 8*(1). Retrieved from http://seminar.net/index.php/volume-8-issue-1-2012/185-storytelling-edu-educational-digital-unlimited (accessed 19 March, 2015).

Hull, G. & Katz, M.-L. (2006). Crafting an agentive self: Case studies of digital storytelling. *Research in the Teaching of English, 41*(1), 43–81.

Johnson, L., Adams Becker S., Estrada, V. & Freeman, A. (2014). *NMC Horizon report: 2014 higher education edition*, Austin, TX: New Media Consortium.

Lambert, J. (2013). *Digital storytelling: Capturing lives, creating community*. New York: Routledge.

Matthews-DeNatale, G. (2008). *Digital storytelling: Tips and resources*. Retrieved from https://net.educause.edu/ir/library/pdf/ELI08167B.pdf (accessed 19 March, 2015).

Meadows, D. (2003). Digital storytelling: Research-based practice in new media. *Visual Communication, 2*(2), 189–193, doi: 10.1177/1470357203002002004.

Robin, B. & McNeil, S. (2012). What educators should know about teaching digital storytelling. *Digital Education Review, 22*, 37–51.

Rushdie, S. (1991, December 12). Excerpts from Rushdie's address: 1,000 days 'Trapped inside a metaphor'. *New York Times*. Retrieved from http://www.nytimes.com/books/99/04/18/specials/rushdie-address.html (accessed 19 March, 2015).

Tertiary Education Quality and Standards Agency. (2012). *About TEQSA*. Retrieved from http://www.teqsa.gov.au/about (accessed 19 March, 2015).

6

STORIES AND NARRATIVES

Using digital stories to learn science

Pauline Ross

Human lives are storms of stories. We live and dream stories. We tell stories and we learn from them. We gratefully collapse into stories after a long day at work. Without stories to organise our experience, our own lives lack coherence and meaning. (Gottschall, 2013)

Context

When we think of the first story ever told we imagine primitive humans in caves, drawing their stories on the walls. When we think of the possibility of using storytelling to learn science, we hesitate – some of us respond by rejecting story-telling. Perhaps we respond like this because combining the words 'science' and 'stories' together is risky, anti-rigour and maybe even anti-science (McWilliam, Poronnik, & Taylor, 2008). After all, the definition of a story is an account of events, which can be true but may equally be fictitious and false, that is, 'it is only a story' (Negrete & Lartigue, 2010, p. 98) – the creative imaginings of a storyteller may not necessarily represent reality. Science, in contrast, is commonly about facts and theories explained using logical and formal discourse and evidenced through experimental testing.

Science is, however, full of stories. The stories in science are historical, stories of discoveries driven by human curiosity. Many rigorous scientific explanations start their life as stories, the products of creative minds (Einstein & Infeld, 1961). Stories in science include the metaphors and the 'what if's', which only reach maturity when they are converted into explanations supported and accepted by the scientific community after thorough testing and collecting empirical evidence (Negrete & Lartigue, 2010). Although science theories are validated through supporting and rejecting hypotheses or predictions, they have creative and dramatic origins. Medawar (1969) reminds us that hypotheses often arise by guesswork, imagination and inspiration, not by linear, deductive thinking. He distinguishes between the creative process and the testing of a hypothesis, which is a strictly logical and rigorous process to ultimately determine the fate of the hypothesis, which is either supported or discarded by the test:

> The purpose of scientific enquiry is not to compile an inventory of factual information . . . We should think of it rather as a logically articulated structure of justifiable beliefs about nature. It begins as a story about a possible world – a story which we invent and criticise and modify as we go along, so that it ends by being, as nearly as we can make it, a story about real life. (Medawar, 1969, p. 59)

Stories in science are about the actions of real-life people and the scientific process such as the discovery of DNA. While the discovery of DNA could be described as a series of experiments by Watson, Crick, Wilkins, Franklin and Pauling, it could alternatively be described as a race among laboratories and a jostling amongst protagonists, ending in rewards for Watson, Crick, Wilkins and lack of recognition for Franklin. The biography written by Brenda Maddox (2003) tells the story of Rosalind Franklin, 'the dark lady of DNA', describing her as single-minded, forthright and tempestuous in her decision to become a scientist at the young age of 15, but whose role in the great discovery was airbrushed out of history, and finally ending in her premature death. Such a story evokes emotion, sympathy and admiration for Franklin. Through stories, students can learn that science is not about a process of verification. When stories are used to learn science, students enjoy the triumph and compare the difficulties, which the scientists experience with their own struggles to understand scientific concepts. In fact, science research is often a very emotional and personal adventure, so students learn about the scientific process by following the twists and turns in the stories and the successes and failures depicted (Solomon, 2008).

Stories in science learning can also include the substantive content and concepts of science in ways that make them relevant to everyday life (Norris, Guilbert, Smith, Hakimelahi, & Phillips, 2005). Take, for example, the following passage, which contains biological concepts from a leading storyteller of science, Richard Dawkins:

> It is raining DNA outside. On the bank of the Oxford canal at the bottom of my garden is a large willow tree, and it is pumping downy seeds into the air . . . DNA whose coded characters spell out specific instructions for building willow trees that will shed a new generation of downy seeds . . . It is raining instructions out there; it's raining programs; it's raining tree-growing, fluff-spreading, algorithms. That is not a metaphor, it is the plain truth. It couldn't be any plainer if it were raining floppy discs. (Dawkins, 1986, p. 111)

This story has a narrator and an agency. The narrator is known and he is asking us to imagine molecular DNA being distributed with a purpose through the air by an agent – the seed. Although the readers may not be located at Oxford University, they can imagine a similar process occurring in their own backyards wherever they are located across the globe. There is a connection and there is a consequence that this DNA rain is sending down instructions just like a computer to create new cells.

We learn from such stories. Stories help us to understand the abstract and impose coherence on a set of events. They help us to imagine and feel the experience of others, and they engage and motivate us. Storytelling stimulates an emotional response that fixes attention and leads to understanding, which may result in better long-term memory. This is perhaps because a story mimics the underlying cognitive structure required to understand the concept (Klassen, 2010). Graesser and Ottati (1995) suggest that for stories to be effective in memory representation they must be accessed at a later point of time to answer questions and be applied to real-life situations. In the immediate term, stories influence people's understandings sufficiently to lead to social change (Avraamidou & Osborne, 2009).

Stories in science are also important because they break the mystique that science content is an objective body of knowledge. Much has been said about the abstracted, disembodied and decontextualised content of science when it is taught as a body of facts that students have to memorise, so common in university science courses. In contrast, the development of science knowledge is often an iterative, personal and emotional process of investigation. In fact the discovery of science knowledge is anything but objective and decontextualised. The mysteriousness and opacity of the traditional way science is taught estranges students because it disconnects them from their everyday experiences and presents science as uncontroversial, unquestionable and unequivocal knowledge that needs to be memorised (Avraamidou & Osborne, 2009). Presenting content to students emphasises the product of a scientific endeavour, but often fails to portray the subjective and nonlinear process of developing this knowledge. The effect of this is that people disappear from science as agents in the story. Students end up positioned outside the theories which science develops, like spectators looking in (Avraamidou & Osborne, 2009). Storytelling breaks this traditional logical and formal style of discourse and mode of knowing commonly used in science learning (Negrete & Lartigue, 2010). The language of stories is unlike any language used in many science classrooms, which is generally objective, authoritative, impersonal and humourless. Stories use everyday language, alien to the world of science, making the science more accessible to students. The rules of language in science remove the emotive and forbid the dramatic. Suspense, mystery and the elements of surprise are also removed (Lemke, 1990). Lemke summarises by stating that the norms of scientific language veto most of the techniques that all good communicators and storytellers know are necessary for engaging the interest of an audience and helping them to identify with the point of view. Much of the alienation is the excision of the personal (Avraamidou & Osborne, 2009), the metaphoric, the sensational and the fictional. A recount of scientific fact in the science classroom is separated from the world of human values, judgements and interests and, as Lemke (1990) concludes, to be a good communicator and teacher of science you need to go against these rules and violate the stylistic norms to humanise the science. If Lemke is correct, then almost all good teachers are also good storytellers, and this has always been apparent to good teachers (Klassen, 2010).

If stories do all these things, then why are stories missing from traditional science teaching? They are missing despite a significant number of authors advocating for a storytelling approach in science learning (Avraamidou & Osborne, 2009; Bickmore & Grandy, 2007; Klassen, 2010; Negrete & Lartigue, 2010; Norris *et al.*, 2005; Solomon, 2008). Many have suggested that we excessively worry about the rigour and objective view of science knowledge to maintain the status of new knowledge. Others have suggested that there are benefits from maintaining the mystique of science and reserving it for the so-called 'student geniuses' with good memories (Lemke, 1990).

Whatever the reason(s), there is now urgency for change in science learning. Enrolments in science, both at secondary and tertiary level, are declining nationally and internationally and government reports indicate a widespread decrease in student engagement (Goodrum, Druhan, & Abbs, 2011; Rice, Thomas & O'Toole, 2009). In addition, technology is causing disruptive changes to pedagogies and in higher education this disruption is acute. With falling attendance of students at lectures and the expectation that learning should be anytime and anywhere (Johnson, Adams Becker, Estrada, & Freeman, 2014), the value of learning content in lectures and the on-campus experience is being questioned. Johnson *et al.* argue that there is a growing shift to students as co-creators of content rather than consumers of content. The ubiquitous presence of personal digital technologies and the rise of a maker-space culture are creating opportunities for new ways to tell science stories creatively.

Creating a digital story has become relatively easy technologically in recent years because of the exponential growth of personal mobile phones and computers preloaded with free movie-making software (Hoban & Nielsen, 2010). This exponential growth coincides with the dual body of research that suggests that storytelling and multimodal representations of science concepts can enhance science learning.

The aim of this chapter is to describe how student-generated digital storytelling can be used to engage students in learning science content. It includes a description of what characterises a story in science, how narratives and storytelling using digital media have been used in tertiary-level biology and environmental science at a major metropolitan university and why storytelling pedagogy may improve student understanding of scientific concepts. The chapter will tell the story of the use of digital media in curriculum design and provide examples on how to implement storytelling in science learning at any education level.

What is a story?

A story in science is an account of a sequence or series of events that are connected either factually or fictitiously. Although some authors create distinctions between a story and a narrative, to distinctly separate stories from narratives is difficult. Solomon (2008) defines stories broadly as narratives with characters that are interlinked through science knowledge. The story has three aspects: a person; the story as a person's thought; a distinct point of view with a teller and listener. Avraamidou and Osborne (2009) describe four types of scientific text, one being the narrative in science textbooks, which either take the form of a 'narrative in science' or a 'narrative in nature'. Narratives in science can be framed through scientists developing a claim supported by data. Narratives in nature are popularising articles where plants or animals are the subjects and their activities are presented as a story. This is a subset of the narrative genre, which describes a series of actions and experiences by real or imagined characters. Klassen (2010) states that, while all stories are narratives, not all narratives are stories, because narratives lack the critical elements found in stories. Klassen further proposes that stories are a temporal sequence of events with a beginning, middle and end and the events possess a causative or intentional element involving action of humans or human-like agents. This is in contrast to the expository text that is most often found in science and its associated textbooks that strive to eliminate the subjective and human. Bruner (1986) states that narratives are stories that order human experience, and makes a distinction between the structure of a story and the meaning and feelings of the narrative, which can evoke sympathy, anger or sadness. Norris *et al*. (2005) provide a framework to construct a narrative requiring particular occurrences or events. This framework has eight elements: (i) a sequence of events; (ii) a narrator that determines the point; (iii) a narrative appetite which creates in readers and listeners a desire to know what will happen; (iv) written in the past tense; (v) a structure which may include imbalances with complications, successes and failures; (vi) an agent that may be human or other; (vii) a purpose to help us imagine or understand the natural world; and (viii) a reader who approaches the text with expectations and anticipation. Table 6.1 presents examples of narratives created in a first-year biology subject.

Avraamidou and Osborne (2009) point out distinctions in the structure of a narrative between Norris *et al*. (2005), Toolan (2001) and Chatman (1978) (cited in Avraamidou & Osborne 2009) especially in terms of tense and agency. All agree that narratives require events, a narrator and agency, be they agent, human or non-human material objects.

For stories to be used in science learning, what narrative elements are valuable? Avraamidou and Osborne (2009) emphasise that narratives should include three main elements: (i) events (i.e. a sequence of events that are connected with a structure where events are temporally related, beginning, middle and end); (ii) a narrator; and (iii) an agency (i.e. human or non-humans that act on each other). Norris *et al*. (2005) also includes the elements *purpose*, which provides the reader with some picture of the scientist's vision of the material world and *time*, which is also considered a central defining element. There is a consensus view that the time frame of a narrative should be in the past, 'someone telling someone that something happened' – like 'once upon a time'. Whether narratives in science need only

TABLE 6.1 Examples of narratives created in first year biology at a large metropolitan university

Narrative context	Narrative task	Narrative prompt questions
You notice you have been in the bath for too long because your fingers and toes are wrinkled in appearance.	In 200 words or less, create a narrative on how water moves into the cells in your fingers and toes. Your explanation should include all of the following biological terms: high concentration, low concentration, random movement of water molecules, diffusion	You can prepare for this task by answering the following questions: • What does the term concentration mean? Does it have a volume or area associated with it? • Are water molecules constantly moving? If so are they moving randomly or along a concentration gradient or both? • Compare and contrast the movement of people into a soccer stadium with the movement of water molecules into your fingers. • Imagine you are the size of a water molecule. How will you manage to pass through the skin layer of a finger or toe? • Zoom up into the macroscopic world of your finger. Why is it wrinkled in appearance? Find out why this does not happen.
You have been given a decaying, wooden log by your teacher. She poses the following question: 'Where does the mass of this dry log come from?'	In 200 words or less, write a narrative to describe where the mass of the tree (solid found in the wood) comes from. Your narrative should include the following biological terms: chlorophyll, chloroplasts, water, carbon dioxides, oxygen, photosynthesis	You can prepare for this task by answering these questions: • Zoom down to focus on a carbon dioxide gas molecule moving along a concentration gradient into the leaf. • Zoom down to focus on an oxygen molecule moving along a concentration gradient out of the leaf. Zoom out and back to the exterior of the leaf.

concern past events is questionable. Science being predictive, a story can hypothetically create a narrative that connects events and by the nature of being a prediction, the events could occur in the future.

Implementation

Narrative explanations and storytelling have been implemented in the curriculum in undergraduate biology, invertebrate biology and environmental science at a major metropolitan university in Sydney for several years. It was less than 20 years ago that digital cameras were supplied to the consumer market. Even in the first decade of the twenty-first century, it was almost impossible to supply sufficient numbers of digital and video cameras to students and ensure equity of access. This was especially the case in large first-year classes where student enrolments where often greater than 700 students.

In the early 2000s, before the tools to create digital media were ubiquitous, students were directed to create narratives to communicate their understanding in fundamental concepts in biology. In large first-year classes, short 100-word narratives were created by students to explain their understanding in cell biology and genetics. Students wrote narratives explaining the cause of their wrinkly fingers and toes, the result of staying too long in the bath, and resolving the mystery of how it could be possible to get "all my mitochondria from my mother" (see Table 6.1). These narratives included some of the components of a narrative, mainly purpose and events. At the same time, in smaller classes, students were directed to create concept cartoons with a narrative basis using PowerPoint. Keogh and Naylor (1999) developed concept cartoons as a strategy to probe student understanding and misconceptions in key conceptual areas. Although cartoons had been used for a number of years in secondary education across a range of disciplines, they were rarely used in tertiary institutions. Keogh and Naylor argue that concept cartoons allow learners to reflect on the science in their everyday experience, so that relevance is given to the ideas being created. In the context of our work with students in invertebrate anatomy, the concept cartoons they created were highly effective, both to explain invertebrate anatomy, and because they contained all the necessary components of a narrative, including structure and events that generate a desire for the reader to know what will happen next. Many of the cartoons created were in the sequence of a cartoon strip. Even though the static nature of cartoon images in some ways limits the ability to bring the stories to life, at least in comparison to animations, the cartoon strips that the students created were high-quality representations that demonstrate creativity and strong conceptual understanding.

With the exponential growth of personal digital technologies, it has become possible to transform non-digital representations into digital narratives and stories as a new way to engage students with science content. Our first attempt involved the use of flash animation, which resulted in a very high-quality product that was time consuming to create, even with extensive software expertise. It was clear from this experience that a different mode of communication was necessary that would allow all students to animate science content using narratives and storytelling. Slowmation (abbreviated from 'slow animation'), a simplified version of claymation, quickly became the most feasible solution (Hoban, 2005; Hoban & Ferry, 2006).

Students in a large second-year environment unit were set the task of creating digital media on a local, national or global issue or event that was/is considered a 'problem' in the environment. They were instructed to construct a narrative by researching, planning, storyboarding, designing models, taking digital photographs and using technologies (Hoban & Ferry, 2006). Students were asked to use some of the key narrative elements described by Norris *et al.* (2005) ensuring that they had a narrator, a sequence of events and structure, a purpose, a narrative appetite and agency and combine this with cartoons. These elements were easily incorporated into describing an environmental issue. As Avraamidou and Osborne (2009) state, narrative text is more appropriate for representing environmental education than the expository text, which has so far dominated science learning. The result was a series of high-quality stories that were uploaded for sharing with peers to YouTube. Students created stories using such resources as Common Craft (http://www.commoncraft.com/). Other students drew images by hand or painted them, which were then animated using stop motion. Others used a mixture of still images, hand-constructed and cartoon-like characters. All included voice-overs.

Discussion

Creating and assessing narratives and stories

The examples presented describe a process of evolution in implementing storytelling and narratives in a range of units across year levels in a tertiary biology curriculum. Written narratives were used to improve student conceptual understanding of concepts in biology. The concepts targeted were those known to be potentially difficult for students to understand and were threshold concepts (Ross *et al.*, 2010). Concept cartoons were used to create narratives about invertebrate anatomy, as anatomy units can be challenging for students to learn because of the volume of language that requires recall.

Digital narratives in flash animation were also used to visualise the methodological steps in an experiment to test predictions about the natural world. Finally and most recently, narratives were used to communicate environmental problems using slowmation, which is a simplified way of making an animation that enables students to create their own as a new way of learning science (Hoban & Nielsen, 2010).

The digital narratives that students created illustrate various ways of representing content and the nature of the illustrations has changed over time depending on the availability and accessibility of technology. Slowmation is the most-recent mode of digital media. In the early 2000s there was insufficient technology available for all students to create digital media. The ownership of personal digital technology has grown exponentially (Hoban & Nielsen, 2010). It is now estimated that there are 6–7 billion mobile devices in the world and it is predicted that the number of mobile devices will exceed the human population by the end of 2014. Many of these mobile devices have a high-quality camera, meaning that the media-making devices are in students' pockets. Access to such technology, therefore, allows students to create and re-create content and share the digital products on social media. In the current study, the students' digital media creations were presented to their peers in class and also posted on YouTube to share with a broader audience. Over a period of one year, the digital media products received collectively over 400 views. Sharing of content via social media is anticipated to accelerate in the next one to two years and fuel the shift from students as consumers of content to students as creators of content (Johnson *et al.*, 2014).

Digital media creations challenge conventional strategies used to learn science. Although the discovery of science knowledge is a creative process driven by human curiosity, the learning of science knowledge at secondary or tertiary levels is often anything but creative. Digital media creation provides opportunities for students to engage in learning content by being metacognitive about the science concepts and how to best represent them. Science teaching is dominated at all levels by a trans-missive-style approach in lectures, which focuses on the passing on of declarative knowledge with the teacher in the role of the knowledge expert (Tobias, 1990; Tytler, 2007). Even in the practical laboratory, recipe-based, cookbook practicals dominate, and heavily weighted end-of-semester exams assess lower-order reasoning skills, requiring little more than rote memorisation. Secondary science students do not choose science at senior levels because it is 'boring' (Goodrum *et al.*, 2011) and the student exodus from tertiary science has been attributed to rigor mortis rather than rigour. Limitations to these approaches have recently received more attention and more-active learning strategies are now coming into the curricula. Creating a digital story about the content of science or the processes of scientific investigation is one way to provide opportunity for creativity in our increasingly technological world.

Assessment of digital media also needs to reward creativity. In our courses, the weighting of assessment tasks of non-digital and digital media ranged from 10–60%. Although the digital creation is a product, the process of creating the stills prior to animation can largely determine the quality of the final digital product making both the product and the process assessable. Digital media, however, can be time consuming to create. Anecdotally, students report spending 30 hours or more to create one slowmation, which only lasts for 3–5 minutes. Some students and academics argue that the amount of time taken to create digital media, including slowmation, is mismatched with the assessment weighting and learning value. The percentage weighting given to individual assessment tasks in science that occur during the semester is traditionally around 10–15%. The greatest percentage in terms of assessment weighting is given to the final exam, which is generally in the 40–65% range. Although academics say they value on-course assessment and new media in general, there remains inaction on appropriately weighting these types of assessable tasks. Instead academics argue that student performance in on-course assessment may not be reflective of what they know, which must be certified by the final examination. Also, academics insist that there is no assurance that the digital media creation was made by the student. While these arguments continue to have credence, the assessment weightings of digital media tasks will remain low. The value of digital media is in the learning gain and the student experience.

Providing instructions to students to design digital media is not straightforward. Hoban and Nielsen (2010) provide technological direction with timing, materials, orientation, technology and purpose. Purpose is one of the eight elements of a narrative described by Norris *et al.* (2005) and the seven elements described by Avraamidou and Osborne (2009). Both frameworks provide useful guidance on structuring digital media, as do the text examples provided by these authors. A framework for assessing slowmation could be constructed using the elements in the tables in both of these publications. In the current study, only three criteria were used to assess student digital media creations: content, creativity and language (see Table 6.2). This rubric helped to simplify the marking and to emphasise creativity equally with content.

Conclusion

Narratives and stories are thought to lead to higher cognitive gains when compared to expository text, the traditional genre of scientific writing. Narrative text is easier to comprehend and remember than expository text. Also, whereas expository texts are hierarchical, narrative texts include a sequential pattern of events. When one part readily evokes the next, the sequence is more similar to the cognitive structure of scientific explanations (Ogborn, Kress, Martins, & McGillicuddy, 1996). When Negrete and Lartigue (2010) taught narrative and expository ways of communicating scientific information to different groups and compared their responses in exams, the researchers found that although performance in the exams was similar for both groups of students, the narrative group retained information longer. Research has also shown that creating digital media improves understanding and recall, perhaps because of the relationship between the representation (digital media) and the referent (the concept or content) (Hoban & Nielsen, 2010). Narratives are also amusing, attractive and enjoyable and connect to students' emotions that are often removed from the objective science world (Sutton & Wheatley, 2003).

Will there be some disadvantages to using narratives and telling stories in science? The answer here is yes. Inevitably there will be some students who feel that they are not being taught genuine science (Lemke, 1990), but breaking this tradition allows more people access to science information. So why use digital stories to provide increased opportunities to represent science? In a recent article, Eagleman (2013) provided a manifesto on why students should be taught to communicate science in different ways. He states that science needs to move from the cloisters of academia into the public sphere. Communicating science into the public sphere will hopefully stem the flow of bad information, inform public policy, clarify what science is and is not and share the raw beauty of the scientific pursuit. It is very difficult for the public to access the information written using

TABLE 6.2 Assessment criteria for a slowmation task

	Standards		
	Does not Meet Criteria	Meets Criteria	More than Meets Criteria
Content	More thought and work is required to translate the content in case study/case report into an electronic resource. □ 1	Content in case study/case report is reasonably translated but needs additional research, thought and application. Issues could be better communicated effectively and engagingly. □ 3	Content in case study/case report is translated by additional research and unique applications. Issues are communicated effectively and engagingly. □ 5
Creativity	More creativity and original/novel thought is required. □ 0	Materials incorporate some use of visual, auditory, animation, video and/or interactive content in creating a resource. □ 7	Materials incorporate substantial use of visual, auditory, animation, video and/or interactive content in creating a polished and professional resources in a novel and interesting manner □ 10
Control of Language	Your text is filled with errors in grammar, spelling and/or punctuation and references that frequently interfere with meaning. □ 0	Your text contains few errors in grammar, spelling and/or punctuation and references and these errors do not interfere with meaning. □ 4	Your text contains no errors in grammar, spelling, punctuation and references. □ 5

the scientific genre without training. The formal structure of a scientific journal article conceals the narrative and story, which are the thought processes that lead to the research and conclusions (Medawar, 1969). Although this is changing and some journals are implementing graphics, video abstracts and audio slides with interactive graphs, there is still some way to go.

We have examples of scientists who are brilliant storytellers, including Attenborough, Dawkins, Medawar, Carl Sagan and EO Wilson, but there will always be many scientists who struggle with translating the findings of their research in understandable ways. To improve this, we need to be better science communicators and part of this is being better storytellers. We are storytelling organisms leading socially and storied lives (Connelly & Clandinin, 1990). Through creating slowmations and other digital media, students at all levels of education can tell these narratives and stories of science.

References

Avraamidou, L. & Osborne, J. (2009). The role of the narrative in communicating science. *International Journal of Science Education, 31*(12), 1683–1707. doi: 10.1080/0950069080 2380695

Bickmore, B. R. & Grandy, D. A. (2007). *Science as storytelling*. Retrieved from http://blogs. evergreen.edu/cpat/files/2013/04/scienceAsStory4_2.pdf (accessed 19 March, 2015).

Bruner, J. (1986). *Actual minds, possible worlds*. Cambridge, MA: Harvard University Press.

Chatman, S. (1978). *Story and discourse: Narrative structure in fiction and film*. Ithaca, NY: Cornell University Press.

Connelly, M. F. & Clandinin, D. J. (1990). Stories of experience and narrative inquiry. *Educational Researcher, 19*(5), 2–14.

Dawkins, R. (1986). *The blind watchmaker*. New York: Norton and Company.

Eagleman, D. M. (2013). Why public dissemination of science matters: A manifesto. *Journal of Neuroscience, 33*(30), 12147–12149.

Einstein, A. & Infeld, L. (1961). *The evolution of physics*. New York: Simon and Schuster.

Goodrum, D., Druhan, A. & Abbs, J. (2011). *The status and quality of year 11 and 12 science in Australian schools*. Canberra: Australian Academy of Science. Retrieved from https://www. science.org.au/sites/default/files/user-content/year-1112-report-final.pdf (accessed 19 March, 2015).

Gottschall, J. (2013). The science of storytelling: How narrative cut through distraction like nothing else. [Weblog post] Retrieved from http://www.fastcocreate.com/3020044/ the-science-of-storytelling-how-narrative-cuts-through-distraction (accessed 19 March, 2015).

Graesser, A. C. & Ottati, V. (1995). Why stories? Some evidence, questions, and challenges. In R. S. Wyer, Jr. & T. Krull (Eds.), *Advances in social cognition (VIII), knowledge and memory: The real story* (pp. 121–132). Hillsdale, NJ: Lawrence Erlbaum.

Hoban, G. & Nielsen, W. (2010). The 5Rs: A new teaching approach to encourage slowma-tions (student-generated animations) of science concepts. *Teaching Science, 56*(3), 33–38.

Hoban, G. F. (2005). From claymation to slowmation: A teaching procedure to develop students' science understandings. *Teaching Science: Australian Science Teachers' Journal, 51*(2), 26–30.

Hoban, G. F. & Ferry, B. (2006). *Teaching science concepts in higher education classes with slow motion animation (slowmation)*. World Conference on E-Learning in Corporate, Government,

Healthcare & Higher Education (pp. 1641–1646). Chesapeake, VA: Association for the Advancement of Computing in Education. Retrieved from http://ro.uow.edu.au/cgi/viewcontent.cgi?article=1910&context=edupapers (accessed 19 March, 2015).

Johnson, L., Adams Becker, S., Estrada, V. & Freeman, A. (2014). *NMC horizon report: 2014 higher education edition*. Austin, TX: The New Media Consortium. Retrieved from http://www.nmc.org/publications/2014-horizon-report-higher-ed (accessed 19 March, 2015).

Keogh, B. & Naylor, S. (1999). Concept cartoons, teaching and learning in science: An evaluation. *International Journal of Science Education*, *21*(4), 431–446.

Klassen, S. (2010). The relation of story structure to a model of conceptual change in science learning. *Science & Education*, *19*, 305–317. doi: 10.1007/s11191–009–9212–8

Lemke, L. J. (1990). *Talking science: Language, learning and values*. Norwood, NJ: Ablex.

Maddox, B. (2003). *Rosalind Franklin: The dark lady of DNA*. London: HarperCollins.

McWilliam, E., Poronnik, P. & Taylor, P. G. (2008). Re-designing science pedagogy: Reversing the flight from science. *Journal of Science Education and Technology*, *17*(3), 226–235.

Medawar, P. B. (1969). *Induction and intuition in scientific thought*. Philadelphia, PA: American Philosophical Society.

Negrete, A. & Lartigue, C. (2010). The science of telling stories: Evaluating science communication via narratives (RIRC method). *Journal of Media and Communication Studies*, *2*(4), 98–110.

Norris, S. P., Guilbert, S. M., Smith, M. L., Hakimelahi, S. & Phillips, L. M. (2005). A theoretical framework for narrative explanation in science. *Science Education*, *89*, 535–563. doi: 10.1002/sec20063

Ogborn, J., Kress, G., Martins, I. & McGillicuddy, K. (1996). *Explaining science in the classroom*. Buckingham, UK: Open University Press.

Rice, J., Thomas, S. M. & O'Toole, P. (2009). *Tertiary science in the 21st century*. Canberra: Australian Council of Deans of Science.

Ross, P. M., Taylor, C. E., Hughes, C., Kofod, M., Whitaker, N., Lutze-Mann, L. & Tzioumis, V. (2010). Threshold concepts: Challenging the way we think, teach and learn in biology. In J. H. F. Meyer, R. Land & C. Baillie (Eds.), *Threshold concepts and transformational learning* (pp. 165–177). Rotterdam, The Netherlands: Sense.

Solomon, J. (2008). Science stories and science texts: What can they do for our students? *Studies in Science Education*, *37*(1), 85–105. doi: 10.1080/03057260208560178

Sutton, R. E. & Wheatley, K. F. (2003). Teachers' emotions and teaching: A review of the literature and directions for future research. *Educational Psychology Review*, *15*(4), 327–358.

Tobias, S. (1990). They're not dumb. They're different: A new 'tier of talent' for science. *Change*, *22*(4), 11–30.

Toolan, M. J. (2001). *Narrative: A critical linguistic introduction*. London: Routledge.

Tytler, R. (2007). *Re-imagining science education: Engaging students in science for Australia's future*. Australian Education Review No 51. Camberwell, Australia: Australian Council for Educational Research.

VIDEO OVERVIEW

Video is a media form that plays moving visual images at 25–30 frames per second to render a fast-moving image. This rapid speed of images can capture the real-time movement of living things and many mobile devices such as phones now come with in-built video functioning. Websites such as YouTube and Vimeo also provide repositories for video sharing and display. The next section of the book provides a wide range of innovative ways that videos have been created by students to learn or communicate science. Most of the videos are narrated to explain science concepts and, hence, are multimodal and display the modes of fast-moving images (the video) accompanied by voice or speech (the narration). These modes can be further enhanced by adding the modes of writing, such as captions, to explain the science or music to enhance meaning of the media.

There are some really innovative ways that students can create videos for science learning and communication. In Chapter 7, Julian Cox explains a way in which students have interviewed and videoed experts in different science disciplines to get a sense of purpose in their undergraduate degrees. In Chapter 8, Gwen Lawrie encourages her students to make video blogs (vlogs) to explain different types of chemical reactions to engage students in learning and communicating key ideas of a chemical reaction. In Chapter 9, Gerry Rayner encourages students to conduct environmental field studies as a way to understand topics such as climate change. Students then summarise their research in a 3–4-minute video. Iouri and Regina Belski take an innovative approach to learning about electronics, by getting students to design and make teaching resources for other students in the form of narrated videos demonstrating dynamic worked examples. This notion of getting students to design teaching resources for other students is a good way to learn because, in making a resource, students think like a teacher in organising the content – they need to understand it themselves, zero in on the key points, organise information in coherent steps and think about the language used for the relevant audience. The value of students learning by designing teaching resources for other students has been substantiated in a recent study in the cognitive sciences (Nestojko, Bui, Kornell & Bjork, 2014). In Chapter 11, Matthew Kearney, Kimberley Pressick-Killborn and Peter Aubbusson show how generating videos can help students understand and communicate science or they can be used as inquiry tools to examine science processes more closely.

References

Nestojko, J. F., Bui, D. C., Kornell, N. & Bjork, E. L. (2014). Expecting to teach enhances learning and organization of knowledge in free recall of text passages. *Memory and Cognition, 42*, 1038–1048.

7

VIDEO INTERVIEWS IN SCIENCE AND ENGINEERING FOR PROFESSIONAL PERSPECTIVES

Julian M. Cox

Context

The story of this approach to learning and assessment began in a highly structured professional degree program in Food Science and Technology at a university in Sydney, Australia. In 1995, the program was, surprisingly, very traditionally academic. Year 1 was filled completely with foundation courses in biology, chemistry and physics. Students felt little connection with the discipline or the program until Year 2. Further, while some upper-level food courses addressed more professionally relevant aspects of industry, such as management, courses were largely technical in their treatment of food science and technology, and assessment by technical assignment and examination was pervasive. There was little focus on the communicative versus technical aspects of written work and, similarly, little if any explicit attention given to many generic skills, such as oral and interpersonal communication and teamwork.

Over the next few years, and in conjunction with colleagues, first one then two courses were introduced in Year 1, with an ultimate focus on technical, social and professional acculturation. The first course introduced students to all of the academic staff associated with the program, providing a sense of belonging to the program as well as, through a lecture series, the diversity of areas that constitute the Food Science and Technology program. The second course, through a range of experiential classes and related assessment tasks, provided instruction and practice relating to a range of professional skills as well as professional acculturation. Of most relevance to the latter, and to this chapter, was a group/team-based video assignment. As a cohort the class discussed and developed a list of various roles and functions needed in the food industry that might be undertaken by a food scientist or technologist. Students self-selected into groups and then, by mutual interest, chose one of the identified aspects of the food industry that most interested them as a group. The task was a first-come, first-served choice where the groups then identified and interviewed a food industry professional in the chosen role or aspect of the industry. Through a compilation of the videos and a peer-review process, the cohort could gain a patchwork perspective of the industry as a whole. Individually, students gained a variety of insights into professional life in food science and technology.

My move to the Faculty of Science as Associate Dean (Education) in 2008 led to the assumption of responsibility (in 2009/10) for Year 1 Faculty of Science (designated SCIF1xxx) courses, designed to provide students with an experience not unlike that in the Food Science and Technology program: broadly speaking, professional perspective and practice. Such courses are compulsory in the Medical Science and Advanced Science programs, and elective in the Bachelor of Science. The SCIF courses are designed, in whole or at least large part, with the following purposes in mind:

- Acculturation of students, at two levels. The first is to ensure a sense of belonging within the respective cohorts, particularly among Advanced Science students, who ultimately undertake a diversity of majors, with the cohort consequently fragmenting in upper years. Second, and of particular relevance here, is early and foundational acculturation to the professional world, interacting with scientists, the community and its practices.
- Professional practice. Through a tutorial component of the SCIF courses, students engage in instructional and experiential activities relating to a range of skills relevant to professional life, including interpersonal and formal oral and written communication, group/team roles, dynamics and processes, ethics and codes of practice.
- Professional perspectives. Students are afforded the opportunity to explore their professional practice in relation to their chosen area of study or intended major, thereby engaging early with their discipline and community, gaining a sense of their professional futures that also personalises their learning. This includes a 'lecture stream' in the Advanced Science course in which students choose to participate in largely research-process activities in the context of the broad area of their discipline. That is, students form a sub-cohort to learn more about their area of interest, such as mathematics, psychology or chemistry.

In 2009, the Advanced Science SCIF1121 course included a 'World-wide Day in Science' assignment, in which individual students would interview a scientist on a given day, the intention being for the whole cohort to gain perspectives about professional scientists and, collectively, the diversity (similarities/commonalities and differences) among a collection of scientists on that one day. This assignment, as well as being individual, was produced largely in written form, with the potential for selected examples to be uploaded to a website and produced as a multimedia piece, with text as the core, augmented with still images and, occasionally, a short video.

Since 2009, the task has evolved into the following assignment, based on the desire to incorporate a group/team-based assessment task and the use of video as the main medium, based on the similar assignment from Food Science and Technology. In Year 1 SCIF courses, a small group (3–4) of students conducts a videotaped interview with a scientist, producing from that interview a video that is then shared with all other students within each specific course, where it is critiqued by the members of two other groups within the cohort. This task speaks to all three purposes of the courses. Students self-select their groups, though they are encouraged to form those groups on the basis of common interest – that is, the task is likely to have most meaning and be of most benefit to all members of the group if they share a common area of scientific interest or even the same intended major, and then select a scientist from that area, discipline or major. This affords students the opportunity to gain valuable professional perspective. I consider this to be the most valuable aspect of the task.

Most recently, a very similar task has been introduced as part of the development of a new (2014) Year 3 course in Mechanical and Manufacturing Engineering (MMAN3000) which, like the FOOD and SCIF Courses, is non-technical, aimed at development or enhancement of professional skills and perspectives. In fact, the triple tag line of the course is 'job-ready, thesis-ready and team-ready'. With that somewhat historical background and providing a broad context, the remainder of the chapter will focus on both pedagogical and production processes in specific courses (FOOD, SCIF and MMAN) in the faculties of Science and Engineering at the University of New South Wales, Sydney.

Implementation

In all three courses, students are made aware through an orientation lecture very early in the semester not only of the mechanistic nature of the task, or what has to be done, but the pedagogical underpinnings – the 'whys' of the task. Instructional sessions and activities on group roles, dynamics and processes are delivered through lectures and/or tutorials and homework (minor assessment tasks). Students are reminded of the video assignment and encouraged to seek connections between the assessment task and group or teamwork as a process, along with delivery of the video as a product.

Group formation

Coincident with these activities, students are required to form groups (of 3–4) as early as possible. In the case of the Year 1 FOOD and SCIF courses, students are permitted to self-select. Given the challenging and critical transitional nature of Year 1, it is considered that working with newly formed relationships is a positive that outweighs group member selection based on a range of other parameters. In the MMAN course, group formation is a directed process (as outlined next), given that students are in Year 3 and need to move beyond working with friends, onto their professional and personal development.

In all cases, group formation and execution of the task is encouraged or selected in part on the basis of mutual interest relevant to the students' possible career. That is, in the case of the FOOD task, groups are encouraged to pursue an aspect of the industry of interest to all group members. Similarly, SCIF students are encouraged to learn about a scientist relevant to their intended major or at least in an area of strong interest. In both cases, relationships may still take precedence during group formation, although topic choice also has an influence. In the SCIF courses, formation of groups aligned with interest facilitates an intermingling of students, enhancing the sense of belonging and student identity, another aim of the course.

The MMAN course is a different matter. In this Year 3 course, groups are formed on the basis of criteria, which in some cases are negotiated, with others specific to the task. The criteria range from availability to meet during the week to having interview skills or video-editing experience. One of the criteria relates to the particular area of study, so mutual interest is still factored in, but as only one facet in the group formation process. Group formation is facilitated through use of CATME, a suite of web-based tools for group formation and group member evaluation, developed in engineering education (http://info.catme.org; Layton, Loughry, Ohland & Ricco, 2010). Based on similarities or differences in student responses to a set of standard and/or custom questions, groups are created to optimise membership based on logistics and roles/functions, rather than existing relationships.

Interviewee selection

The decision around the choice of interview subject is dictated in part by differences in the nature and aims of the task and in part by the nature of the student group, as well as a thematic priority of each course. In all three courses, selection of an interviewee is driven by the intended professional destination (broadly defined) of the students. For example, in the FOOD and MMAN courses, the professional destination is seen as industry, so the expectation is that the student groups interview a subject based in industry. This is particularly important in the MMAN course, as the interview task may also assist students in finding an industrial training placement, a compulsory component of their program. In SCIF1121, in which Advanced Science students are seen as future research leaders, the subject must be a research scientist and, given their Year 1 status, students are permitted to interview on campus (which is logistically much easier). More specifically, finer selection is based on consensus or unanimous agreement, which is in turn based on 'plan', intended major or area of interest – in the case of SCIF1121, for example, this might be psychology, physics or microbiology.

The interview

The interview process is only loosely guided, in that a short series of questions are provided as a prescribed starting point. This provides a base level of consistency across the interviews, assisting teachers in assessment, but also facilitating comparative insights for students. Students are strongly encouraged to formulate additional questions and be prepared to generate questions as the interview proceeds, based on responses from the subject. Further, students are required to seek resources providing advice on effective interview techniques to enhance their process.

The duration of the interview itself is not prescribed. This is a negotiation between the students, in formulating their strategy and questions and, in turn, between the group and their subject. Thus, groups have the opportunity to generate as much raw footage as they are afforded with the cooperation of the subject. The duration of the video for presentation is set at 5–10 minutes, as a broad guideline. The duration may vary, with viewability contingent upon the talent of the subject, though 10 minutes appears to be a duration suitable for conveying a clear picture of the subject to the audience (other students in the course). To some extent, duration is also determined by production values; the higher the quality of the video (as well as the subject), the easier the viewing and the longer the video can be.

The location for the interview is not prescribed, but students in FOOD and MMAN courses are encouraged to interview 'on location' or in conjunction with a site visit, to gain perspectives of place additional to perspectives from the subject. For example, a FOOD interview might take place, in part, at or close to a manufacturing plant, so students gain a sense of the smell, noise and other sensory characteristics of the workplace. Such experiences are memorable and lend authenticity.

Technical considerations

The interview is, of course, produced on video. While availability and ownership of devices for video capture are increasingly pervasive, the device used can have a significant impact upon the quality of the final product. This is especially true if the resolution of the device, and thus the raw footage, is inferior. It is much easier to view, and for a longer period, a video in which high production values are evident. In Science, the Faculty Learning and Teaching Unit has invested in HD video cameras to ensure the raw footage is of high quality and to ensure groups have access to a camera if one is not available among the group membership.

On occasion, subject to availability of expertise, students have been given instruction and advice on video making, including use of cameras and production values. Provision of such advice is highly recommended, as the overall and average quality of the final product seems to improve with such input. Students are responsible for the editing of raw footage into a final movie. At the most basic level, students undertake no or minimal editing, typically reflecting little overall effort in completing the task. Many students edit footage down to fit the guideline time frame and also add simple elements such as titles and credits. From discussions with students, such editing is achieved using commonly available software such as iMovie (Mac) and Movie Maker (Windows). From feedback, this is the most frustrating part of the task, though this also represents an opportunity for students to develop new specific skills and engaging with new techniques (as is common in STEM disciplines). As well, students develop personally through perseverance with this specific task, as the assignment in general often requires this.

Typically, videos have been uploaded to UNSW TV. Through the use of settings, privacy can be maintained (a constraint often placed by the subject) and access restricted to members of the course. Templates can also be used to drive further and automated processing, and to include elements such as faculty branding and copyright conditions. Videos are viewable from a streaming server that uses automated transcoding and allows for a range of formats across a range of bandwidths. Current (2014) iterations of the SCIF and MMAN courses are making use of a new activity within Moodle, the Media Collection, in which students, as individuals or teams, can create a gallery of audio, image or video files for display or assessment (https://moodle.org/plugins/view.php?plugin=mod_mediagallery). This activity links seamlessly to YouTube videos, with unlisted videos providing both access and privacy. A new version of UNSW TV, currently in production, will see cloud storage of content and access to that content via Moodle Media Collection.

An interview transcript

While a video cannot be presented here, the task can be exemplified through the excerpts, here drawn from a 2014 interview of Professor Michael Archer. While the simplest examples present the interview alone, a number of videos start with a novel introduction or, as here, an introduction of the subject:

> [Introduction: voice-over, showing footage of Mike at his desk, taking measurements of a piece of fossilised skull.]

> Mike Archer is a Professor of Paleontology in the School of BEES at UNSW. Some notable projects that he has been involved in are the Thylacine Project and the Lazarus Project, which aim to bring extinct species back to life. He has also been involved in many fossil excavations and discoveries in the Riversleigh site in northern Australia.

One of the major aims of the task is to get a sense of what the subject's job involves generally and Professor Archer's words offer unique insight into his work:

> I'm a Professor in the School of BEES, Biological, Earth and Environmental Sciences, but I was the Dean of Science here [at UNSW Australia]. So, I have fairly eclectic interests across a wide range of sciences, and a little beyond the sciences, the science fiction around the science part. When I retired as Dean in 2009, I then became a full-time research professor. So, I'm teaching, about half my time is teaching, and about half is doing research on a whole range of different initiatives, and I'm having fun [smiling broadly].

And specifically:

> I started the Thylacine Project, which was kind of a hope for effort to recover DNA of the extinct Tasmanian Tiger or Thylacine. I started that work in

about 2000 when I was Director of the Australian Museum. The technology was nowhere near the point at which, even if we did get the DNA, that we could use that to bring the Thylacine back. Geneticists said it would never keep that DNA intact, considering that the specimen that I started with had been collected in 1866. Suffice to say, that everything we put up, every geneticist said was impossible, we smiled and tried it anyway, and it did work. There was DNA. Contrary to what they said, that we couldn't use the polymerase chain reaction [PCR], which is molecular cloning, to get enough of what you've recovered to be able to work with . . . And at first it didn't work but then [named scientist], one of the people on the team, just put her thinking cap on and figured a way around the problem and discovered that she could do PCR. So all the barriers were knocked over one after another and that was, I think, probably one of the first de-extinction projects tried anywhere in the world. So I started thinking about the gastric brooding frog, a frog that went extinct about 40 years ago [video produced 2014], but people knew about it enough to know how exciting it was. It was the only frog in the world that swallowed its fertilised eggs and then gave birth using its stomach to fully formed frogs, which is amazing. And we are at the point where we have got embryos back of this extinct frog. Science lurches ahead.

Including the best and worst aspects:

It's hard to think of any worst aspects. I guess the only worst aspect is the bureaucracy of the university, all the filing out of forms, the explosion of paperwork. You can't do anything these days without filling out a ridiculous number of forms and checklists and things, and this really slows us down. Even research, you could be spending fifty percent of your time writing research grants, only some of which will succeed. The good part . . . is discovery. It's just so much fun, not just to find out, test what you already know, and just corroborate ideas and concepts but to . . . I guess in paleontology, I get this all the time . . . [picks up rock] . . . this particular rock for example, I pick it up in the field, I don't know what's in that rock. It's just so exciting to think what might be there.

In the case of Year 1 courses, it is desirable for students in transition to understand how professionals experienced that time:

I went to Princeton University first. My first year in Princeton, I have to say was, in some ways, disappointing. Since I was 11, I really knew where I was going. I mean, I was a classic nerd. Man, I was deep into fossils and geology, deep into animals. I wasn't interested in people. I don't even remember how many courses I might have had at Princeton, but there would have been probably hundreds . . . I have no idea. So we had a lot of little courses. This is more typically American Ivy League-type education. So, you're introduced, you're considered to be broadened by this. You're given everything from ancient art to Greek, German, every conceivable course . . . right across the spectrum . . . First year philosophy . . . I loved that. But here we don't do that. Here we tend to channel students fairly quickly into a career path. And I'm not sure what is the better way to go.

There is a desire to have students gain a sense of the whole person, often asking subjects about their life or interests outside of work:

I have to say, most of my work interests flow over into all the time I've got. There's a big overlap. But, inserted in the middle, at nearly every chance I get, are movies. I mean, it's not the present world we live in isn't sufficient, it is, but there's people who have imagined alternative worlds, different ways of thinking about things. It's a bit like an obsession with reading, but for me I can't stand sitting there doing nothing, reading a book. But I can be doing exercise and watching a movie. When I'm in the car, I'm listening to audio books all the time, reading me wonderful stories. I guess most of the external activities, intellectual ones, involve listening to the wisdom coming out of others' people's heads, podcasts from science shows and things like that. So there's a steady stream of that around me all the time.

Further, subjects often provide advice, whether or not solicited through questioning:

I think the biggest advice I could give . . . well, two bits of advice . . . In terms of pursuing a career . . . It's trite, though on the other hand it's the kind of truism that we all know about in terms of seeking a partner for life, is that you do not marry for money. Sometimes you can marry for money and love, and that's not bad, but on the other hand, if you have to make a choice, then it has to be for love. And I think choosing a career is exactly the same. You should not, and I see too many people who do, choose a career because they or their parents think it's going to be good, there's lots of money in it. And yet you get to the end of your life and you can have a traumatic epiphany, a moment when you realise you just wasted your life. You've just done what you are not fascinated by, something you didn't love and you're sick of it. Why did you spend your only single life you have doing what you didn't love?

The second bit of advice, which I think is really critical, is do not listen to old farts who tell you what can't be done. There's no more debilitating thing, and yet no more common thing you hear, from academics, particularly after they get to be about 50 or so. They've run their life, they've done their research in particular ways and they have preconceptions. They're getting more and more locked in. They're less and less inclined to subject to questioning everything they took for granted, and they inflict this on you. They want you to accept their understanding of what's going on. And they want you to accept that there's no point in going there, because that won't work or there's no point in trying this because we're pretty sure that won't work. Your job is to know when you're hearing crap from an old fart who is basically so locked in to what they think, trying to indoctrinate you with their same inhibitions about what's possible to be done. Don't let anybody tell you what can't be done.

And final words . . .

We discover our comfort zones, and for me, it's always been the natural world, and it will continue to be. I very much feel a part of the natural world, and that's my comfort zone, past, and future, and present.

Discussion

In terms of the nature of this task, the use of media described elsewhere in this book deals largely with student-generated media to support learning of technical, discipline-based content. While in other tasks, it may be implicit, the emphasis here is explicitly upon development of success skills (teamwork, interpersonal and other communication skills) as well as development of professional perspectives. This aligns very well with the aims of the courses and, indeed, broader imperatives. The regulatory landscape for higher education, underpinned by the requirements of peak community or accrediting bodies such as the Higher Education Standards Panel and Engineers Australia, places greater emphasis on development of skills and competencies beyond the technical knowledge and skills base. The Learning and Teaching Academic Standards for science (Jones & Yates, 2011) dictate that graduates from a bachelor degree program in science will be able to communicate science effectively by "communicating scientific results, information, or arguments, to a range of audiences, for a range of purposes, and using a variety of modes" (p. 11) and to work "effectively, responsibly and safely in an individual or team context" (p. 11). Similarly, the *Stage 1 Competency Standard for Professional Engineer* (Engineers Australia, 2013) requires "effective oral and written communication in professional and lay domains . . . [and] . . . effective team membership and team leadership" (p. 2). The task provides for some warranty in both of these areas of competency. Further, the task has the potential to raise awareness of a range of other competencies, through appropriate questioning of the subject and observation of surroundings.

The major inherent benefit of this form of assessment task, as identified by many students, is the opportunity to meet with and discuss the career of a professional scientist, technologist or engineer. In all courses, the subject is, typically, a professional of long standing. Consequently, this affords students the opportunity to gain insights into their potential future. In many cases, students receive a balanced view, understanding that there are positives and negatives in any career. It is considered important that students gain a realistic view of what it means to be a professional, rather than pursuing a perception. The feedback from students demonstrates excellent alignment with the major objectives of the courses and activity articulated above, to ensure students gain a sense of their professional future. Research into the generation of professional identity in a diversity of fields, primarily human service professions, ranging from nursing (Anderson, 1993) to teaching (Timoštšuk & Ugaste, 2010), suggests that early engagement with professionals or the profession affords students a better or more-accurate perspective of professional life.

The process of producing a video can be, from the student perspective, a limitation; at the least, some students find the actual process of producing and uploading the video to be frustrating. From the instructor's perspective, the technological aspects of movie production and upload offer several benefits. As budding STEM professionals, students need to realise that they will engage with new methods, techniques and experiences throughout their careers and these may not always seem directly relevant. Further, communication using a range of modes is now considered a critical graduate capability, based on the frameworks described above. The challenges presented by this aspect of the task also engender personal development, in areas such as perseverance.

Like many of the activities in the FOOD, SCIF and MMAN courses, the group video assignment provides for personalised learning. At the level of the group, in FOOD and SCIF courses, students have the opportunity to self-select membership, with one driver being the choice of scientist to be interviewed. Taking SCIF as an example, students with personal interest in, say, microbiology can form a group and find and interview a microbiologist. Even if group membership is mixed, and a given student does not identify particularly with the interview subject, that student still has the opportunity to include questions that have personal significance. Thus, at best, the professional perspective gained is directly relevant to *all* group members. At worst, it is directly relevant to a majority (a group is unlikely to select a scientist who is not relevant to most members), while providing to other members more generic perspectives on the life of a STEM professional.

At finer granularity, the interview itself is open to personalisation. The assignment in a given course requires all groups to ask, as a starting point, the same set of questions; this is to ensure a baseline consistency across all interviews, ensuring the inclusion of a range of perspectives, which allow students from all groups to contrast and compare. Even for those questions, the students can decide how the questions are asked. Beyond the core set of questions, students have the opportunity to ask any questions they wish – they are encouraged to use interview techniques that extend from the core, as well as including distinct questions.

This activity and, indeed, the relevant SCIF and MMAN courses in general have implications for learning within the respective programs of study in Science and Engineering, respectively, at UNSW Australia. Unlike much more content-rich courses, the courses described here are not designed to provide a technical underpinning. That said the overall theme of driving independent learning hopefully impacts the approach students take to those content-rich courses. It is hoped that the range of skills developed or, more likely, enhanced in these courses equip or enable students to perform better in a range of tasks, based on the instruction, exploration and practice of a range of success skills. The task supports identity and belonging within the cohort, typically seeing group membership bridging a range of differences, facilitating the forging of relationships between students. The comfort afforded students, particularly those in transition through acculturation to cohort and community, provides a safer environment in which to foster independence and self-efficacy (Krause, Hartley, James & McInnis, 2005), addressing an important paradox in higher education (McInnis & James, 1995).

With respect to the video interview, the task supports professional and personal development, providing a professionally relevant opportunity to practice oral and interpersonal communication as well as group or teamwork skills. It also speaks to other professionally relevant concepts, such as ethics and codes of practice. Further, the insights or perspectives gained through the process should provide students with a much greater ability to understand their place in what they perceive as their community, or even in their program. At worst, and most relevant to Year 1 students, these perspectives enable students to make an informed choice about continuing with their present program of study (there is no point wasting their time). Of course, at best, understanding place should enhance the affective domain of student learning, providing an emotional boost and greater motivation to study, in turn, enhancing resilience or reducing attrition.

The production of student-generated videos documenting aspects of the career path and activity of a STEM professional has benefits for students, teachers and the community. Enhanced awareness of their professional future can impact positively upon the cognitive and affective domains of student learning. This, in turn, can enhance student engagement and the classroom experience for both students and teachers. By driving early student engagement with the professional community and giving them a vision for their careers, the readiness of graduates can be enhanced, as they have gained a better understanding of what it means to be a professional in their respective areas. Being more career-aware and ready can enhance cognition, aptitude and attitude in the workplace.

References

Anderson, E. P. (1993). The perspective of student nurses and their perceptions of professional nursing during the nurse training programme. *Journal of Advanced Nursing, 18*(5), 808–815.

Engineers Australia (2013). *Stage 1 competency standard for professional engineer.* Retrieved from http://www.engineersaustralia.org.au/sites/default/files/shado/Education/Program%20 Accreditation/130607_stage_1_pe_2013_approved.pdf (accessed 24 March, 2015).

Jones, S. & Yates, B. (2011). *Learning and teaching academic standards project: Science learning and teaching academic standards statement.* Sydney: Australian Learning and Teaching Council.

Krause, K., Hartley, R., James, R. & McInnis, C. (2005). *The first year experience in Australian universities: Findings from a decade of national studies.* Canberra: Australian Department of Education, Science and Training.

Layton, R. A., Loughry, M. L., Ohland, M. W. & Ricco, G. D. (2010). Design and validation of a web-based system for assigning members to teams using instructor-specified criteria. *Advances in Engineering Education, 2*(1), 1–28.

McInnis, C. & James, R. (1995). *First year on campus: Diversity in the initial experiences of Australian undergraduates.* Canberra: Australian Government Publishing Service.

Timoštšuk, I. & Ugaste, A. (2010). Student teachers' professional identity. *Teaching and Teacher Education, 26*(8), 1563–1570.

8

VIDEO BLOGS

A vehicle to support student-generated representations and explanations in chemistry

Gwen Lawrie

Context

Video blogs (or vlogs) offer a new dimension in multimodal learning because they are forms of student-generated media that require learners to actively participate in the process of developing explanations. A vlog is a video that involves the student narrating visual media as a result of reflection about the content or understanding (Parkes & Kajder, 2010). As in the case of a blog, a vlog enables the individual to communicate an explanation, perspective or position; however, this is generally without the interactive feature of an audience providing feedback through an online comments field.

Scientists, and chemists in particular, rely on multiple representations to support the depiction or explanation of models, processes and concepts. Learning chemistry requires acquisition and application of multiple symbols, language and representations that are inherent to the discipline. Expert chemists proficiently translate between different representations because their mental models are well developed and they are competent in their spatial abilities (Hoffman & Laszlo, 1991; Kozma & Russell, 1997; Waldrip & Prain, 2012).

Theoretical basis

The triadic model of a sign (semiotic) system for representations in science (Peirce, 1931/1955) has been successfully applied in the context of student-generated videos as a framework for media-enhanced learning in science (Hoban, Loughran & Nielsen, 2011; Hoban & Nielsen, 2012). A 'semiotic progression' is enacted as students move from researching initial content for their video (referent) into the process of creating a storyboard, then generating and sequencing models (representations), taking photographs and, finally, narrating the concepts/processes (interpretant). Developing this sequence is how students make meaning from their representations as they revisit the content many times through changing from one mode of communication to another. This framework has been applied to video blogs in chemistry (Lawrie & Bartle, 2013) in the context of novice learners. In this study, students selected a molecule or substance that had personal significance and then sought relevant information (referent), constructed a visual aid in the form of a structural model (representation) and created a video in which they explained how the structure related to its properties and function (interpretant). To explain this further, and to illustrate the instructional design for vlogs, the elements of semiotics have been adapted to identify the processes that students must complete in creating their video blogs, as shown in Figure 8.1.

The relationships shown in Figure 8.1 indicate three principal affordances of video blogs that enhance the process of learning concepts in chemistry including: engagement with multiple representations; expression of internal mental models; and development of explanations. Evidence is growing to indicate that student-generated representations and explanations are far superior for individual learning in comparison to passive engagement with either expert-generated representations (e.g. textbook diagrams) or explanations provided during didactic lecture delivery. These ideas are explored further in the following to demonstrate the utility of video blogs as learning vehicles in chemistry.

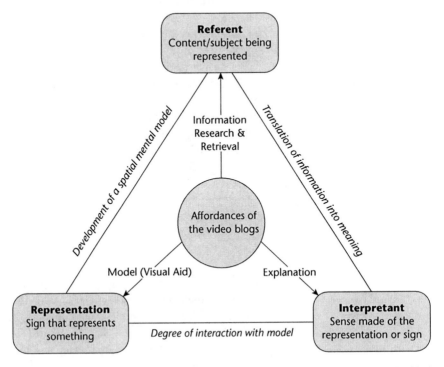

FIGURE 8.1 A schematic representation of the affordances of video blogs embedded onto an adaptation of Peirce's semiotic triad (Peirce, 1931) to illustrate how this media supports students in their development of meaning-making

Video blogs enable learners to engage with multiple external representations across the three domains in the semiotic triad (Figure 8.1). First, learners are required to research the subject/content of their vlog (referent). This requires appraisal of multiple representations to filter information and identify the key features that they intend to explain. Second, learners must interpret and translate the expert-generated content into their own representation using other modes such as writing, image, voice or music. Third, learners need to interpret their own representations to support the intended meaning (interpretant).

Interpretant: Making meaning of representations

An integral component of the process of creating a vlog for a perceived audience is that the learners must first generate an explanation for themselves, also known as self-explanation (Chi, de Leeuw, Chiu & LaVancher, 1994). During this process of self-explanation, learners move iteratively between internal and external representations (Zhang, 1997) to develop the explanation. The extent of a student's understanding of the concepts underpinning the external representations becomes apparent when they formulate an explanation. In creating the representations, learners must acquire and apply disciplinary language to translate meaning from their internal representations and understanding into the perceived language of the audience (Prain, 2002; Yore & Treagust, 2006). Thus, self-explanation is a powerful approach that teachers can use to their advantage in order to increase students' awareness of the mental models they make. An example of this pedagogical practice is in engaging learners in explaining causal diagrams (e.g. textbook diagrams), texts, multimedia/multiple representations and problem solving (Cho & Jonassen, 2012; Villalta-Cerdas & Sandi-Urena, 2014). Others have recognised that the actual process of explaining a mental model can change the existing mental model (Brooks, 2009; Gilbert, Boulter & Rutherford, 1998a).

External representations and models become a scaffold for thinking and understanding when learners have been involved in their construction (Hoban et al., 2011; Waldrip & Prain, 2012; Waldrip, Prain & Carolan, 2010). Video blogs have potential to exploit a haptic dimension, in which the student interacts with their visual aid (representation). This has been found to further enhance students' explanations and provides important insights for instructors into the depth and accuracy of the students' understanding (Lawrie & Bartle, 2013).

Representation: The role of visual aids

As noted earlier, chemists rely on multiple external representations that are often multimodal to depict or explain models, processes and concepts. Expert chemists proficiently translate between different representations because their mental models are well developed and they are competent in their spatial abilities (Hoffman & Laszlo, 1991; Kozma & Russell, 1997; Waldrip & Prain, 2012). Novice chemistry learners must acquire and apply the symbols, language and representations inherent to the discipline, and learn to translate among the different representations.

Any scientist's ability to translate between representations depends on the sophistication of their internal representations (concepts, principles and mental models), which involves generating external representations (elemental symbols, chemical formulae, graphs and equations) to support their explanations (Kozma & Russell, 2005). Zhang (1997) suggested that internal and external representations are inextricably linked and so it is perhaps unsurprising that researchers spend substantial effort in attempting to gain insight into an individual's mental models by analysing external representations (Gilbert, 2005). There is a vast body of science education literature in representations and visualisation that is beyond the scope of this chapter. However, key studies are cited to demonstrate the overwhelming evidence, indicating that active engagement with multiple external representations assists learners to develop and refine their mental models.

Student-generated representations include oral and written language, mono-modal and multimodal texts, observational and conceptual drawings, graphs, annotated self-explanations, visual summaries, video productions, animations and 3D models. The framework of representational construction affordances (Prain & Tytler, 2012) reinforces the position that the process of learning concepts requires representational competence in science discourse to achieve science literacy. Using models as explanatory tools requires active engagement with related representations, rather than passive encounters, to maximise the benefits to student learning. Learners generate their mental models through making a connection between the observed phenomena and the scientific explanation (Gilbert et al., 1998a).

As they transition from primary school, through secondary school and into the tertiary curriculum, learners are able to test and adapt their existing mental models, resulting in an increase in the sophistication of their understanding. However, there is also evidence to suggest that low-knowledge learners engaging with representations that are static images or texts (symbols and structures) tend to focus on superficial aspects, such as shapes and colour, rather than the underlying concepts being represented (Corradi, Elen, Schraepen & Clarebout, 2014). In addition, a learner's spatial ability is a significant factor in the success of the successful application of a model (Dori & Barak, 2001). Indeed, learners' conceptions of scientific models are consistent with a naïve realist epistemology (Treagust, Chittleborough & Mamiala, 2002) – learners often believe that representations display physical copies of reality rather than embodying consensus views of scientists or different theoretical perspectives.

Implementation

As previously discussed, student-generated digital video projects are important in engaging learners with representations and explanations and represent assessment tasks that can also support student gains in enhanced literacy skills and authentic communication practices (Hoban et al., 2011; Hofer & Owings-Swan, 2005; Kearney & Schuck, 2006; Keast, Cooper, Berry, Loughran & Hoban, 2010). A carefully considered pedagogical strategy is necessary to reduce the likelihood that students might create a video that involves simple regurgitation of retrieved information. Our instructional strategy involves four key criteria or elements as part of the design of the vlog as an assessment task to ensure student engagement with the task:

1. students must incorporate structural models or representations as visual aids into the explanation;
2. technology skills are scaffolded as required to enable the process of making a video and reduce barriers to the production;
3. assessment criteria are developed specifically to support learning gains; and,
4. evidence of student learning from the task is gathered.

Student interaction with their visual aids (representations) in vlogs

Learners develop richer explanations when they engage interactively with their structural models so the instructional design needs to embed this through assessment. Marks are allocated based on the extent to which the students interact with their visual aid. Evidence suggests that this interaction may be further enhanced if there is a haptic element to the interaction, such as hands-on kinaesthetic manipulation (Bivall, Ainsworth & Tiball, 2011; Talley, 1973). Research indicates that learners who interact with physical models (actional-operational) demonstrate better learning outcomes than those who engage with static diagrams (visual-graphical) (Dori & Barak, 2001; Wu & Puntambekar, 2012).

Raising learners' awareness of the different forms of visual aid and how the interaction is important can be achieved when the instructor explicitly models explanations during lectures or in the classroom. There are a number of approaches that instructors can incorporate in their teaching, either in the forms of representation or nature of resources provided to students:

- *Static images sourced online*, for example, through Google image searches for electronic or molecular structures as visual/graphical representations (Wu & Puntambekar, 2012).
- *Interactive 3D visualisation tools* of molecular structures are available online (e.g. through open-source tools such as JMol). These sophisticated representations can be manipulated in real time to enhance students' spatial visualisation skills and provide a more-dynamic representation of molecular structure.
- *Handmade physical models and structures* that are created synchronously with explanations are actional-operational representations (Wu & Puntambekar, 2012). Physical models enable students to use gestures to interact with the model/structure as they highlight the feature being explained. Learners who engage in constructing plastic molecular models in parallel with virtual models demonstrate better understanding and spatial ability than those in a control group exposed only to graphical representations (Dori & Barak, 2001). Lawrie and Bartle (2013) observed that meaning was most effectively conveyed in the visual aid when learners applied hand gestures as part of their explanations,

regardless of whether they were interacting with a physical model or a hand-drawn or static image.

- *Hand-drawn structures*: Multiple studies examine the process of drawing representations by hand in enhancing student understanding in science (Ainsworth, Prain & Tytler, 2011; Brooks, 2009). Chemists also explain and understand structures better when they draw them by hand (Kozma, Chin, Russell & Marx, 2000). Indeed, drawing representations of molecular level processes enabled learners to better link observable phenomena to concepts than those who worked only with online dynamic visualisations (Zhang & Linn, 2011).

Examples of individual student vlogs and how they have incorporated these various types of representations and models into supporting their vlog explanations are provided in Figure 8.2a–d.

Interaction with static images is difficult for students to achieve in a video format unless they either annotate or interact with the images synchronously with their narration. Animation of PowerPoint images can provide a dynamic element. For example, in Figure 8.2a the narrator describes the structure of brass where arrows fly in to point to features mentioned. The screenshot shown in Figure 8.2a is accompanied by the narration, "the ions form a lattice structure while the electrons are allowed to play freely around these ions. These ions are held together in place due to the mutual attraction to the surrounding sea of electrons".

Hand-made clay, ball-and-stick molecular models (Figures 8.2b and 8.2c) are simple yet very effective as visual aids because they enable students to interact with a physical structural model that helps them to explain key structural features or properties. Students can opt to annotate a static photo of their structural model embedded in the video using animation to enhance their explanation. In the example shown in Figure 8.2b, the narrator explains, "Ethanol is the simplest form of alcohol, which means it is an organic compound in which a hydroxyl group is bound to a carbon atom or bound to other hydrogen and carbon atoms" and the atoms are highlighted individually on the ball-and-stick model by animation as the narrator speaks. A

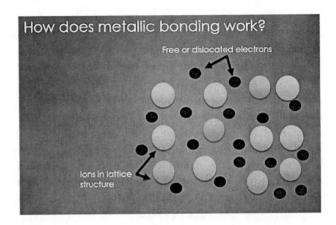

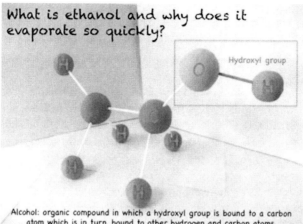

What is ethanol and why does it evaporate so quickly?

Hydroxyl group

Alcohol: organic compound in which a hydroxyl group is bound to a carbon atom which is in turn, bound to other hydrogen and carbon atoms.

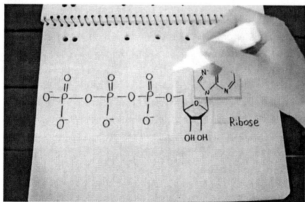

Ribose

OH OH

FIGURE 8.2 a-d Examples of visual aids that students typically adopt to support their vlog explanations: (a) animated PowerPoint schematic; (b) clay ball-and-stick structure annotated in the video to highlight features; (c) clay ball-and-stick model used interactively by narrator to explain structure; and (d) synchronous hand-drawn chemical structures further annotated to support explanation

more-haptic approach is where students opt to manipulate the physical structural model themselves during their explanation. Figure 8.2c shows a screenshot from a sequence where the narrator holds, rotates, arranges and points to the ball-and-stick structures that he has created. His narration explains the arrangement:

> ...one carbon atom bonding covalently to three others in a trigonal planar [geometry] resulting in very strong flat sheets or layers. These sheets have no set length and width but rather they extend expansive[ly]. Each layer is one gigantic molecule, which is arranged in parallel to the other sheets one above the other like a pack of cards. The molecules can slide over one another easily.

Hand-drawn structural representations can elicit deeper explanations because the narrator has to have a clear mental model in order to translate the mental model into a structure being drawn in real-time. In the screenshot vlog example in Figure 8.2d, the narrator explains "next there is a series of three phosphate groups and this is essentially where the potential energy of ATP is stored or more precisely between the terminal phosphate and the oxygen to its right". Simultaneously, the narrator is using a highlighter to denote the key functional groups to support the explanation. This generally results in a rich explanation that also reveals the level of the student's understanding of the underlying concepts.

Scaffolding learners' technology skills

Students who have low technology skills can quickly be overwhelmed by the task of creating movies, even if they are familiar with using their mobile devices to record videos. The instructor can reduce this cognitive load through providing appropriate scaffolding for the processes of planning, video editing and online video sharing. This can take the form of providing digital cameras, instructions for movie editing (for both Windows and iOS systems), exemplars and access to technical support (particularly in saving movies in a format appropriate for sharing). Students may also express anxiety in sharing their video blog publicly, so use of video sharing sites such as YouTube and Vimeo are recommended, which provide the settings options to host uploaded videos as 'unlisted'. This means that students can choose who has access to them by virtue of a unique URL for access to the videos. Under these conditions, the videos remain private and in the control/possession of the individual student. It is not surprising that some students take pride in their video product and subsequently share their links with family members or add their video into an e-portfolio of creative works. This could also be an option for assessing the vlogs.

Assessment criteria that reflect the intended learning outcomes

Well-written assessment criteria can assist learners to move out of the domain of descriptive and causal explanations and into the higher-level interpretive and intentional explanations. Criteria should be framed to incorporate the anticipated learning outcomes so that learners are encouraged to engage iteratively in each of the three active components of the meaning-making triad (Figure 8.1). Suggested criteria include communication and explanation (using appropriate language and symbols), content (that supports meaning-making), visual presentation (interacting with a visual aid) and technical aspects (visual and audio clarity, and length). Requiring a short video (2–3 minutes) encourages learners to translate and reframe information efficiently to be precise in their explanations.

In the process of generating video blogs, learners are required to translate the language of science into their own language in order to understand the concept (self-explaining) during information retrieval. They subsequently translate this self-explained meaning into a language suitable for their perceived audience (Prain, 2002; Yore & Treagust, 2006). The perceived audience has an important impact on how learners communicate their understanding (Gunel, Hand & McDermott, 2009). In considering their potential audience for the video blogs, some learners were reluctant to share their videos with their peers; however, they believed that they could gain useful feedback through the same process (Lawrie & Bartle, 2013). Peer review is thus an attractive option for assessment to enhance learners' awareness of their own thinking as they critically appraise how other learners applied a visual aid to support the explanation in the vlog. Peer review also influences how students construct their videos out of awareness for their perceived audience (Keast *et al.*, 2010). Learners are, thus, more likely to consider how to engage the audience in their vlog through creative visual presentation and use of more-sophisticated visual aids (Kearney & Schuck, 2006).

How do we know students are learning?

Explanations are often elicited in the form of responses to questions that can be placed on a continuum of explicit–implicit. In considering different types of explanations (Gilbert *et al.*, 1998a) proposed that elements of causal typology could be mapped onto Martin's (1972) typology of explanations: intentional explanation (justification of actions); descriptive explanation (explanation of meaning); interpretive explanation (citation of theory); causal explanation (causation); and predictive explanation (deduction of future event). Very young learners transition from functional explanations to connectedness explanations and finally to mechanistic explanations (Gilbert, Boulter & Rutherford, 1998b). This typology of explanations continues to be relevant in categorising learner explanations (Talanquer, 2010). Consideration of the typology of explanations in parallel with representational competences illustrates how an instructor can evidence these in video media (Table 8.1) as well as link these to visual-aid examples set in the context of chemistry (Lawrie & Bartle, 2013). The level of representational competence in the student-generated visual aids can readily be categorised (Kozma & Russell, 2005) and mapped against common representations adopted as visual aids used in a video blog as shown in Table 8.1.

TABLE 8.1 Representational competences to support student explanations in chemistry in their vlogs

Characteristics of the Application of a Structural Visual Aid in Explanation	Representational Competences (Kozma & Russell, 2005)	Types of Explanation (Martin, 1972)
The model or structure is described in simple descriptive terms using categorisation and enumeration such as the identity and number of atoms (in molecules) or number of electrons and orbitals (in atoms or ions).	(1) Representation as depiction. (2) Early symbolic skills.	Functional Descriptive
The structure or model is used to explain a property (such as the shape or polarity of the molecule).	(3) Syntactic use of formal representations. (4) Semantic use of formal representations (applying meaning).	Causal/mechanical Interpretive
The explanation of structure is extended to relate physical properties to the specific function of the molecule/ substance (for example, how shape affects binding in a receptor site, solvency or material properties)	(5) Reflective rhetorical use of representations.	Intentional (teleology) Predictive

Analysing student vlogs for learning gains

Evaluation of whether the vlogs have enhanced learning outcomes for a particular cohort of students requires a strategy for analysing the vlogs beyond application of the assessment criteria, particularly if marking is completed by tutorial assistants or through peer review. Lawrie and Bartle (2013) inductively developed categories for coding the content of vlogs. The categories include: personal relevance (connection to the molecule/substance chosen); language (correct terminology); information processing (multiple sources and correct concepts); visual aid (accuracy); and explanation of structure (correct representations). These categories align with the assessment criteria standards for the task.

The visual aids adopted by students can also be categorised as: student-generated; actional-operational physical model (handmade or hand drawn); or visual-graphical representation (static printed diagrams or animations sourced online). The vlogs make student thinking visible, allowing instructors to gain deeper insight into students' existing conceptions which, in turn, can inform teaching practice. Evidence of alternate conceptions that emerge through student explanations can also lead to adjusting other course activities. Alternate conceptions appear to be more prevalent among students who do not engage actively with a visual aid but rely on describing static images reproduced from online sources (Lawrie & Bartle, 2013).

Discussion

Student-generated representations in digital explanations reflect the process of translating between referents (information), representations of structure and the narration, providing instructors with a mechanism for gaining insight into learners' understanding (Lawrie & Bartle, 2013). Analysis of the videos (and assessment of the vlogs by the whole class) enables identification of alternate conceptions held by learners. Engaging learners in critical appraisal of multiple structural representations as they develop their own visual aids avoids overdependence on any single model (Kieg & Rubba, 1993).

One of the most significant potential roles of video blogs in chemistry learning is for learners who have limited prior knowledge and must complete intensive bridging or introductory tertiary courses (Lawrie & Bartle, 2013). The process of researching information, generating a structural model and explaining structure–property relationships gives students the opportunity to immerse themselves in the language and symbolism of chemistry. Interacting with multiple representations further assists them to form coherent mental models, although there is always a risk of learners acquiring alternate conceptions if they engage only with the superficial features in the representations. As noted earlier, novice learners often imply meaning from the shapes and colours rather than focus on the underlying conceptual information (Corradi *et al.*, 2014; Kozma & Russell, 1997). Additional scaffolding is strongly recommended, perhaps in the form of an active-learning workshop, to introduce learners to multiple external representations of chemical structures.

A key benefit for learners in generating physical models of structures is enhanced visuospatial skills that are important in the science, technology and mathematics disciplines (Harle & Towns, 2011; Wu & Shah, 2004). Further, because learners choose a molecule of personal relevance as the subject of the video blog task, they identify the role of chemistry in their own lives even if their professional aspirations lie in another STEM or health-related discipline.

One of the limitations of video blogs is the ability of the instructor to review and mark multiple individual videos for large-enrolment classes. The solution is to have teams of students create video blogs. Participating in a team effort may reduce the individual benefit for particular students to some extent because they may not fully engage in all of the aspects of the learning process represented in Figure 8.1 when the task is divided among team members. However, students still gain additional benefit through explaining concepts to other team members as they move toward the collective product.

References

Ainsworth, S., Prain, V. & Tytler, R. (2011). Drawing to learn in science. *Science, 333*, 1096–1097.

Bivall, P., Ainsworth, S. & Tiball, L. A. E. (2011). Do haptic representations help complex molecular learning? *Science Education, 95*, 700–719.

Brooks, M. (2009). Drawing, visualization and young children's exploration of 'Big Ideas'. *International Journal of Science Education, 31*(3), 319–341. doi: 10.1080/09500690802595771

Chi, M. T. H., de Leeuw, N., Chiu, M.-H. & LaVancher, C. (1994). Eliciting self-explanations improves understanding. *Cognitive Science, 18*, 439–477.

Cho, Y. H. & Jonassen, D. H. (2012). Learning by self-explaining causal diagrams in high-school biology. *Asia Pacific Education Review, 13*, 171–184. doi: 10.1007/s12564-011-9187-4

Corradi, D. M. J., Elen, J., Schraepen, B. & Clarebout, G. (2014). Understanding possibilities and limitations of abstract chemical representations for achieving conceptual understanding. *International Journal of Science Education*, *36*(5), 715–734. doi: 10.1080/09500693. 2013.824630

Dori, Y. J. & Barak, M. (2001). Virtual and physical molecular modelling: Fostering model perception and spatial understanding. *Educational Technology & Society*, *4*, 61–74.

Gilbert, J. K. (2005). Visualization: A metacognitive skill in science and science education. In J. Gilbert (Ed.), *Visualization in science education: Models and modelling in science education* (pp. 9–27). Dordrecht, The Netherlands: Springer.

Gilbert, J. K., Boulter, C. & Rutherford, M. (1998a). Models in explanations, Part 1: Horses for courses? *International Journal of Science Education*, *20*(1), 83–97. doi: 10.1080/09500 69980200106

Gilbert, J. K., Boulter, C. & Rutherford, M. (1998b). Models in explanations, Part 2: Whose voice? Whose ears? *International Journal of Science Education*, *20*(2), 187–203. doi: 10.1080/0950069980200205

Gunel, M., Hand, B. & McDermott, M. (2009). Writing for different audiences: Effects on high-school students' conceptual understanding of biology. *Learning and Instruction*, *19*, 354–367.

Harle, M. & Towns, M. (2011). A review of spatial ability literature, its connection to chemistry, and implications for instruction. *Journal of Chemical Education*, *88*, 351–360.

Hoban, G., Loughran, J. & Nielsen, W. (2011). Slowmation: Preservice elementary teachers representing science knowledge through creating multimodal digital animations. *Journal of Research in Science Teaching*, *48*, 985–1009.

Hoban, G. & Nielsen, W. (2012). Using 'slowmation' to enable preservice primary teachers to create multimodal representations of science concepts. *Research in Science Education*, *42*, 1101–1119.

Hofer, M. & Owings-Swan, K. (2005). Digital moviemaking: The harmonization of technology, pedagogy and content. *International Journal of Technology in Teaching and Learning*, *1*(2), 102–110.

Hoffmann, R. & Laszlo, R. (1991). Representation in chemistry. *Angewandte Chemie*, *30*, 1–16.

Kearney, M. & Schuck, S. (2006). Spotlight on authentic learning: Student developed digital video projects. *Australasian Journal of Educational Technology*, *22*(2), 189–208.

Keast, S., Cooper, R., Berry, A., Loughran, J. & Hoban, G. (2010). Slowmation as a pedagogical scaffold for improving science teaching and learning. *Brunei International Journal of Science and Mathematics Education*, *2*(1), 1–15.

Kieg, P. F. & Rubba, P. A. (1993). Translation of representations of the structure of matter and its relationship to reasoning, gender, spatial reasoning and specific prior knowledge. *Journal of Research in Science Teaching*, *30*(8), 883–903.

Kozma, R. B., Chin, E., Russell, R. & Marx, N. (2000). The roles of representations and tools in the chemistry laboratory and their implications for chemistry learning. *Journal of the Learning Sciences*, *9*, 105–143.

Kozma, R. B. & Russell, J. (1997). Multimedia and understanding: Expert and novice responses to different representations of chemical phenomena. *Journal of Research in Science Teaching*, *34*(9), 949–968.

Kozma, R. B. & Russell, J. (2005). Students becoming chemists: Developing representational competence. In J. K. Gilbert (Ed.), *Visualization in science education: Models and modelling in science education* (pp. 121–146). Dordrecht, The Netherlands: Springer.

Lawrie, G. A. & Bartle, E. (2013). Chemistry vlogs: A vehicle for student-generated representations and explanations to scaffold their understanding of structure–property relationships. *International Journal of Innovation in Science and Mathematics Education, 21*(4), 27–45.

Martin, M. (1972). *Concepts of science education: A philosophical analysis.* London: Scott, Foresman.

Parkes, K. A. & Kajder, S. (2010). Eliciting and assessing reflective practice: A case study in Web 2.0 technologies. *International Journal of Teaching & Learning in Higher Education, 22,* 218–228.

Peirce, C. (1931/1955). Logic as semiotic: The theory of signs. In B. Justus (Ed.), *Philosophical writings of Peirce (1893–1910)* (pp. 98–119). New York: Dover. (Original work published 1931.)

Prain, V. (2002). *Learning from writing in secondary science: Some theoretical implications.* Paper presented at the Ontological, Epistemological, Linguistic and Pedagalogical Considerations of Language and Science Literacy: Empowering Research and Informing Instruction Conference, Victoria, BC, Canada.

Prain, V. & Tytler, R. (2012). Learning through constructing representations in science: A framework of representational construction affordances. *International Journal of Science Education, 24*(17), 2751–2773. doi: 10.1080/09500693.2011.626462

Talanquer, V. (2010). Exploring dominant types of explanations built by general chemistry students. *International Journal of Science Education, 32*(18), 2392–2412. doi: 10.1080/09500690903369662

Talley, L. (1973). The use of three-dimensional visualization as a moderator in the higher cognitive learning of concepts in college level chemistry. *Journal of Research in Science Teaching, 10,* 263–269.

Treagust, D. F., Chittleborough, G. & Mamiala, T. L. (2002). Students' understanding of the role of scientific models in learning science. *International Journal of Science Education, 24*(4), 357–368. doi: 10.1080/09500690110066485

Villalta-Cerdas, A. & Sandi-Urena, S. (2014). Self-explaining effect in general chemistry instruction: Eliciting overt categorical behaviours by design. *Chemistry Education Research and Practice, 15,* 530–540. doi: 10.1039/C3RP00172E

Waldrip, B. & Prain, V. (2012). Learning from and through representations in science. In B. J. Fraser, K. Tobin & J. McRobbie (Eds.), *Second international handbook of science education* (pp. 145–155). Dordrecht, The Netherlands: Springer.

Waldrip, B., Prain, W. & Carolan, J. (2010). Using multi-modal representations to improve learning in junior secondary science. *Research in Science Education, 40,* 65–80.

Wu, H.-K. & Puntambekar, S. (2012). Pedagogical affordances of multiple external representations in scientific processes. *Journal of Science Education and Technology, 21,* 754–767.

Wu, H.-K. & Shah, P. (2004). Exploring visuospatial thinking in science education. *Science Education, 88,* 465–482.

Yore, L. & Treagust, D. (2006). Current realities and future possibilities: Language and science literacy – empowering research and informing instruction. *International Journal of Science Education, 28,* 291–314.

Zhang, H. Z. & Linn, M. C. (2011). Can generating representations enhance learning with dynamic visualisations? *Journal of Research in Science Teaching, 48*(10), 1177–1198.

Zhang, J. (1997). The nature of external representations in problem solving. *Cognitive Science, 21,* 179–217.

9

STUDENT-GENERATED VIDEOS FOR INQUIRY-ORIENTED PROJECTS IN ENVIRONMENTAL SCIENCE

Gerry M. Rayner

Context

The use of digital media to enhance student understanding of science has largely been through instructor development of course-specific materials, such as simulations, visualisations and games, and the integration of web-based media. Although there have been constraints on the potential of these resources to maximise student learning outcomes (Dutton, Hope Cheong & Park, 2004), they continue to grow across the educational landscape at all levels. Whilst these resources may be valuable, the use of student-generated digital artefacts is less common and may provide a powerful means to enhance student knowledge and understanding of complex environmental issues. This is likely a consequence of the immediacy, increased sophistication and capability of the technology (Hoban, 2013a), and also through the participation of millennial-style learners, who possess the devices (e.g. smartphones) and technology (rapidly evolving applications) and, if not, the assumed levels of know-how or sophistication (Herold, 2012). In a recent study of undergraduates' use of and familiarity with digital media, Kumar, Liu and Black (2012) commented on the lack of evidence about student use of novel technologies in study-related contexts. Initiatives that integrate emergent technologies in undergraduate curricula and which demonstrate enhanced learning and skills outcomes in students thus provide useful examples for further scholarly endeavour.

Student-generated digital media that are contextually relevant to serious environmental challenges have considerable potential to generate deeper learning by students and prevent the formation of misconceptions, which are commonplace for difficult concepts and processes, particularly in science disciplines (Burgoon, Heddle & Duran, 2011). As Gee (2013) contends,

... global warming, environmental degradation, growing massive inequality, and rapid technological changes – for example new tools to redesign viruses and make new forms of life – all set a context that is relevant to what young people should know and be able to do in the future, if they are to have one. (p. 20)

An example of the potential of digital media to impact perspectives on a broad scale has been provided by Lowe *et al.* (2006), who described the significant effect of an environmental disaster movie on viewers' concern about climate change and other environmental risks.

The use of digital media in environmental biology is founded on the new literacies studies approach of Gee (1990), who defines 'literacy' as something that is done in the context of society and which, thus, has a sociocultural perspective. At the primary-school level, Gee (2010) described the positive impact of a worked example of digital media on children's language development, and Klopfer, Sheldon, Perry and Chen (2012) reported on the positive impact of an educational game on students' interest in academic content. In a study traversing primary and secondary education and across a range of disciplines, Kearney and Schuck (2006) reported on the authenticity of student-generated digital video in enhancing student learning and engaging with peers. In secondary settings, Harness and Drossman (2011) provided an example of how students' production of videos enabled them to become more environmentally aware and encouraged more-responsible behaviours. Further, O'Toole (2012) engaged senior secondary students in generating videos of chemistry procedures and techniques, and students reported a broadly enhanced learning experience, based on increased collaboration, leadership, critical thinking, problem solving and communication.

While student use of digital media is an emerging area of academic scholarship at the primary and secondary school levels, it appears to be less common at the tertiary level, with isolated examples in marketing and accounting (Greene & Crespi, 2012), bioethics (Willmott, 2014), biochemistry (Ryan, 2013) and public health and health promotion (Shuldman & Tajik, 2010). However, there appear to be very few examples of student-generated digital media to develop their scientific literacies regarding environmental issues, in particular 'big ticket' items such as anthropogenic climate change. One exception is that reported by Wilson, Niehaus, White, Rasmussen and Kuchel (2009), who described student video documentary-making in first-year ecology, a process that encouraged students to engage with scientists and motivated their greater interest in ecological and environmental issues.

While student use of digital media increasingly forms part of course-related assessment tasks and skills development (e.g. Campbell, 2012; Hakkarainen, 2011), it is less common in problem-based and inquiry-orientated settings. Paradoxically, these are contexts where digital media may have the greatest pedagogical impact. The nature of scientific endeavour provides a framework in which students have opportunities to ask questions, research contextually relevant topics and work collaboratively to investigate such questions and present their findings. As Pasquali (2007) contends, the process involved in filming an activity, followed by editing the video into a clear sequence and adding audio or other materials, has considerable potential to enhance student understanding of the scientific method. Further, student-generated video is considered eminently suitable for science education, as it is captures "the active, experimental and visual nature of science" (Hilton, 2011, p. 311). However, the use of student-generated digital video for learning may also enhance students' critical thinking skills (Brandon & Hollingshead, 1999; Resnick, 2007) and problem-solving abilities, both of which can be optimised through group collaboration (Sawyer, 2006).

Scientific research is demonstrating how human-mediated climate change is affecting patterns of rainfall and temperature across Australia, generating knock-on effects to flowering times in plants and breeding cycles and migration movements of animals. These are components of species' phenologies, which describe life-cycle events of organisms and how these are influenced by seasonal and inter-annual variations in climate. The impacts of climate change on the distribution and behaviour of plants and animals provide a strong contextual basis for student activities in environmental science. ClimateWatch (CW), which provides the foundation for this student activity, was developed by Earthwatch (www.earthwatch.org), together with the Australian Bureau of Meteorology and Australian universities, to gain a more-thorough understanding of the impacts of temperature and rainfall changes on the biology and behaviour of Australia's biota. This chapter explores the considerable pedagogical value of field-based activities that incorporate inquiry-oriented learning, teamwork and collaboration, the collection, analysis and synthesis of data and, importantly, provision of opportunities for students to present the results of their inquiries in creative and interesting ways, using a range of digital media options.

Implementation

This study focused on a first-year environmental biology subject with student enrolments of 242 and 253 in 2012 and 2013, respectively. In each cohort, most students were enrolled in a Bachelor of Science degree at an Australian university in Melbourne, with the rest comprising students from a Bachelor of Environmental Science (~50 students) and a range of double degrees (e.g. BA/BSc, BEd/BSc, BEng/BSc). The course curriculum encompasses themes such as biodiversity, energy flow and biochemical cycling, plant and animal evolution and adaptation, and human impacts on the environment, including themes such as extinction, deforestation, pollution and anthropogenic climate change.

In the context of climate change, students were tasked with a semester-long team project to research and gather observational data on a self-selected ClimateWatch indicator species and integrate it with existing information to predict how climate change might impact on the species. In order to provide students with sufficient time to design, develop, revise and finalise their presentation, the project rationale was introduced in Week 2 of the semester. In that session, students were presented with the overall structure and aims of the ClimateWatch program, and three short videos were shown, providing background information about ClimateWatch and instructions on how to download and install ClimateWatch smartphone applications with which to record and log observations. Students were also provided with a rationale about how these team projects integrated with the broader ClimateWatch program and information regarding the value of accurate, real-time data collection in supplementing longer-term phenological information about the ClimateWatch indicator species.

Information in the form of descriptions, images and distributional data sets, including locations on the university campus, was provided about the indicator species available for study. Examples of methods of data collection and input into the ClimateWatch database, and the chronology for project evaluation and presentation, were also provided. Each team was given time to select an indicator species (no two teams in a session could study the same species), brainstorm their approach and delegate tasks, at which point they received feedback about their plans from teaching staff. Teams also received advice about the value of team-based projects, including recognition of their own efforts in the project, and the importance of individual roles in the overall success of the team. Each team was given freedom to select their study site(s), conduct field observations and record and analyse resultant data. The culminating part of the assignment included the design and development of a digital media presentation on their species, and while video production was encouraged, the final choice of media was made by each team.

In Week 10, 2 weeks prior to final presentations, student teams submitted a draft storyboard or outline of their presentation for review, feedback and discussion with a teaching associate. This provided an opportunity for each team to further refine its approach to the presentation, and review the proposed content and timing of the presentation. Assessment of draft presentations was based on four criteria: (i) evidence of research (>2 peer-reviewed references); (ii) provision of information about the indicator species, including images, text and distributional data; (iii) evidence of data gathering and preliminary analysis (e.g. bar charts, derivation of means); and (iv) storyboard development as a draft video, PowerPoint or text document. These assessment criteria were judged against three performance levels – good, moderate and poor – with a final grade allocated out of four marks, comprising 20% of the total marks for the activity.

The remaining 80% of marks for this project were based on the quality of team presentations, conducted in Week 12. Each presentation was limited to 10 minutes, with a further 5 minutes allocated for questions and discussion. A weighted mean of tutor and peer assessments (70 and 30%, respectively), based on provided rubrics, determined the grade for each presentation. Assessment criteria comprised: (i) the quality and extent of research; (ii) explanation of terms and concepts; (iii) structure and cohesiveness; (iv) proficiency in the use of digital media; and (v) use of evidence and argumentation. These assessment criteria align strongly with those of Langan *et al.* (2005), but with the added criterion related to the proficient use of innovative digital media. The provision of feedback by tutors and peers enabled students to reflect on the structure and content of their presentations, which is considered to be a feature of well-designed, authentic learning activities (Reeves, Herrington & Oliver, 2002).

Specific example

A blended digital media approach was used by one team of students to describe the phenology of the crested pigeon (*Ocyphaps lophotes*), a mid-sized, seed-eating bird that inhabits grassland and other open-vegetation types across much of mainland Australia. This team designed their presentation as a narrated movie, combining a range of video, audio and drawing tools to describe and illustrate the species, together with aspects of its distribution and behaviour, in the context of the ClimateWatch program. For example, the team used drawing tools to describe key features of the species, including its distinctive crest, body colour and wing patterning (see Figure 9.1a). Further, by integrating an interview with a veterinarian into the presentation (Figure 9.1b), the team was able to generate key points about the biology and behaviour of the species, and used textual prompts to impart these to the audience. The team also summarised their data into a number of key figures, and included these, with audio narratives, to indicate broad trends in analyses of their observations (Figure 9.1c).

This team also demonstrated a high degree of collaboration and effectiveness in data gathering and, by integrating it with pre-existing data, they were able to make informed predictions about the effects of climate change on their target species. The team used distribution maps, together with audio and drawing tools, to visually describe the likely impacts of climate change on the distribution of the species and how this might potentially impact on its interactions with other species, including predators (see Figure 9.1d).

They walk they don't hop, so they've evolved to be on the ground

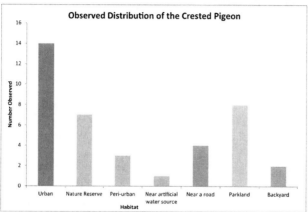

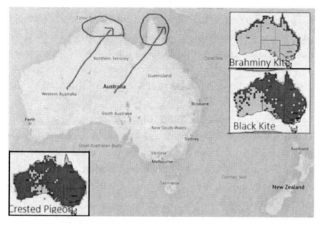

FIGURE 9.1 Students use of (a) drawing tools to illustrate important features of the species; (b) text of key points; and figures for (c) distributional data, and (d) to indicate the effects of climate change on a species' distribution and potential interactions with other species

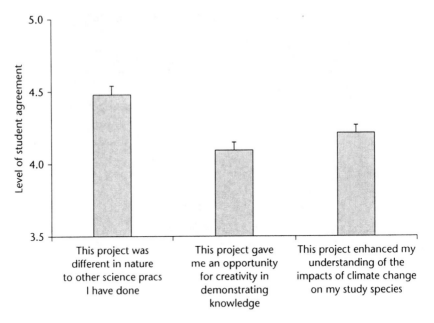

FIGURE 9.2   Students' levels of agreement with three aspects of the ClimateWatch project

Data collection

Student perceptions of this activity were gathered through a post-presentation survey that sought their level of agreement with statements about the pedagogical nature of the task, its uniqueness and its effectiveness in enhancing a range of skills and capabilities, including observation and recording, critical thinking, teamwork and the use of digital media. As shown in Figure 9.2, high proportions of students considered that the ClimateWatch project was different in nature to other science practical activities they had undertaken, that it provided an opportunity for creativity in demonstrating their knowledge and, importantly, that it enhanced their understanding of the impacts of climate change on their chosen indicator species. When students were asked about which aspects of the project they found enjoyable or interesting, 44% of the 258 comments specifically mentioned 'observations in the field' or 'data collection'.

In response to a question about what was enjoyable or interesting about the presentation-related components of the ClimateWatch project, 14 students commented specifically about working on or creating a digital presentation, and 18 of their comments related to "the presenting", or the "teaching and learning from other students" as elements of the presentations, as summarised in Table 9.1.

Many students made unsolicited comments about the distinctive nature of the ClimateWatch project. For example:

Was different to other assignments – awesome!

It was fun from both social and educational.

This unit practical is the most enjoyable of all!

It was very different to anything I've ever done. I liked how it spanned many weeks.

Through the field-study observations and data gathering, students appeared to gain a more-realistic understanding of what is required to undertake fieldwork. For example, one student commented that this, "Was a very good prac, gave some insight into what biologists are faced with in the field and doing their own research".

A number of students commented positively on the freedom and independence they had in designing the project fieldwork and in being creative in the presentation. For example:

Interesting amounts of independence was allowed which I also liked.

The ability of the students to undertake their own research was both liberating and interesting.

I enjoyed getting to be creative and getting to do field work.

When students were asked which aspect of the project they found most enjoyable, a consistent theme was that they enjoyed learning about the use of multimedia and the creativity involved in producing a digital media presentation. For example:

Learning and seeing different presentations.

Being able to use multimedia to present.

Putting together a creative presentation, and the opportunity for a self-guided, controlling, extended investigation.

TABLE 9.1 NVivo analysis of major themes in student feedback regarding presentation-related elements of their ClimateWatch project

Comments about Creating the Presentation	Comments about Presenting, Teaching and Learning from Other Students
• Putting our movie together (×4) • Making/developing a presentation (×3) • Using digital media to make the presentation (×2) • Putting together a sweet PowerPoint • Putting together a creative presentation self-guided • Recording the poem • The videos + images of species • Using different media	• ClimateWatch presentations – learning about other species (×9) • Presenting (×3) • The presentations at the end were really interesting (×3) • Listening in on the challenges faced by others – as highlighted by other groups • Finding the species and hearing how others fared with theirs • What you presented was your actual findings and observations to the class

Evolution of media forms

When first implemented in 2012, 74% of team presentations were PowerPoint or Prezi-based, largely comprising combinations of still images, figures, maps and text. Some teams (19%) used PowerPoint, but also integrated small snippets of video and/ or audio. Among the 2012 presentations, only 6.5% were digital videos. However, in 2013, digital video presentations comprised 18% of total presentations, an almost threefold increase from 2012. PowerPoint presentations incorporating video and/or audio comprised 30% of productions, and 52% were solely PowerPoint or Prezi.

Discussion

Of the wide range of benefits to students from this initiative, perhaps the most important was students' contextual framing of a contemporary 'wicked issue' (Lorenzoni, Jones & Turnpenny, 2007) with major implications not only for their own futures but for the persistence of many species. Linking contextually relevant practical activities to wicked issues such as climate change has considerable potential to enhance student scientific literacy, given the accepted link between scientific literacy and an understanding of science in the news (McClune & Jarman, 2012). Hakkarainen (2011) showed that engagement in video production promoted students' domain-specific knowledge and skills via the cognitive and social processes involved in designing a subject-related video. Further, engaging students in socio-scientific news can enhance their critical thinking skills, particularly where such interactions require argumentation (Lin, 2013), which is a feature of student ClimateWatch presentations. This initiative may address calls by Sellmann and Bogner (2012) for environmental education programs that enable students to resolve misconceptions about climate change, and remains an area of further potential investigation and evaluation.

Students also valued the project because it afforded them an opportunity to be creative in demonstrating their knowledge through the use of their own technologies. There is considerable value in providing students with opportunities for creativity in explaining their results and demonstrating their knowledge in their own chosen way, particularly when their own scientifically valid contributions to such knowledge lead them to a deeper understanding of the underlying issues. This is consistent with Abd-El-Khalick, Bell and Lederman (1998) who argued that subjectivity, creativity and imagination are integral to scientific investigation. In fact, Sawyer (2006) contends that in today's knowledge-based society, situated, collaborative activities are the most-effective forms of educational practice and best align with the social nature of contemporary innovation. Collaboration in the creation of artefacts has been shown to provide a unique opportunity to advance knowledge and, in some cases, form a knowledge-building community (Scardamalia & Bereiter, 1994). The current project encompasses this and, further, enables the generation of new knowledge (student-derived data) through its integration with other data and the presentation of such to a broader audience.

Students appreciated the team-based nature of the project because it was considerably different to anything most of them had previously done in their undergraduate studies. In the sciences, student practical activities are often dominated by recipe-driven, laboratory-based experiments, requiring validation of concept at the expense of creativity and innovation. Whilst there will always be a role for this type of science learning, students also appreciate being given opportunity to be creative in how they represent their science understandings using their own technologies. The recently adopted Australian Learning and Teaching Academic Standards (LTAS) in science (Jones & Yates, 2011) aim to provide student-centred, active learning opportunities. In this sense, the framing of an inquiry approach to student discovery, where students generate real data that can be used to inform future decision making, is of considerable pedagogical value and strongly aligns with the intent of the LTAS for the sciences. This project's approach is based on student-generated research questions together with the gathering, analysis and interpretation of data and communication of results. This approach is consistent with that of Ernst, Buddle and Soluk (2014), who used a similar method in a foundation field biology course at McGill University. However, the current study also fostered students' creativity and use of contemporary digital technologies, further enhancing the pedagogical value of the teaching strategy.

That students very much enjoyed the field-based nature of the project, away from lecture theatres, tutorial rooms and labs is encouraging, and consistent with other reports of similar approaches (Boyle et al., 2007; Hochuli & Banks, 2008). Given the considerable pedagogical value of fieldwork, it is concerning that the amount of time students spend engaged in such activities has declined substantially over the past two decades (Barker, Slingsby & Tilling, 2001; Phillips, Baudains & van Keulen, 2002; Smith, 2004). The increasing disconnectedness of people from nature and their acceptance of biologically impoverished environments (Cheesman & Key, 2007), demand that undergraduates acquire the requisite knowledge and skills so that, as graduates, they are better placed to impact and inform future discovery and policy development. Activities such as the one reported in this study, which incorporate fieldwork, data gathering and analysis, as well as teamwork and the use of digital media, engages students in doing real science coupled with creativity in how they represent their findings by creating digital media. This provides an important foundation for further tertiary studies that build on and further refine field-based knowledge and skills.

Assessment structures that enable immediate feedback through discussion and the asking of questions, and which incorporate elements of peer and academic evaluation, have considerable potential to enhance individual and collaborative learning (Griesbaum & Görtz, 2010; Reeves et al., 2002). Such structures allow students to make dynamic, scaffolded adjustments to their reasoning and understanding of complex issues and enhance their ability to apply higher-order thinking to their learning. Peer assessment of student work, under suitable conditions of time and context, is considered to be as valuable as that provided by the more-skilled and knowledgeable teacher (Topping, 2009). The use of peer assessment is both novel and extremely current, as tertiary educators grapple with the dual demands of increasing enrolments in science and diminishing teaching budgets. In relation to this, an increasing body of literature about peer assessment indicates its potential to reduce academic marking loads but, additionally, enhance learner independence and raise the overall standard of learning (Liu & Carless, 2006; MacAlpine, 1999).

Implications for science learning other subjects and skill development

The implications of this assignment and other contemporary approaches that embed the use of media making in student activities are potentially game changing in that they are much more student-centred, have the capacity to be more authentic and use accessible technologies and methods to generate hands-on, collaborative learning. There have been claims that technology has not disrupted academic teaching practices to any considerable extent and, where technology has been implemented, it has had the result of replicating provision of content and enhancing administration (Blin & Munro, 2008). However, as the current study shows, when technology is placed in the hands of the learners, and focused on a contextually relevant assignment, there is considerable potential to enhance learning, nurture skills such as teamwork and numeracy and develop new skills and understandings. This approach could be implemented in a similar way in other undergraduate science disciplines, such as earth sciences (on field trips), in biology, chemistry or physics (for laboratory activities and research projects) or mathematics and statistics, through peer collaboration and development of digital media around conceptually difficult numerical or quantitative theorems. In fact the media making by students could in essence be a 3–5-minute product that summarises the methods, results and conclusions of an authentic science activity. This is much easier to mark than a 50-page report!

The next steps in this initiative involve enhancing aspects of site location and data gathering for ClimateWatch projects and in supporting student use of more-advanced digital media for their project presentations. In regard to the first of these, on-campus resources will be improved through provision of a virtual ClimateWatch campus trail. This will be done through digital mapping of ClimateWatch indicator species (plants, birds and mammals) currently on campus, with implementation of an active planting program of indicator plants to supplement the current list. In this way, students can engage more fully in on-campus ClimateWatch activities and, in addition to collecting relevant data, monitor the growth and health of plant species, thus providing benefits for the university grounds staff.

In future, student use of digital video will be scaffolded through development of support materials and tutorials to enhance the students' technical skills. Targeted tutorials have been shown to enhance student skills in the use of blended media (Hoban, 2013b). Through such training and resources, it is anticipated that, in future, an increasing proportion of teams will prepare presentations in digital video or blended media formats. This is an important consideration, as we should not assume that our undergraduates' membership of the so-called 'Net Generation' is synonymous with an ability to use technology to optimise their learning (Caruso & Kvavik, 2005). In this regard, students must be given contextually relevant, scaffolded opportunities, such as the one described in this chapter, to integrate technology with their learning and apply the use of technology tools using a range of modalities to demonstrate their science knowledge and understanding.

Acknowledgements

The author thanks Kate Howard for NVivo software analysis of student survey data, Chris Wilson for assistance in developing curriculum materials and the unit's teaching associates, who provided valuable input during development of the project and feedback on its structural and assessment elements. Finally, I would like to thank the 2012 and 2013 first-year cohorts of Environmental Biology students, who embraced this initiative and through creativity and initiative demonstrated their knowledge in amazing ways. Importantly, these students have added valuable phenological and distributional information about ClimateWatch indicator species to the national Atlas of Living Australia.

References

Abd-El-Khalick, F., Bell, R. L. & Lederman, N. G. (1998). The nature of science and instructional practice: Making the unnatural natural. *Science Education, 82*(4), 417–436.

Barker, S., Slingsby, D. & Tilling, S. (2001). *Teaching biology outside the classroom: Is it heading for extinction? A report on biology fieldwork in the 14–19 curriculum.* Field Studies Council (FSC) Occasional Publication, 72. Shrewsbury, UK: Field Studies Council/British Ecological Society.

Blin, F. & Munro, M. (2008). Why hasn't technology disrupted academics' teaching practices? Understanding resistance to change through the lens of activity theory. *Computers and Education, 50*(2), 475–490.

Boyle, A., Maguire, S., Martin, A., Milsom, C., Nash, R., Rawlinson, S. . . . Conchie, S. (2007). Fieldwork is good: The student perception and the affective domain. *Journal of Geography in Higher Education, 31*(2), 299–317.

Brandon, D. P. & Hollingshead, A. B. (1999). Collaborative learning and computer supported groups. *Communications Education, 48*, 109–126.

Burgoon, J. N., Heddle, M. L. & Duran, E. (2011). Re-examining the similarities between teacher and student conceptions about physical science. *Journal of Science Teacher Education, 22*(2), 101–114.

Campbell, L. O. (2012). If you give a kid a video camera. *Learning and Leading with Technology, 39*(5), 30–33.

Caruso, J. B. & Kvavik, R. (2005). *ECAR study of students and information technology 2005: Convenience, connection, control, and learning.* Boulder, CO: EDUCAUSE Center for Applied Research. Retrieved from http://net.educause.edu/ir/library/pdf/ers0506/rs/ERS0506w.pdf (accessed 24 March, 2015).

Cheesman, O. D. & Key, R. S. (2007). The extinction of experience: A threat to insect conservation? In A. J. A. Stewart, T. R. New & O. T. Lewis (Eds.), *Insect conservation biology. Proceedings of the 23rd Symposium of the Royal Entomological Society* (pp. 322–348). Wallingford, UK: CABI.

Dutton, W. H., Hope Cheong, P. & Park, A. (2004). An ecology of constraints on e-Learning in higher education: The case of a virtual learning environment. *Prometheus*, *22*(2), 131–149.

Ernst, C. M., Buddle, C. M. & Soluk, L. (2014). The value of introducing natural history field research into undergraduate curricula: A case study. *Bioscience Education*. Posted online 5 Feb 2014. doi:10.11120/beej.2014.00023.

Gee, J. P. (1990). *Social linguistics and literacies*. London: Falmer.

Gee, J. P. (2010). *New digital media and learning and an emerging area and 'worked examples' as one way forward*. Cambridge, MA: MIT Press.

Gee, J. P. (2013). *Digital media and learning: A prospective retrospective*. Retrieved from http://www.jamespaulgee.com/node/67 (accessed 20 March, 2015).

Greene, H. & Crespi, C. (2012). The value of student created videos in the college classroom: An exploratory study in marketing and accounting. *International Journal of Arts and Sciences*, *5*(1), 273–283.

Griesbaum, J. & Görtz, M. (2010). Using feedback to enhance collaborative learning: An exploratory study concerning the added value of self- and peer-assessment by first-year students in a blended learning lecture. *International Journal on E-Learning*, *9*(4), 481–503.

Hakkarainen, P. (2011). Promoting meaningful learning through video production-supported PBL. *Interdisciplinary Journal of Problem-based Learning*, *5*(1), 34–53. doi: 10.7771/1541-5015.1217

Harness, H. & Drossman, H. (2011). The environmental education through filmmaking project. *Environmental Education Research*, *17*(6), 829–849.

Herold, D. (2012). Digital natives: Discourses of exclusion in an inclusive society. In E. Loos, L. Haddon, & E. A. Mante-Meijer (Eds.), *Generational use of new media* (pp. 71–86). Farnham, UK: Ashgate.

Hilton, G. (2011). Rehearsing for an audience: Students learning science through video production. *International Journal of Innovation & Learning*, *9*(3), 311–324.

Hoban, G. (2013). Engaging with content and language using student-created blended media. *International Journal on Education*, *1*(1), 1–6.

Hoban, G. & Nielsen, W. (2013). Learning, explaining and communicating science with student-created blended media. In M. Sharma & A. Yeung (Eds.), *Proceedings of Australian Conference for Science and Mathematics Education* (pp. 148–153). Canberra: Australian National University.

Hochuli, D. F. & Banks, P. B. (2008). Selection pressures on zoology teaching in Australian universities: Student perceptions of zoological education and how to improve it. *Australian Zoologist*, *34*(4), 548–553.

Jones, S. & Yates, B. (2011). *Learning and Teaching Academic Standards Project: Science learning and teaching academic standards statement*. Sydney: Author.

Kearney, M. & Schuck, S. (2006). Spotlight on authentic learning: Student developed digital video projects. *Australasian Journal of Educational Technology*, *22*(2), 189–208.

Klopfer, E., Sheldon, J., Perry, J. & Chen, V. H. (2012). Ubiquitous games for learning (UbiqGames): Weatherlings, a worked example. *Journal of Computer Assisted Learning*, *28*(5), 465–476.

Kumar, S., Liu, F. & Black, E. W. (2012). Undergraduates' collaboration and integration of new technologies in higher education: Blurring the lines between informal and educational contexts. *Digital Culture & Education*, *421*, 248–259.

Langan, A. M., Wheater, C. P., Shaw, E. M., Haines, B. J., Cullen, W. R., Boyle, J. C. . . . Preziosi, R. F. (2005). Peer assessment of oral presentations: Effects of student gender, university affiliation and participation in the development of assessment criteria. *Assessment & Evaluation in Higher Education*, *30*(1), 21–34.

Lin, S.-S. (2013). Science and non-science undergraduate students' critical thinking and argumentation performance in reading a science news report. *International Journal of Science and Mathematics Education, 12*(5), 1023–1046.

Liu, N. & Carless, D. (2006). Peer feedback: The learning element of peer assessment. *Teaching in Higher Education, 11*(3), 279–290.

Lorenzoni, I., Jones, M. & Turnpenny, J. R. (2007). Climate change, human genetics, and post-normality in the UK. *Futures, 39*(1), 65–82.

Lowe, T., Brown, K., Dessai, S., de França Doria, M., Haynes, K. & Vincent, K. (2006). Does tomorrow ever come? Disaster narrative and public perceptions of climate change. *Public Understanding of Science, 15*(4), 435–457.

MacAlpine, J. M. K. (1999). Improving and encouraging peer assessment of student presentations. *Assessment & Evaluation in Higher Education, 24*(1), 15–25.

McClune, B. & Jarman, R. (2012). Encouraging and equipping students to engage critically with science in the news: What can we learn from the literature? *Studies in Science Education, 48*(1), 1–49.

O'Toole, M. (2012). *How can student video production affect teaching and learning in my chemistry class?* Unpublished MSc thesis, Dublin City University, Republic of Ireland.

Pasquali, M. (2007). Video in science. *EMBO Reports, 8*(8), 712–716.

Phillips, R., Baudains, C. & van Keulen, M. (2002). An evaluation of student learning in a web-supported unit on plant diversity. In *Proceedings of the 19th ASCILITE Conference*, Auckland, New Zealand. Retrieved from www.ascilite.org.au/conferences/auckland02/proceedings/papers/161.pdf (accessed 24 March, 2015).

Reeves, T., Herrington, J. & Oliver, R. (2002). Authentic activities and online learning. In A. Goody, J. Herrington & M. Northcote (Eds.), *Quality conversations: Research and development in higher education, Volume 25* (pp. 562–567). Jamison, Australia: HERDSA. Retrieved from http://www.ecu.edu.au/conferences/herdsa/papers/ref/pdf/Reeves.pdf (accessed 30 March, 2015).

Resnick, M. (2007). Sowing the seeds for a more creative society. *Learning and Leading with Technology, 35*(4), 18–22.

Ryan, B. (2013). A walk down the red carpet: Students as producers of digital video–based knowledge. *International Journal of Technology Enhanced Learning, 5*(1), 24–41.

Sawyer, R. K. (2006). Educating for innovation. *Thinking Skills and Creativity, 1*(1), 41–48.

Scardamalia, M. & Bereiter, C. (1994). Computer support for knowledge-building communities. *Journal of Learning Sciences, 3*(3), 265–283.

Sellmann, D. & Bogner, F. X. (2012). Education in global climate change at a botanical garden: Students' perceptions and inquiry-based learning. In W. Leal Filho (Ed.). *Climate change and the sustainable use of water resources* (pp. 779–787). Berlin: Springer-Verlag.

Shuldman, M. & Tajik, M. (2010). The role of media/video production in non-media disciplines: The case of health promotion. *Learning, Media and Technology, 35*(3), 357–362.

Smith, D. (2004). Issues and trends in higher education biology fieldwork. *Journal of Biological Education, 39*(1), 6–10. doi: 10.1080/00219266.2004.9655946

Topping, K. J. (2009). Peer assessment. *Theory into Practice, 48*(1), 20–27.

Willmott, C. J. R. (2014). Teaching bioethics via the production of student-generated videos. *Journal of Biological Education.* Published online: 3 Apr 2014. doi: 10.1080/00219266.2014.897640.

Wilson, R. S., Niehaus, A. C., White, J., Rasmussen, A. & Kuchel, L. (2009). Using documentary video-making to enhance learning in large first-year biology classes. *Integrative and Comparative Biology, 49*, e325.

10

STUDENT-GENERATED DYNAMIC WORKED EXAMPLES AS VIDEOS TO ENHANCE LEARNING IN STEM

Iouri Belski and Regina Belski

Context

Successful learning in science, technology, engineering and mathematics (STEM) requires effective integration of conceptual and procedural knowledge (Rittle-Johnson & Alibali, 1999; Schneider & Stern, 2010). In order to 'know how' to establish the amount of time it will take a ball dropped from a height of 10 metres to reach the ground, a learner needs to 'know what' to expect when the ball is released and a learner must be aware of the concept of gravitation. Similarly, the comprehension of gravitation requires knowledge of how to apply Newton's second law of motion.

One effective method that can be used for integrating conceptual and procedural knowledge is studying worked examples (WE). WE have been used by STEM educators for a long time – most textbooks in these disciplines contain numerous WE that students can study on their own. The effectiveness of WE as an instructional device for a novice to integrate conceptual and procedural knowledge in semantically rich domains of STEM disciplines is not wholly unexpected. In professional settings STEM graduates are usually required to apply 'standard' procedures (productions) that are the most appropriate in 'standard' situations (Simon, 1996). WE offer 'expert' solutions that unveil the expert choices of the appropriate productions and the ways experts apply these productions to solve problems. In essence, by studying WE students learn to emulate the experts' strategies and gradually acquire skill in both recognising standard situations ('knowing what') and choosing and applying appropriate standard solution procedures in different situations ('knowing how').

The educational success of WE stems from the fact that using WE imposes a lower cognitive demand on the learner than conventional problem solving. This was first reported by Sweller and Cooper (1985), who compared the impact of WE and conventional problem solving on acquisition of problem-solving skills by students studying algebra. They found that students studying WE needed less time to acquire certain types of knowledge compared to students learning by solving problems (Sweller & Cooper, 1985). Studying WE absorbed fewer cognitive resources and, therefore, resulted in more-efficient student learning. Since 1985, similar conclusions have come from multiple areas of learning including: geometry (Paas & van Merriënboer, 1994), computer science (Schwonke *et al.*, 2009), physics and electrical engineering (Moreno, Reisslein & Ozogul, 2009). It has also been reported that the effectiveness of WE may depend on the domain expertise of the learners and it is likely that WE suit novices the most (Kalyuga, Chandler, Tuovinen & Sweller, 2001).

Until recently, most WE supplied to students were 'static' and were distributed by academics as printed media, pdf or MS Word files. Static worked examples (SWE) usually contain a problem statement, diagrams and pictures showing how to appropriately categorise the problem, the steps to solve the problem and, on some occasions, offer comments on the solution process. Recent rapid developments in IT have created opportunities for educators to offer students 'dynamic' worked examples (DWE) – solutions that present the static information but also visual elements contained in the SWE can incorporate spoken instructions that can be watched repeatedly (Belski, 2011; Belski & Belski, 2013; Moreno & Mayer, 1999; Patel & Feinson, 2005; Wandel, 2010).

Many studies on DWE report improvements in student satisfaction with their studies as well as greater engagement in learning. For example, student surveys by Patel and Feinson (2005) showed that video illustrations were not only more effective in engaging students studying statistics in using spreadsheet applications, but they also helped students enjoy statistics. Comparing end-of-semester student survey results when the videos were available to those when videos had not been offered, Patel and Feinson discovered that: (i) student enjoyment of statistics more than doubled (20% in 2003 up to 46% in 2004); (ii) more students felt that statistics was important for their career success (30% up to 72%); and (iii) the number of students regularly using the statistics software grew substantially (35% up to 65%). Wandel (2010) used DWE in his classes on thermodynamics and found that students perceived the DWE to be very helpful for their learning. Moreover, he found that students liked the videos more than the static snapshots of the videos that were offered as pdf prints. Belski (2011) compared student perceptions of 10 WE that were offered to students studying electronics as both DWE and SWE. He discovered that students liked DWE more than SWE and used the former more often than the latter both during the semester and while preparing for the final examination. It was also reported that DWE significantly enhanced students' unit knowledge as compared to SWE (Belski, 2011). Moreover, Belski and Belski (2013) compared students' performance in the same unit over 4 consecutive years where DWE were introduced in order to compensate for the loss of 12 hours of face-to-face tutorial classes. They reported that students' examination performance significantly improved with the addition of DWE, and demonstrated that this improvement came specifically as a result of the boost in knowledge transfer.

The success in student learning reported by Belski and Belski (2013) triggered the authors' interest in engaging students to design and generate their own DWE to further enhance learning. The authors were interested to discover: (i) whether students learn new material effectively while they record DWE and (ii) whether the DWE recorded by the students can help their peers to learn effectively. This chapter presents two sample cases of students developing DWE and the observed impact on student learning and engagement. In the first case, a student developed two DWE on how to build and simulate electronic circuits with PSpice, which is a circuit simulation software program. In the second case, 75 students created a short DWE on the analysis of digital electronic circuits with PSpice as a part of their unit assessment.

Why DWE on PSpice?

Students in both cases were involved in developing DWE that deployed the electronic circuit simulation software – PSpice. PSpice is a PC version of the SPICE software (Simulated Program with Integrated Circuit Emphasis) that was developed for mainframe computers. PSpice has been used by engineers and scientists for over 30 years and permits users to draw an electronic circuit and to simulate behaviours of the circuit across a number of variables such as time, frequency or temperature. PSpice is considered a standard industry tool for circuit simulation. As a rule, every electronic circuit needs to be simulated and 'improved' before it can be manufactured.

The choice of recording PSpice simulations as DWE was purposeful. It was expected that deciding on the appropriate circuits to simulate, explaining PSpice simulation procedures and simulating circuit behaviours for others would effectively enhance integration of conceptual and procedural knowledge of electronics and result in substantial knowledge gain. Having the students design and create a DWE is based on the following principles:

- PSpice simulation engages students in activities that require sound knowledge of electronics basics. These activities include: (i) deciding on the appropriate circuit topology; (ii) choosing the most suitable circuit components; and (iii) determining the most-effective simulation strategies;
- PSpice simulation usually needs to be validated by hand-drawn estimations and, thus, is likely to engage students in additional theoretical work that is closely related to the simulated circuit. Therefore, the students developing DWE are required to conduct substantial theoretical work in order to ensure that their DWE are accurate;
- PSpice simulation offers various output options that require sound comprehension of electronics basics for adequate interpretation. Simulation results can be confusing, especially for a novice. Therefore, interpretation of the simulation results requires learners to study unit material more thoroughly and even to search elsewhere for more information about the circuit under construction; and,
- Although sketching a circuit in PSpice is usually straightforward, programming the chosen PSpice analysis may be challenging and typically requires sound comprehension of the expected circuit behaviour as well as a good understanding of basic definitions and circuit theorems.

Screen-capture software tools

In order to record the DWE, students were asked to use software for recording a computer screen. There are numerous freely available software tools for capturing videos of a computer screen that could be learnt quickly (e.g. Ezvid, CamStudio, Webinaria). Most of these software tools have an important drawback – they offer limited or no editing capabilities. Commercially available Camtasia Studio software allows recording and editing the video content and can also be made interactive by inserting quizzes that are then available when viewing the video via a web browser.

Implementation

Case example 1

To investigate whether being involved in the development of DWE enabled a student to learn new material effectively and whether the DWE recorded by the student could help his peers to learn effectively, an engineering student (let us call him David) was asked to develop two DWE on the PSpice simulation for novices as part of a fourth-year design project supervised by one of the authors. David's original knowledge in PSpice was limited and required substantial enhancement. He had not recorded educational videos before. It was expected that he would produce two DWE of 15–20 minutes duration, and that these DWE would contain quizzes and be narrated by a 'teacher' and a 'student'. To enable this, David was provided with a Camtasia Studio software licence. Figure 10.1 shows screen prints of two sections of David's DWE that have been merged into one image by the authors. The section on the left in Figure 10.1 is devoted to practical hints on how PSpice simulation can help in establishing voltage and current values that are required to replace a complex circuit by its simplified representation – the Thevenin's equivalent. The section on the right in Figure 10.1 shows a result of a quiz (completed by the author) that has been embedded into David's DWE in order to help students in assessing their comprehension of the DWE material.

After completing his work David was asked to reflect on his learning as a result of the video development. Overall, David assessed the DWE development as a sound learning experience:

> I learnt a lot from developing PSpice video tutorials. It was not as easy to develop tutorials as people say. Patience, time management and creativity are very important in developing tutorials . . . This deepened my knowledge of electronics and electrical engineering, and enhanced my understanding of each component's behaviour. My mind was broadened by the creation of the video tutorials.

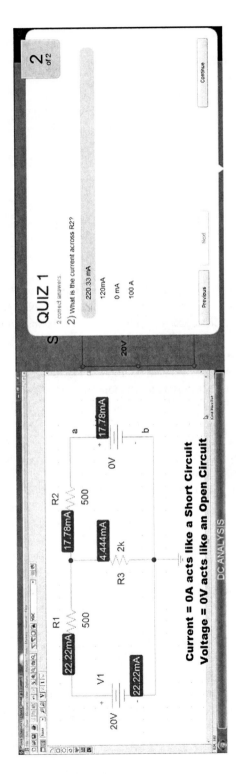

FIGURE 10.1 A screen print of David's DWE (used with permission)

In David's opinion, scripting and editing DWE were the most challenging activities of DWE recording (*What were the most challenging issues while developing videos?*):

> Writing the scripts and editing the video and audio files . . . I spent lots of time revising the tutorial scripts and producing the video tutorials.

Moreover, these activities in David's opinion resulted in the most effective learning (*Which stage of the video development was the most useful for your individual learning?*):

> Preparing the script was very important because this . . . enhances your creativity, vocabulary and . . . knowledge about electronic components . . . Preparing narration was similar to preparing the script. My creativity was also improved in this stage.

David also reflected on extremely effective learning while developing quizzes:

> Developing quizzes gave me a broader understanding of what I was doing. For example, I created a script and chose the circuits that I wanted to discuss. Then, by constructing a similar circuit with different values [of components] for the quizzes allowed me to elaborate on the topic.

David's feedback demonstrates that he felt engaged in his learning, and improved his knowledge, skills, confidence and creativity through the process of developing DWE for his peers.

Both videos recorded by David were made available to students enrolled in a third-year unit in electronic engineering, who were later surveyed on the DWE quality, and the impact of these DWE on their learning. The survey (SurveyMonkey, web-based) was prepared and conducted by David. Sixty students participated in the survey. His fellow students found David's DWE helpful for their learning. Table 10.1 presents data from the student responses to a number of the survey questions that were related to the influence of David's DWE on their learning.

TABLE 10.1 Survey responses (n = 60; Scale: 5 = strongly agree, 3 = not sure, 1 = strongly disagree)

	Mean	Std. Dev.
Q1 I am able to learn more per hour spent, with traditional teaching, rather than using an interactive multimedia approach.	2.62	1.22
Q2 After completing a multimedia tutorial on PSpice, I feel very confident to use PSpice to simulate the circuit shown.	4.13	0.81
Q3 I am inspired to do more simulations by multimedia based tutorials.	4.00	0.80
Q4 The step-by-step process of creating the circuit and simulating it is well explained and shown by the video tutorial.	4.27	0.71

TABLE 10.2 Survey responses (n = 60; Scale: 5 = excellent, 4 = good, 3 = average, 2 = satisfactory, 1 = poor)

	Mean	Std. Dev.
Q5 How would you rate the video tutorial based on video and audio quality?	3.78	1.18
Q6 How would you rate the information delivered and the prepared quiz?	3.98	0.97

Table 10.2 presents the survey data on students' perceptions of the DWE video and audio quality as well as the adequacy of the quizzes that were embedded in the DWE produced by David.

Student opinions on the videos were positive:

> I found it very informative and much better than other material available on the Internet. They are well prepared and easy to understand. I was surprised by how clear it was. Good quality and easy to understand. Great video.

David was surprised by the positive feedback, as while he felt that he had learnt a lot in the process, he did not anticipate that viewers would be satisfied with audio and video quality of his DWE:

> I was also convinced that the challenging part of video tutorials is to produce a better quality audio and video that satisfies them.

David also established that viewers assessed the quizzes as useful:

> . . . the most useful part of video tutorials were the quizzes. Because based on student feedback, after watching the video tutorials they have the chance to apply what they have learnt.

Case example 2

To investigate whether the findings of enhanced learning through the production of DWE from David's example could be translated to a larger group of students, the authors incorporated the production of DWE into a unit assessment task for a whole class. Seventy-five students (fourth-year undergraduate and postgraduate) enrolled in a unit on advanced circuit simulation with PSpice were given 2 weeks to record a 5–10-minute DWE on digital electronic circuit simulation. The DWE corresponded to 25% of the unit's total assessment. Although the unit activities covered numerous advanced topics of circuit simulation, no classes were held on digital simulation. It was expected that students would learn digital simulations while preparing and recording their DWE.

Most of the students had never created educational videos or been involved in the development of educational materials. Only one student indicated that he had used screen capture software in the past to record a simple procedural video. Students were made aware of numerous available software tools for capturing video from a computer screen that could be learnt quickly and downloaded for free. Students had to make their own choices of software to use. Figure 10.2 shows a small section of one student-generated DWE, which incorporated extensive audio explanations covering both the operation of a traffic light and its simulation in PSpice.

The left half of the screen in Figure 10.2 depicts the digital circuit that models the behaviour of the traffic light. The right half of the screen contains a state diagram of the traffic light. The state diagram is a graphical representation of all the states that the traffic light can be in (e.g. 'the green light to pedestrians and the red light to cars' or 'the red light to pedestrians and the yellow light to cars'). This state diagram defines the conditions for all possible states of the traffic light and how they occur.

After student marks were released, they were asked to reflect on their learning during the development of the DWE videos by participating in a web-based survey (Qualtrics). The survey consisted of 10 questions, two of which were open-ended. Twenty-one students completed this survey. Table 10.3 presents the opinions of students on the development of DWE and the impact of this development on their learning.

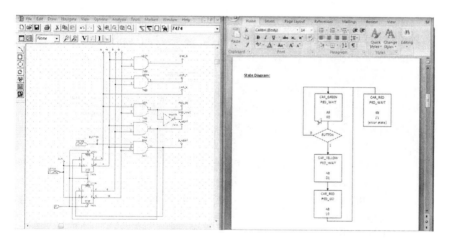

FIGURE 10.2   A screen print of a student's DWE (used with permission)

TABLE 10.3   Survey responses (n = 21, Scale: 10 = fully agree, 5 = not sure, 0 = fully disagree)

		Mean	Std. Dev.
Q1	I enjoyed developing PSpice video tutorial	7.52	2.27
Q2	Developing PSpice video tutorial helped me to learn digital simulations very effectively	6.30	2.16
Q3	Developing PSpice video tutorial was much more useful for my learning than the lecture classes	4.47	2.01
Q4	I wish to have more video assignments in my future study	5.68	3.69

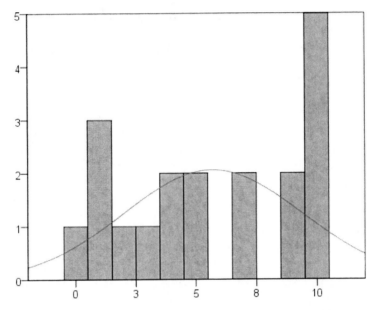

FIGURE 10.3 Distribution of students' opinions for Question 4 in Table 10.3

Figure 10.3 presents the actual distribution of student responses to Question 4 in Table 10.3, the only question in Table 10.3 that revealed an unusually high standard deviation.

The following is a selection of typical student responses to the survey questions that identify how activities in DWE development impacted on their learning.

What aspects of developing your video were most efficient for your learning?

I had to think like a teacher. Researching and gathering all the relevant information. Most efficient learning while developing video was to understand the topic and showing it stepwise rather than putting the facts randomly. Using most of the techniques taught in lectures and labs in the project in the given time of less [than] 10 minutes.

What aspects of developing your video challenged you the most?

Organising language to express the idea. Oral English and professional language. To deliver the audience with more information not only on the circuit and simple simulation, but also some extended knowledge. That needs good understanding not only of electronic circuits, PSpice itself and also the ability to think clearly. The narration of the video. Completing the video within 5 minutes was the most challenging. There was so much I wanted to say but could not finish it in 5 minutes. So at the end [I] had to minimise my video contents.

It is important to note that some student responses to the latter question identified that they experienced problems that were related to editing their DWE:

> Editing the video with the software chosen. [I] spend 90% time on . . . learning how to record video and editing . . . ! Most challenging part of developing video was to dub [and] show at the same time.

Students' concern with the editing was later clarified by face-to-face discussions with a smaller group (n = 10). It was confirmed that some students chose screen capture software that either did not offer an editing facility or had a poor one. Therefore, in order to make their videos free of errors and glitches, many students had to re-record their videos several times.

Discussion

Student opinions from both case examples suggest that the first research question, whether students learn new material effectively while they produce DWE, appears to have a positive answer. There were, however, some differences between the two cases. It seems that David, who devoted more time to plan, record and edit his DWE, was more certain of his learning gains than the average student in the second example. David believed that the DWE development deepened his knowledge of electronics and broadened his mind. This outcome is in line with the authors' expectations on the use of PSpice DWE as the means for integrating conceptual and procedural knowledge. This outcome also supports the suggestions of Hoban and Nielsen (2013), that individual learning can be enhanced through engaging students in producing educational videos.

Most of the students involved in Case Example 2 enjoyed the experience (Question 1, Table 10.3: *I enjoyed developing PSpice video tutorial*; Mean = 7.52/10; SD = 2.27). Despite that enjoyment, students were less excited about their learning gains on the new topic of digital circuit simulation. The 'average' opinion of the 21 students on their learning while developing DWE was just positive (Question 2 in Table 10.3: *Developing PSpice video tutorial helped me to learn digital simulations very effectively*; Mean = 6.30/10; SD = 2.16; 5 – not sure). The difference in student opinions in questions 1 and 2 may be explained by their frustration with the limitations of the screen capture tools. More specifically, as mentioned, some students were unhappy with the very-limited capabilities to edit the recorded video offered by the software tools that were available for free. These software limitations required students to record their DWE numerous times in order to ensure that the final DWE would be of acceptable quality. This resulted in additional time investment that could have been avoided if proper editing features were available.

Interestingly, students in the second example assessed the impact of the DWE development on their learning as nearly on a par with the face-to-face learning (Question 3 in Table 10.3: *Developing PSpice video tutorial was much more useful for my learning than the lecture classes*; Mean = 4.47/10; SD = 2.01). During the semester the 'lecture' classes that were conducted for 2 hours a week were very practical. They consisted of short periods of theoretical introductions (5 minutes) followed by practical exercises (students were given tasks to simulate on their own laptops that usually required 20 minutes of practical work and discussions). Therefore, students' opinions revealed by their responses to Question 3 can be considered as a strong indication of the learning effectiveness of individual video-development activities. Although students viewed the face-to-face classes as a little more effective than video development, it is likely that the dominance of face-to-face learning can be attributed to the previously mentioned students' frustration with the limited editing capability of free software for screen capture. Thus, it would be of interest to investigate the matter further and to establish whether students who use a friendlier screen capture tool would assess the video-development activities as more effective for their learning than the face-to-face classes.

Taking into account students' reported enjoyment of the development of DWE, their modest enthusiasm to have more video assignments was unexpected (Question 4 in Table 10.3: *I wish to have more video assignments in my future study*; Mean = 5.68/10; SD = 3.69). It is important to note that the standard deviation of the latter result was very substantial. Analysis of the individual student responses to Question 4, shown in Figure 10.3, reveals a nearly equal division of the students – nine of them wanted to develop more videos, eight were against it. It is likely that the low enthusiasm to video assignments was also directly related to the substantial amount of time required to record quality videos. In other words, it is likely that the students who had chosen the screen capture software without editing capability were more pessimistic about further engagement in video-based assignments.

Even with the technical limitations students faced, there was a positive impact of DWE on student learning. While developing DWE, David and the students in the second example constructed representations as a semiotic progression (Hoban & Nielsen, 2013). Student responses on the survey reveal that whilst developing DWE they had to: (i) research their task; (ii) decide on and prepare circuit diagrams for the simulations; (iii) decide on the appropriate simulation strategy and the simulation output; (iv) simulate the circuit and check the validity of the simulation results; (v) interpret the simulation results; and (vi) prepare a script and narration. Seemingly, these activities engaged students in integrating conceptual and procedural knowledge and resulted in sound knowledge gains.

To consider the second research question of whether the DWE recorded by the students can help their peers to learn effectively, the survey data from Case Example 1 are informative. Opinions from the 60 students surveyed in the first case example suggested that student-generated DWE could help other learners. The student responses to Question 4 in Table 10.1 (*The step-by-step process of creating the circuit and simulating it is well explained and shown*) (Mean = 4.27/5, SD = 0.71) indicate strongly that the DWE created by David were easy to follow. Moreover, the students perceived that they had learnt from the DWE. Their answers to Question 2 in Table 10.1 (*After completing a multimedia tutorial on PSpice, I feel very confident to use PSpice to simulate the circuit shown*) confirm their learning gain (Mean = 4.13/5, SD = 0.81). Furthermore, the responses to Question 3 in Table 10.1 shows that DWE motivated the students to use PSpice further (*I am inspired to do more simulations, by multimedia based tutorials*) (Mean = 4.00/5, SD = 0.80). Essentially, student opinions confirmed: (i) that they were able to follow the DWE comfortably; (ii) that they gained knowledge from DWE that improved their self-confidence in PSpice; and (iii) that they were motivated to do more simulations on their own as a result of watching DWE.

It is important to note that the positive conclusion relating to the second research question is further validated by the students' response to Question 1 in Table 10.1 (*I am able to learn more per hour spent, with traditional teaching, rather than using an interactive multimedia approach*) (Mean = 2.62/5, SD = 1.22). Such a response to this question positions the learning effectiveness of the DWE on PSpice above that of the traditional face-to-face teaching and needs to be critically considered by STEM educators. This positive student opinion on DWE further supports the results on the impact of DWE on student learning that were presented in the opening section of the chapter. Therefore, providing STEM students with DWE that focus on areas that are known to create the highest student confusion is likely to result in enhancement of student learning.

The information contained in Table 10.2, as well as student opinions presented previously, confirmed the adequate quality of the DWE (*How would you rate the video tutorial based on video and audio quality?*) (Mean = 3.78/5, SD = 1.18). In essence, students who accessed David's DWE suggested that useful educational multimedia resources need to be judged on content but not on the video/audio quality. Extending this result to instructor-generated resources, this means that STEM educators need not worry too much about the quality of DWE they record and that they can use free or inexpensive software tools like iMovie, Windows Movie Maker and Camtasia Studio to create DWE. Furthermore, this student opinion implies that educational videos created by students with slowmation (Hoban & Nielsen, 2012) or Camtasia Studio that do not offer 'superior' video quality can be effectively used as teaching aids by other learners.

In accordance with David's opinion presented in the 'implementation' section of this chapter, developing quizzes was very beneficial for his personal learning. Students who watched David's DWE also had positive opinions about the quizzes (*How would you rate the information delivered and the prepared quiz?*) (Mean = 3.98/5, SD = 0.97). This positive assessment of the quizzes embedded into DWE by fellow students, though, did not reveal the true educational impact of the quizzes on their learning. Therefore, the influence of embedding quizzes into DWE on the learning of the DWE viewers needs further investigation.

The case examples presented in this chapter have certain limitations. Case Example 1 involved a single student video-creator. David had positive reflections on his learning with DWE, but of course he is only one student. David's assessment of the educational effectiveness of developing the DWE was corroborated by the Case Example 2 students. Thus, we cautiously suggest that engaging STEM students in developing DWE is a sound educational strategy. It could also be argued that only 21 students involved in the second example completed the survey and that the outcomes of the survey would be more statistically generalisable if the survey had been completed by at least 30 students. At the same time, 21 responding students represent a statistically acceptable sample out of a class of 75 who were invited to participate in a non-compulsory web-based survey via email after the unit was complete. Accordingly, the outcomes of the statistical analysis of survey responses of students from Case Example 2 can also be accepted as validating the educational effectiveness of engaging STEM students in DWE development.

Conclusion

In the two case examples discussed, DWE enabled students to learn new skills and gain new knowledge both through developing the DWE and in watching those produced by others. Whilst students reported enjoying the experience overall, those students using freely available screen capture software found the lack of editing options a frustration as it required them to re-record the video numerous times. This likely contributed to mixed opinions on whether they would favour future assignments requiring student-generated video production. Considering the increasing availability of software that enables students to be engaged in the production of learning resources to benefit themselves and their peers, the authors would recommend that other STEM educators consider utilising student-produced DWE in their study units – but taking care to ensure suitable editing software is available for student use.

References

Belski, I. (2011). Dynamic and static worked examples in student learning. In Y. M. Al-Abdeli & E. Lindsay (Eds.), *Proceedings of the 22nd AAEE Conference* (pp. 396–401). Fremantle, Australia: Engineers Australia.

Belski, I. & Belski, R. (2013). Impact of dynamic (videotaped) worked examples on knowledge transfer. In C. Lemckert, G. Jenkins & S. Lang-Lemckert (Eds.), *Proceedings of the 24th AAEE Conference* (pp. 3A2, 1–8). Nathan, Australia: Griffith University.

Hoban, G. & Nielsen, W. (2012). Using 'slowmation' to enable preservice primary teachers to create multimodal representations of science concepts. *Research in Science Education*, 42(6), 1101–1119.

Hoban, G. & Nielsen, W. (2013). Learning science through creating a 'slowmation': A case study of preservice primary teachers. *International Journal of Science Education*, 35(1), 119–146.

Kalyuga, S., Chandler, P., Tuovinen, J. & Sweller, J. (2001). When problem solving is superior to studying worked examples. *Journal of Educational Psychology*, 93(3), 579–588.

Moreno, R. & Mayer, R. E. (1999). Cognitive principles of multimedia learning: The role of modality and contiguity. *Journal of Educational Psychology*, 91(2), 358–368.

Moreno, R., Reisslein, M. & Ozogul, G. (2009). Optimizing worked-example instruction in electrical engineering: The role of fading and feedback during problem-solving practice. *Journal of Engineering Education*, 98(1), 83–92.

Paas, F. G. W. C. & van Merriënboer, J. J. G. (1994). Variability of worked examples and transfer of geometrical problem-solving skills: A cognitive-load approach. *Journal of Educational Psychology, 86*(1), 122–133.

Patel, R. & Feinson, C. (2005). Using PHStat and Camtasia Studio 2 in teaching business statistics. *Journal of College Teaching & Learning, 2*(9), 53–58.

Rittle-Johnson, B. & Alibali, M. W. (1999). Conceptual and procedural knowledge of mathematics: Does one lead to the other? *Journal of Educational Psychology, 91*(1), 175–189.

Schneider, M. & Stern, E. (2010). The developmental relations between conceptual and procedural knowledge: A multimethod approach. *Developmental Psychology, 46*(1), 178–192.

Schwonke, R., Renkl, A., Krieg, C., Wittwer, J., Aleven, V. & Salden, R. (2009). The worked-example effect: Not an artefact of lousy control conditions. *Computers in Human Behavior, 25*(2), 258–266.

Simon, H. A. (1996). *The sciences of the artificial* (3rd ed). Cambridge, MA: MIT Press.

Sweller, J. & Cooper, G. A. (1985). The use of worked examples as a substitute for problem solving in learning algebra. *Cognition and Instruction, 2*, 59–89.

Wandel, A. P. (2010). Student usage of videos containing worked solutions. In A. Gardner & L. Jolly (Eds.), *Proceedings of the 21st AAEE Conference* (pp. 301–306). Sydney: University of Technology.

11

STUDENTS' USE OF DIGITAL VIDEO IN CONTEMPORARY SCIENCE TEACHER EDUCATION

Matthew Kearney, Kimberley Pressick-Kilborn and Peter Aubusson

Context

Learner-generated digital video (DV) projects are widely used in school classrooms to support or modify pedagogy and curriculum outcomes (Bull & Bell, 2010). The popularity of these tasks has been inspired by a burgeoning choice of easy-to-use, accessible digital cameras and editing facilities, with expanding possibilities for seamless creation and online dissemination of video products. DV tasks can enhance a wide range of learning outcomes, from the development of traditional and new literacy skills to affective benefits. They can support a rich, authentic learning experience that encourages student autonomy and ownership, and meaningful student roles and interactions, especially when students are given an opportunity to discuss and celebrate their products with a relevant audience (Schuck & Kearney, 2006). However, the use of DV projects in the context of initial teacher education is under-theorised and has typically focused on the analysis of classroom-based footage of teaching practices (Yerrick, Thompson, McLaughlin & MacDonald, 2011).

The purpose of this chapter is twofold. First, an alternative way of framing the use of DV in teacher education is presented, drawing on Schuck and Kearney's (2006) two main modes or types of student-generated digital video across the school curriculum. In this framework, Type 1 DV tasks are used primarily as a *communication tool* to facilitate students' communication, while Type 2 DV tasks are used primarily as an *inquiry tool* to enhance students' observation and analysis of performance or phenomena (Schuck & Kearney, 2006). The second purpose of this chapter is to employ this framework to analyse and discuss how DV tasks are used by prospective teachers in science teacher education. We present illustrative case snapshots developed from a national Australian project called Teaching Teachers for the Future for this purpose. This project aimed to develop student teachers' digital competencies and pedagogies. The discussion incorporates implications for science teacher education and directions for future research.

Type 1 DV tasks as communication tools

Discussion of DV projects in teacher education has typically focused on their use as an inquiry tool into teaching practices, rather than more-immersive, generative DV types of tasks where student teachers communicate information, understandings and emotions (Type 1a) or distil thinking (Type 1b) (Martin & Siry, 2012; Wong, Mishra, Koehler & Siebenthal, 2007).

Use by pre-service teachers to express understandings and emotions (Type 1a)

DV tasks can mediate students' communication and expression of ideas and are typically used to communicate science knowledge. Sample genres of Type 1a DV tasks include video essays (Norton & Hathaway, 2010), concept videos (Hechter & Guy, 2010), slow animations or slowmations (Hoban, 2007), 'ideas-based' videos or iVideos (Kearney, 2013; Wong et al., 2007) and role-plays (Yerrick, Doster, Nugent, Parke & Crawley, 2003). A strong theme throughout this literature is the engagement of cognitive and affective processes, facilitated by the emotional investment demanded in the tasks (Hakkarainen, 2009). Student teachers can develop discipline-specific content knowledge through the process of generating video products (Hakkarainen, 2009) and they can display their knowledge of specific science concepts through these video-based representations (Hoban, Loughran & Nielsen, 2011; Yerrick, Ross & Molebash, 2005). Type 1a DV tasks help student teachers to develop confidence and professional identity as teachers of science (Hechter & Guy, 2010), as well as multimodal literacy and creativity skills (Hoban et al., 2011), aesthetics and authentic expression (Girod, Bell & Mishra, 2007).

Hechter and Guy (2010) have investigated how pre-service elementary (primary) teachers communicate their understanding of core science concepts by making instructional science 'concept videos', which are essentially 3–5-minute demonstrations or role-plays. The video making requires the pre-service teachers to think deeply about the target science concepts, with video products becoming representations of their science views. Products were used to address student teachers' alternative science conceptions. Yerrick et al. (2003) used video role-plays to help student teachers understand the history of science. Student teachers videorecorded interviews with local community members who applied science in their everyday lives and made DV autobiographies about how they use science themselves. They began to 'see themselves as scientists' and to appreciate the ubiquity of science in their everyday lives. In Norton and Hathaway's (2010) research, student teachers created video essays on a given topic (similar to concept videos) for the children in their classes during practicum. Results evidenced content learning and engagement (by K–12 learners) while student teachers developed their professional identities. Another sample genre is a form of animation where learners create slow-motion animations to explain a science concept. Like Hechter and Guy's (2010) study, Hoban (2007) found that making slowmations with the purpose of representing and accurately explaining science content to an audience enhanced the student teachers' motivation to understand target concepts. Finally, Wong *et al.* (2007) provide a rationale for supporting the use of iVideos ('ideas-based videos'). The process of making these short, advocacy-style videos in teacher education can be a catalyst for deep consideration of subject matter, creativity and aesthetics.

Use by pre-service teachers to distil thinking (Type 1b)

Type 1b DV tasks have been used in teacher education as a metacognitive tool to distil thinking, usually in the contexts of video-based journaling, (personal) digital storytelling and e-portfolios. Clarke (2009) reported on student teachers keeping DV reflective reports while on school practicum. Although there was minimal video editing in these 'video-diaries', students perceived that they were making more-honest reflective posts and were able to convey emotions and complexity that would be difficult through the mode of written text. The student teachers believed that the video reflections provided more intimacy, liveliness and entertainment, and gave them the ability to visually represent school-based artefacts as stimulus for their posts. Similarly, Lambert and Cuper (2008) reported on student teachers' DV reflections on their learning. They concluded that the DV medium was a creative outlet for student reflection and that rich metacognitive comments were elicited.

Yerrick *et al.* (2011) reported on student teachers' engagement in reflective practices such as post-teaching journalling. The 'video confessional' technique used video to document and analyse reflective discourse prompted by an instructor. Yerrick *et al.* (2011) emphasised modelling how to 'video confess' and be a critical thinker, making time to connect informally and capitalised on video snippets to extend learning. Increased levels of self-awareness were evident, since the process provided students with: 'a mirror to see themselves and to practice critical reflection' (Yerrick *et al.*, 2011, p. 128). Similarly, the use of personal digital storytelling (Robin, 2006) has been used to support pre-service teacher reflection and professional empowerment. Professional identity development (Roby, 2010) and reflection on experience have been reported as outcomes – including support for reflective processes during e-portfolio development (Cheng & Chau, 2009; Finger & Russell, 2005). For example, Kearney (2009) reported on student teachers using digital storytelling to present a reflective piece around selected artefacts in a coherently packaged, visually compelling 'personal story of their learning'. Developing these stories facilitated the early stages of the reflection process: returning to the experience and attending to associated emotions (Boud, Keogh & Walker, 1985). Student teachers were able to distil their thinking mediated by their (personal) digital story of learning, integrating deeper analyses of their experiences and appraisal of their learning.

Type 2 DV tasks as inquiry tools

Learner-generated digital video has been reported in science teacher education as an observation and analysis tool in two ways, which we label as two types in this discussion: for examining science phenomena to enhance science content knowledge development (Type 2a); and to analyse science teaching performance, usually to support development of science pedagogical knowledge (Type 2b). Both types of DV tasks can include the use of sophisticated analysis software and annotation tools (Rich & Hannafin, 2009; Zahn, Pea, Hesse & Rosen, 2010) to interrogate video data of phenomena for science inquiry purposes or field-based science teaching events for the purposes of pedagogical inquiry.

Use by pre-service teachers to observe and analyse science phenomena (Type 2a)

Type 2a DV tasks give science learners sophisticated tools to observe and analyse dynamic science phenomena in intricate detail. The observation and analysis of real-life science phenomena can make science more relevant to learners and help them build links between their prior experiences and abstract models and principles (Escalada & Zollman, 1997). Our human 'window' into the natural and physical world is limited and much phenomena of interest to science learners exists as scales beyond our temporal, perceptual or experiential limits (Kozma, 2000). Video can help overcome these barriers by showing dangerous, difficult, expensive or time-consuming demonstrations not normally possible in the laboratory (Bell, Juersivich, Hammond & Bell, 2011). For example, video can create the illusion of slowing down or speeding up time. This facility is particularly useful when considering time-dependent phenomena prevalent in many examples of science concepts.

Digital video-based laboratory (VBL) software can be used to gather and analyse data about science events and phenomena, allowing students and teachers to capture video of experiments they perform themselves. Students can then use this software to efficiently generate graphs and other representations to analyse and model their video 'data'. Many studies have shown that these video-based laboratories are motivating and authentic experiences for learners (Rubin, Bresnahan & Ducas, 1996). More recent examples in teacher education contexts include prospective science teachers' use of VBL to investigate real-world problems to build conceptual understanding (Bryan, 2010).

Park (2010) makes a strong argument for Type 2a DV tasks in science teacher education. Although much of his discussion focuses on developing pedagogies with existing, published video to promote inquiry environments, Park also advocates developing student teachers' capabilities with learner-generated video to record interesting events, interpret data, test models and raise questions for inquiry. Bell *et al.* (2011) emphasise the importance of prospective science teachers understanding the benefits and constraints for learning from digital video and other dynamic visual representations such as simulations, animations, dynamic graphs and virtual manipulatives. These representations can be more effective for learning than direct experience, especially for abstract concepts involving difficult-to-observe phenomena. As much of science learning is about understanding dynamic and abstract processes, this (Type 2a) use of DV tasks to closely scrutinise science phenomena is important for student teachers to understand.

Use by pre-service teachers to observe and analyse science teaching events or experiences (Type 2b)

Type 2b DV tasks allow student teachers to critically observe and analyse a science teaching event or experience in order to conduct a pedagogical inquiry. This includes videorecording and editing of theirs and others' teaching episodes for observation and analysis purposes, for example, to critique teaching performance (Martin & Siry, 2012). Video data can capture the rich complexities and immediacy of classroom activities as a representation of a teacher's practice that can be analysed later (Zhang, Lundeberg, Koehler & Eberhardt, 2011).

Prospective teachers have traditionally observed and analysed externally created recordings of expert teachers (e.g. video cases) who are modelling exemplary teaching practices. However, the recording and analysis of one's own teaching can offer opportunities to closely examine classroom interactions, especially when student teachers edit their own video footage (Yerrick et al., 2011). The process helps student teachers to observe and analyse their own teaching 'from a distance', to objectively critique their own practice and to obtain detailed feedback from peers and supervisors (Zhang et al., 2011).

This type of DV task (Type 2b) has been used to target student teachers' own beliefs about science and science teaching. Yerrick et al. (2005) investigated science student teachers editing and creating videos of their own teaching and found this process was more effective than watching videos featuring others. The student teachers firstly used DV tasks to explore children's thinking by probing the children's core science ideas in an interview (e.g. seasons, moon phases, heat transfer) before editing selected footage to produce a digital video to communicate children's science beliefs. de Mesquita, Dean and Young (2010) also worked in science education contexts to help student teachers sharpen their observation and analysis skills and reflect on pertinent facets of their teaching. One focus for de Mesquita et al., similar to Yerrick et al. (2005), was to use DV to elicit naïve science conceptions and confront novice teachers' science views. de Mesquita et al. emphasised the use of annotation software to help in this process, for example, to add text features (captions, quotes, written critiques) to easily integrate and link specific events in a video.

Student teachers' Type 2b video products have been 're-used' to facilitate the development of professional communities of learners (Sherin, 2004; van Es, 2012) and as a 'means to re-think, re-value and re-consider teaching practices' (Girod et al., 2007, p. 23). For example, Yerrick et al. (2011) reported positive findings regarding the development of teacher identities through the sharing of video artefacts, discussion and critique of each other's teaching, which involved the exchange of perspectives.

Summary

There is a growing contemporary literature base shedding light on the benefits of pre-service teachers constructing and sharing their own digital videos (Hathaway & Norton, 2012). DV tasks in science teacher education can be categorised into two types, drawing on the framework reported by Schuck and Kearney (2006) in school contexts. The use of each type matches a characteristic purpose and target audience (see Table 11.1) and includes a variety of genres discussed in the literature.

Although Type 2b DV tasks feature frequently in science teacher education literature, there is a need to revisit and further explore more-immersive, creative Type 1 and 2a DV tasks to develop student teachers' science content and peda-gogical understandings, new literacies and leverage metacognitive processes. In the next section, we use our framework to present case illustrations from our science teacher education practice to highlight and contextualise these types.

TABLE 11.1 Summary of types of use of learner-generated digital video in science teacher education

Type/Main Purpose	Examples/Main Audience	Sample References
1. Communication Tool		
a. To express ideas, understandings and emotions	Video essays, concept videos, iVideos, reports, role plays, documentaries, slowmations, instructional videos, video 'anchors' Target audience: Peers, community – possibly school students	Dickinson & Summers, 2010; Hechter & Guy, 2010; Hoban, 2007; Norton & Hathaway, 2010
b. To enhance metacognition/ distillation of thinking	Video-based journal, blogs, personal digital stories (of learning), video-based e-portfolios Target audience: Self, peers, teacher	Cheng & Chau, 2009; Finger & Russell, 2005; Kearney, 2009
2. Inquiry Tool		
a. To analyse phenomena (conceptual inquiry)	Observation and measurement of natural science events, such as analysis of motion Target audience: Self, peers	Bell et al., 2012; Bryan, 2010; Park, 2010
b. To analyse teaching and learning (pedagogical inquiry)	Observation and feedback on practice such as the teaching and/ or learning episodes of oneself and others (on campus or during school professional experience) Target audience: Self, peers	de Mesquita et al., 2010; Martin & Siry, 2012; Yerrick et al., 2005, 2011

Implementation

The Teaching Teachers for the Future project was a government-funded initiative, implemented over 2011–2012, targeting the ICT proficiencies of pre-service teachers in Australian universities. Science education was a specific context for our institution's participation. The case examples that follow are drawn from this project and the teaching initiatives that have subsequently been inspired by it. The case examples are from our undergraduate primary education program and emphasise the rich and contextualised discipline-specific use of DV that is part of our pedagogy. Each of the examples comes from inquiry-based science teacher education contexts, designed with a social constructivist underpinning. These case narratives illustrate how our previously discussed framework (Table 11.1) can be employed to analyse and interpret the use of learner-generated DV practices in teacher education. Since much discussion of DV projects in science teacher education has focused on analysis of science teaching events and critique of teaching performance (Type 2b), the following case snapshots mainly focus on DV of Types 1 and 2a.

Case snapshot 1: DV as stimulus for children's investigating or designing and producing

This case consists of two examples illustrating pre-service primary teachers' use of DV as a communication tool (Type 1a), with a focus on expressing ideas to create a context for, and to promote, school students' engagement in science learning. In the first example, the student teachers chose to create short video clips as a teaching resource for their professional experience placements in primary classrooms. The purpose of making these 'video anchors' was to introduce and provide an engaging context for children to conduct their own science investigations or to design and produce a video. For example, one student teacher chose to create an original video in which she played a role as presenter of an imaginary television program, Aussie Backyard Science (see http://youtu.be/LshIDdz0z9k). In her clip, the student teacher speaks directly to her K–6 students and poses a number of questions that relate to key science concepts, in the local astronomy context of relationships between the Earth, Moon and Sun. The questions posed in the clip are intended as a starting point for the school children's own subsequent science investigations. These questions included: 'Why do we have months?', 'Why do we have years?' and 'Why do we have leap years?' A second example involved a small group of three pre-service teachers who created a video that was subsequently shown to children during a Design and Produce Day at a local partner primary school. The student teachers collaboratively made a DV clip of a fictional news bulletin, which highlighted issues related to fresh water as a limited resource and the need to conserve water in the local school community (see http://youtu.be/ajP67PULal4). The clip was used as an 'anchor' both to contextualise and deliver the design brief to the children, in a way that was novel and aimed to make the design task immediately relevant to them.

Case snapshot 2: DV as an introductory context for pre-service teachers' own science inquiry

This case also consists of two examples drawn from workshops for a unit framed using a 'learners' questions approach' (Faire & Cosgrove, 1988), focusing on light and sound (Example One) and kitchen chemistry (Example Two). The examples highlight Type 2 DV generation. The student teachers in the first example made video recordings around the university campus using mobile devices. In pairs, they recorded different examples of light and/or sound as observed or experienced as they moved around the buildings and campus grounds (Type 2a). When the class engaged in discussion about how to best share their video, one student teacher suggested using Instagram. The footage was then used as stimulus for further class discussion in which the pre-service teachers were encouraged to pose questions about the phenomena observed in the shared video. The questions guided their subsequent investigations, which they designed and undertook in small collaborative groups of four (formed by combining two pairs) during their weekly tutorials. For example, one group of student teachers focused on why some shadows were 'fuzzy' while other shadows were more sharp and dark in appearance. All groups shared their findings with classmates on campus in the form of 'hands-on' activity stations, with the pre-service teachers in the imagined role of 'explainers' in a science museum. Thus, while the DV products captured science phenomena for immediate analysis and discussion amongst the student teachers, the creation of a DV was embedded in an inquiry sequence that promoted subsequent investigation and explanation.

In a second (Type 2) example, student teachers observed a lecturer's demonstration of popping corn, in the introductory workshop of a unit focused on kitchen chemistry and, more specifically, the concept of heat causing change. As part of this workshop the student teachers made a video recording of a glass-lidded electric frypan on their mobile phones, so that they subsequently could more closely observe and scrutinise the phenomenon. The lecturer later reflected that not only did the video afford the student teachers with an opportunity to review the science phenomenon (Type 2a), it also gave them a Type 2b opportunity to review the lecturer's teaching, providing a model in this context. The questions the lecturer asked, her role in drawing student teachers' attention to particular features during the process and her responses to student teachers' comments to develop the discussion were all recorded and available for subsequent analysis (Type 2b).

Discussion

This paper addresses the need identified by Hathaway and Norton (2012) to further explore the rapidly changing teaching and learning developments with DV, particularly in discipline-specific contexts such as science education. It presents a framework that builds on the taxonomy identified by Schuck and Kearney (2006), to interpret and understand contemporary practices with learner-generated DV in science teacher education. Type 1 DV tasks are used to communicate information, ideas and emotions (1a) or to distil thinking (1b), and Type 2 DV tasks are used to observe and analyse science phenomena (2a) or science teaching and learning events (2b). Although Type 2b DV tasks feature frequently in the science teacher education literature base, a need was identified to revisit and further explore more-immersive, creative Type 1 and Type 2a DV tasks specifically, to help in the development of student teachers' science content and pedagogical understandings.

The case snapshots shared in this chapter reflect the complexity of science teacher education contexts in which DV tasks are embedded in inquiry-based approaches. The emphasis has been on student teachers collaboratively creating their own products for an authentic audience, to share their ideas and understandings with peers, staff and school students, to report on the designs and findings of science investigations, to inquire into science phenomena and to develop pertinent pedagogical approaches. The case snapshots highlight a mixture of types currently being used in our teacher education practices. For example, Case 2 set out to use Type 2a video to interrogate science phenomena (relating to the popcorn context) but, on another level, the videos became Type 2b artefacts for inquiring into the art of demonstrating.

Creative ways of disseminating the final video products was a feature of the pedagogy adopted in the cases (Kearney, 2011), including the learner-driven choice and use of social media to share digital artefacts and exchange student ideas. Re-use of the final videos as teaching resources in school-based settings was emphasised. For example, the student teachers in Case 1 used their final (Type 1) video product as a resource to stimulate children's science-based inquiry while on professional experience, akin to the creation of video 'anchors' for project-based learning approaches reported in Dickinson and Summers (2010). Future directions for our science teacher education practice include using shared DV to which others can add annotations, in relation to the science phenomena. The purpose of such practice would be to promote collaborative critical analysis and discussion of subtle conceptual modifications, and to elicit questions about their students' understandings as a catalyst to conduct further investigations.

How pre-service teachers re-use their DV artefacts to promote constructivist school-based learning environments, both physical and virtual, warrants further attention. For example, further research is needed to investigate the value of pre-service teachers using their video products as 'anchors' in online constructivist environments, incorporating teaching models such as the 5Es approach (e.g. see Dennis, 2012). Further studies also need to investigate how these types of collaborative, design-based 'deep-play' experiences (Koehler et al., 2011) impact on pre-service teachers' school science teaching, as well as their students' learning outcomes and motivation in STEM. To avoid STEM learning experiences being seen by coming generations as a throwback to a past age, it is imperative for pre-service science teachers to become familiar with the digital landscape of the twenty-first century, including creative use of emerging DV technologies, and become knowledgeable about their meaningful integration into the science curriculum.

Acknowledgements

The Teaching Teachers for the Future project was funded by the Australian Government Department of Education, Employment and Workplace Relations (DEEWR) through the ICT Innovation Fund. Thank you to the UTS students who gave us permission to make specific reference to their student-generated DV productions. Thank you also to the academic colleagues who have collaborated with us in implementing and researching these teaching innovations.

References

Bell, L., Juersivich, N., Hammond, T. C. & Bell, R. L. (2011). The TPACK of dynamic representations. In R. N. Ronau, C. R. Rakes & M. L. Niess (Eds.), *Educational technology, teacher knowledge, and classroom impact: A research handbook on frameworks and approaches* (pp. 103–135). Hershey, PA: IGI Global.

Boud D., Keogh, R. & Walker, D. (1985). Promoting reflection in learning: A model. In D. Boud, R. Keogh & D. Walker (Eds.), *Reflection: Turning experience into learning* (pp. 18–40). New York, NY: Nichols.

Bryan, J. A. (2010). Investigating the conservation of mechanical energy using video analysis: Four cases. *Physics Education, 45*(1), 50–57.

Bull, G. L. & Bell, L. (Eds.). (2010). *Teaching with digital video: Watch, analyze, create.* Eugene, OR: International Society for Technology in Education.

Cheng, G. & Chau, J. (2009). Digital video for fostering self-reflection in an ePortfolio environment. *Learning, Media and Technology, 34*(4), 337–350.

Clarke, L. (2009). Video reflections in initial teacher education. *British Journal of Educational Technology, 40*(5), 959–961.

de Mesquita, P. B., Dean, R. F. & Young, B. J. (2010). Making sure what you see is what you get: Digital video technology and the preparation of teachers of elementary science. *Contemporary Issues in Technology and Teacher Education, 10*(3), 275–293.

Dennis, C. (2012). Learning in LAMS: Lesson from a student teacher exploring gene ethics. In C. Alexander, J. Dalziel, J. Krajka & E. Dobozy (Eds.), *Teaching English with technology, 12*(2), 74–87.

Dickinson, G. & Summers, E. J. (2010). (Re)Anchored, video-centered engagement: The transferability of pre-service training to practice. *Contemporary Issues in Technology and Teacher Education, 10*(1), 106–118.

Escalada, L. T. & Zollman, D. (1997). An investigation on the effects of using interactive digital video in a physics classroom on student learning and attitudes. *Journal of Research in Science Teaching, 5*(34), 467–489.

Faire, J. & Cosgrove, M. (1988). *Teaching primary science.* Hamilton, New Zealand: Waikato Education Centre.

Finger, G. & Russell, G. (2005). *ICTs and teacher education: Digital portfolios, digital storytelling, reflection and deep learning.* Conference paper presented at Australian Teacher Education Association Conference, Surfers Paradise, Australia.

Girod, M., Bell, J. & Mishra, P. (2007). Using digital video to re-think teaching practices. *Journal of Computing in Teacher Education, 24*(1), 23–29.

Hakkarainen, P. (2009). Designing and implementing a PBL course on educational digital video production: Lessons learned from a design-based research. *Educational Technology Research & Development, 57*(2), 211–228.

Hathaway, D. & Norton, P. (2012). Video production and classroom instruction: Bridging the academies and the realities of practice in teacher education. *Journal of Technology and Teacher Education, 20*(2), 127–149.

Hechter, R. P. & Guy, M. D. (2010). Promoting creative thinking and expression of science concepts among elementary teacher candidates through science content movie creation and showcasing. *Contemporary Issues in Technology and Teacher Education, 10*(4), 411–431.

Hoban, G. (2007). Using slowmation to engage preservice elementary teachers in understanding science content knowledge. *Contemporary Issues in Technology and Teacher Education, 7*(2), 1–9.

Hoban, G., Loughran, J. & Nielsen, W. (2011). Slowmation: Pre-service elementary teachers representing science knowledge through creating multimodal digital animations. *Journal of Research in Science Teaching, 48*(9), 985–1009.

Kearney, M. (2009). Investigating digital storytelling and portfolios in teacher education. In G. Siemens & C. Fulford (Eds.), *Proceedings of World Conference on Educational Multimedia, Hypermedia and Telecommunications 2009* (pp. 1987–1996). Chesapeake, VA: AACE.

Kearney, M. (2011). A learning design for student-generated digital storytelling. *Learning, Media and Technology, 36*(2), 169–188.

Kearney, M. (2013). Learner-generated digital video: Using ideas videos in teacher education. *Journal of Technology and Teacher Education, 21*(3), 321–336.

Koehler, M. J., Mishra, P., Bouck, E. C., DeSchryver, M., Kereluik, K., Shin, T. S. & Wolf, L. G. (2011). Deep-play: Developing TPACK for 21st century teachers. *International Journal of Learning Technology, 6*(2), 146–163.

Kozma, R. (2000). The use of multiple representations and the social construction of understanding in chemistry. In M. Jacobson & R. Kozma (Eds.), *Innovations in science and maths education: Advanced designs for technologies of learning* (pp. 11–46). Mahwah, NJ: Lawrence Erlbaum.

Lambert, J. & Cuper, P. (2008). Multimedia technologies and familiar spaces: 21st-century teaching for 21st-century learners. *Contemporary Issues in Technology and Teacher Education, 8*(3), 264–276. Retrieved from http://www.citejournal.org/vol8/iss3/currentpractice/article1.cfm (accessed 24 March, 2015).

Martin, S. & Siry, C. (2012). Using video in science teacher education: An analysis of the utilization of video-based media by teacher educators and researchers. In B. Fraser, K. Tobin & C. McRobbie (Eds.), *The second international handbook of science education* (pp. 417–433). Dordrecht, The Netherlands: Springer.

Norton, P. & Hathaway, D. (2010). Video production as an instructional strategy: Content learning and teacher practice. *Contemporary Issues in Technology and Teacher Education, 10*(1), 145–166.

Park, J. (2010). Digital video in science education. In G. Bull & L. Bell (Eds.), *Teaching with digital video: Watch, analyze, create* (pp. 81–106). Eugene, OR: International Society for Technology in Education.

Rich, P. & Hannafin, M. J. (2009). Video annotation tools: Technologies to scaffold, structure, and transform teacher reflection. *Journal of Teacher Education, 60*(1), 52–67.

Robin, B. (2006). The educational uses of digital storytelling. In C. M. Crawford, R. Carlsen, K. McFerrin, J. Price, R. Weber & D. A. Willis (Eds.), *Proceedings of Society for Information Technology and Teacher Education International Conference 2006* (pp. 709–716). Chesapeake, VA: AACE.

Roby, T. (2010). Opus in the classroom: Striking CoRDS with content-related digital storytelling. *Contemporary Issues in Technology and Teacher Education, 10*(1), 133–144.

Rubin, A., Bresnahan, S. & Ducas, T. (1996). Cartwheeling through CamMotion. *Communications of the ACM, 39*(8), 84–85.

Schuck, S. & Kearney, M. (2006). Capturing learning through student-generated digital video. *Australian Educational Computing, 21*(1), 15–20.

Sherin, M. (2004). New perspectives on the role of video in teacher education. In J. Brophy (Ed.), *Using video in teacher education* (pp. 1–27). New York, NY: Elsevier Science.

van Es, E. A. (2012). Examining the development of a teacher learning community: The case of a video club. *Teaching and Teacher Education, 28*(2), 182–192.

Wong, D., Mishra, P., Koehler, M. J. & Siebenthal, S. (2007). Teacher as filmmaker: iVideos, technology education, and professional development. In M. Girod & J. Steed (Eds.), *Technology in the college classroom*. Stillwater, OK: New Forums.

Yerrick, R. K., Ross, D. & Molebash. P. (2005). Too close for comfort: Real-time science teaching reflections via digital video editing. *Journal of Science Teacher Education, 16*(4), 351–375.

Yerrick, R. K., Thompson, M., McLaughlin, S. & MacDonald, S. (2011). Collected from the cutting room floor: An examination of teacher education approaches to digital video editing as a tool for shifting classroom practices. *Contemporary Issues in Technology and Teacher Education, 11*(1), 118–148.

Yerrick, R. K., Doster, E., Nugent, J. S., Parke, H. M. & Crawley, F. E. (2003). Social interaction and the use of analogy: An analysis of pre-service teachers' talk during physics inquiry lessons. *Journal of Research in Science Teaching, 40*, 443–463

Zahn, C., Pea, R., Hesse, F. W. & Rosen, J. (2010). Comparing simple and advanced video tools as supports for collaborative design processes. *Journal of the Learning Sciences, 19*, 1–38.

Zhang, M., Lundeberg, M. A., Koehler, M. J. & Eberhardt, J. (2011). Understanding affordances and challenges of three types of video for teacher professional development. *Teaching and Teacher Education, 27*(2), 454–262.

SLOWMATION OVERVIEW

Slowmation (abbreviated from 'slow animation') is a simplified way for school or university students to make a 3–5-minute narrated stop-motion animation to explain a science concept. The process was created 10 years ago by one of the book authors, Garry Hoban, whilst looking for new ways for pre-service teachers to engage with and explain science concepts (Hoban, 2005). The animation process is simplified by using any form of model (e.g. paper, plastic, plasticine, real objects), that is usually laid flat on a table or the ground and then the creator makes small, manual movements whilst taking digital still images. The images are then uploaded into a free movie-making program (iMovie on a Mac or Windows Movie Maker on a PC) and played at two frames/second providing a slow-moving image that can be narrated, hence the name 'slowmation'. Further details and free instructions on the making process are available at www.slowmation.com and www.digiexplanations.com. There are also several thousand examples available by searching YouTube using the term 'slowmation'.

Slowmation is a simplified form of multimedia whereby students can combine several modes of communication – still images, slow-moving images, writing, music and voice or speech to create a multimodal representation. When making a slowmation to explain a science concept, it is important for the creator to consider the purpose, audience and context of the media. Research has shown that creating a slowmation is a good way for students to learn a science concept because they have to engage with content in order to understand it, design a sequence of coherent 'chunks' or steps in explaining the concept, make models to represent the concept and use technology to integrate the different modes to make a clear explanation (Hoban, Loughran & Nielsen, 2011; Hoban & Nielsen, 2013). The creation process is also a good way for students to generate discussion to expose their science ideas that may be right or wrong, and to evaluate their ideas during the construction process (Hoban & Nielsen, 2014).

The examples of implementation presented in the following three chapters provide different ways to use the approach. In Chapter 12, Stephen Keast and Rebecca Cooper from Monash University in Australia present an innovative way to link their university science method course with the pre-service teachers' practicum in schools. In the course, pre-service teachers make a slowmation to explain a science concept to develop an understanding of the making process and then follow this with teaching school students to make one in four lessons whilst on practicum. Upon return to the science method course at university, the pre-service teachers then present their experiences of implementing slowmation, which provides opportunity for rich discussions, as the pre-service teachers have all implemented the same teaching approach but in their different practicum schools. In Chapter 13, Gillian Kidman from Monash University in Australia provides an interesting analysis of different levels or orders of learning and shows how slowmation can influence each of three orders, which she has applied in method courses for both senior secondary teachers and primary science students. Chapter 14, by Ruth Amos and Sandra Campbell from the Institute of Education at the University of London, provides a stimulating account of pre-service teachers making slowmations to explain common misconceptions, which are then peer reviewed to analyse the strategies employed in the digital explanation. The pre-service teachers reflect upon the correctness of the explanation and strategies used providing insights into what makes a good teaching resource, in particular, what makes a good narration including words and sequences of words that they should use for explaining science to school children.

References

Hoban, G. (2005). From claymation to slowmation: A teaching procedure to develop students' science understandings. *Teaching Science: Australian Science Teachers' Journal, 51*(2), 26–30.

Hoban, G., Loughran, J. & Nielsen, W. S. (2011). Slowmation: Engaging preservice elementary teachers with science knowledge through creating digital animations. *Journal of Research in Science Teaching, 48*(9), 985–1009.

Hoban, G. & Nielsen, W. (2013). Learning science through designing and making a narrated stop-motion animation: A case study of preservice teachers conceptual change with slowmation. *International Journal of Science Education, 35*(1), 119–146.

Hoban, G. & Nielsen, W. (2014). Generating science discussions through creating a narrated stop-motion animation: The affordances of slowmation. *Teaching and Teacher Education, 42*, 68–78.

12

DEVELOPING PEDAGOGICAL KNOWLEDGE OF PRE-SERVICE SCIENCE TEACHERS USING SLOWMATION AS A SHARED EXPERIENCE

Stephen Keast and Rebecca Cooper

Context

This chapter explores the work being conducted in General Science Methods in Science Teacher Education at Monash University, Australia into how slowmation (abbreviated from 'slow animation') can help pre-service secondary teachers to develop pedagogical knowledge. The General Science Method course is where pre-service teachers learn how to teach science in the final year of their education degree when they complete teaching placements in two 5-week blocks during the middle of each semester, one in semester one and one in semester two. This chapter explores pre-service secondary teachers' use of slowmation as a teaching procedure with secondary school science students during their second placement.

General Science Method is a year-long course for pre-service secondary school teachers who are planning to teach science for years 7–10, and covers a range of concepts, ideas and issues relevant to science teaching and covers a variety of science topics. Every effort is made to cover topics from a variety of science disciplines so as to best represent a general science curriculum and to make pre-service teachers aware of the breadth of knowledge that they need to consider when teaching a general science class. The level of knowledge across our pre-service teachers is often significantly different; some come with PhDs in particular areas while others may not have studied a particular discipline beyond a Year 10 standard.

We see a need for pedagogical reasoning as a step toward developing pedagogical content knowledge. In our course we promote the concept of pedagogical content knowledge and hope that our students will work toward developing pedagogical content knowledge as they become more-experienced teachers. By introducing, discussing and having pre-service teachers make their pedagogical reasoning explicit as they use slowmation, we are putting them on the path toward considering the development of their expertise as science teachers. Further, they are beginning to think critically about their teaching of specific science topics and to explore the many facets of pedagogical knowledge that make up teaching practice. We hope that this will, in turn, begin the development of pedagogical content knowledge.

Pedagogical reasoning

Shulman (1987) suggested that particular actions were necessary if teachers want to transform their own understandings of content into forms that might usefully support students' learning. According to Shulman (1987) and Wilson, Shulman and Richert, (1987), pedagogical reasoning comprises a cyclical process as outlined here and illustrated in Nilsson's (2009) model (shown in Figure 12.1):

- *Comprehension*: teachers first need to understand the content in their own way and understand how the ideas within their discipline are interrelated and connected. Teachers also need to understand the aims and purposes of teaching the given content.
- *Transformation*: teachers then need to transform their own content understanding into forms that are pedagogically powerful and flexible so that the content might be understood despite the diversity of students' learning styles.
- *Instruction*: working with students to help improve their understanding of the content, through the use of effective teaching strategies.
- *Evaluation*: checking students' understanding or alternate conceptions and providing supportive feedback that students can act on. Also, evaluation is about looking at the teaching and deciding if the right strategies have been used or if they need to be changed, possibly during the lesson.
- *Reflection*: looking back at the teaching and learning that has occurred and considering what has been achieved for both teacher and students, inclusive of the emotions involved.

The process of pedagogical reasoning then cycles back to influence new comprehension as a result of the learning achieved through the previous experiences.

We draw particularly from Peterson and Treagust (1992, 1995, 1998) who explored how pre-service teachers' pedagogical reasoning ability was developed and refined by using problem-based learning. Nilsson (2009) modelled the process of pedagogical reasoning and action (as in Figure 12.1) to help pre-service teachers understand their developing pedagogical knowledge as a cycle (see Nilsson, 2009, p. 244 for an extensive explanation). Within Teaching Concerns we ask our pre-service teachers to explore different critical incidents, the experience of which helps to develop deeper understandings of the complex task of learning to teach secondary science.

Pedagogical knowledge

We have adapted Morine-Dershimer and Kent's (1999) model of pedagogical knowledge for our own purposes (illustrated in Figure 12.2). It was important for us to include assessment practices and feedback in our model, since they were

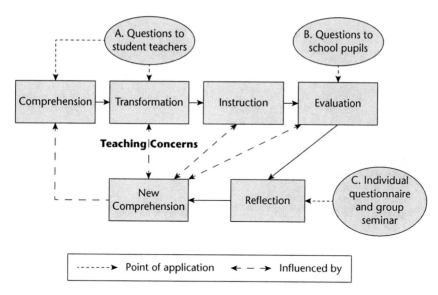

FIGURE 12.1 The process of pedagogical reasoning and action (Nilsson, 2009, p. 244, used with permission)

missing in the model by Morine-Dershimer and Kent. Further, we agree with Corrigan and Gunstone (2011), who suggested that interactions between the facets of general pedagogical knowledge influence each other, represented by double-headed arrows in the diagram. The subtle changes in the representation are important in redefining the interactions within both general pedagogical knowledge and personal pedagogical knowledge. The new model (RMPK – Revised Model of Pedagogical Knowledge) provides a framework for tracking development of pedagogical knowledge by pre-service teachers. It highlights several of the important competencies pre-service teachers need to develop, as well as giving due consideration to their personal beliefs/perceptions and personal practical experience, which is unlike other models of pedagogical knowledge. Teachers bring these perceptions and experiences to the classroom naturally but do not necessarily consider them formally when articulating their teaching practices. Through linking facets, the model of pedagogical knowledge recognises the influence of a teacher's personal beliefs/perceptions and personal practical experiences and suggests that by personally reflecting on these, in combination with what they understand about teaching practice generally, teachers can begin to develop context-specific knowledge.

Relating these ideas to our use of slowmation, we refer to the work of Zeichner (1995), who argued strongly that student teachers' critical awareness must grow out of their own experiences "by drawing attention to certain elements of their practice" (p. 17). In our case, the elements of pre-service teachers' practice are those outlined in RMPK and, more specifically, the instructional strategy in slowmation. The strategy is a simplified way for students to create a stop-motion animation to represent a science concept, whereby images of the model are played slowly at two

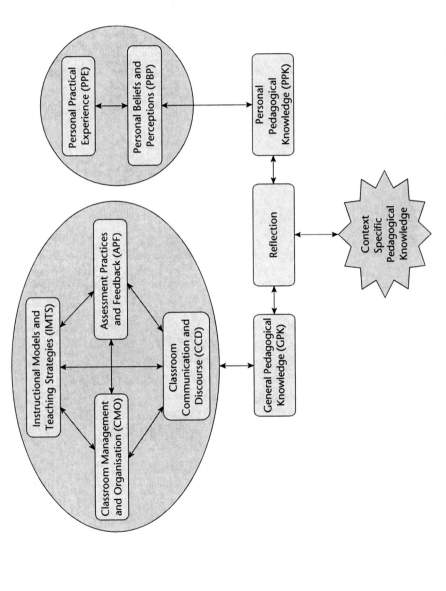

FIGURE 12.2 Revised Model of Pedagogical Knowledge (RMPK), adapted from Morine–Dershimer and Kent (1999)

frames per second to show models moving in slow motion (Hoban, 2005; Hoban, Loughran & Nielsen, 2011). We ask our pre-service teachers to engage in the cycle of pedagogical reasoning to action (outlined previously in Figure 12.1) by making their pedagogical reasoning explicit through the implementation of slowmation in their practicum placement classrooms, subsequent analysis of their experiences and, finally, in a presentation to their peers. In this way, our instructional strategy encourages pre-service teachers to share with peers their general pedagogical knowledge and all its aspects, including beliefs, as outlined in the RMPK model (Figure 12.2). Making explicit their pedagogical knowledge to others helps consolidate their own development, while listening to others make explicit their pedagogical reasoning gives insight to different pedagogies and beliefs. Thus the RMPK model (Figure 12.2) combined with the cycle of pedagogical reasoning (Figure 12.1) drive our work with slowmation to help our students think carefully about and begin to articulate their developing knowledge of teaching science.

Implementation

Purpose for the media making

For the past 8 years, we have used slowmation as part of the learning and teaching in the General Science Method course. Our purpose for using slowmation is two-fold: (i) we want our pre-service teachers to explore an area of content by making a slowmation and (ii) follow it up by using slowmation as a teaching strategy in a secondary school classroom while completing their practicum placement. Pre-service teachers attend placement in separate schools, teaching science classes on their own under the supervision and guidance of an experienced mentor teacher.

The task: Pre-service science teachers exploring an area of content using slowmation in their science method course

We spend one tutorial session at the end of first semester (approximately 2 hours) having the pre-service teachers make slowmations. They work in groups of 3–4 on a topic they choose and by the end of the tutorial session have made a slowmation of about 1–2 minutes duration. The emphasis is not on the product but rather on the process of creating slowmations and what can be learnt about quality learning and the development of pedagogical knowledge. This tutorial session plants the seed for considering the many ways that slowmation can be used to support learning in science and, in particular, how slowmation can be used to improve student understanding of science concepts where alternate conceptions may be at play.

Pre-service science teachers using slowmation in secondary school science classes

At the end of semester 1, the pre-service teachers are set the task to use slowmation with their students while on placement during semester 2. This task is set several weeks before they go on placement because the pre-service teachers need time to think about how to use slowmation, including time to ask questions during other tutorials.

The pre-service teachers are expected to include slowmation as a teaching strategy in a unit of work that they teach in science to any year level they feel appropriate. They are asked to identify any alternate conceptions, assess their students' work and are asked to keep copies of their students' work. In completing this task, the pre-service teachers have many important decisions to make regarding the use of slowmation, such as whether or not a topic is suitable, which aspects should be assessed (and how) as well as matters raised by the use of group work. Part of using slowmation on placement includes having pre-service teachers negotiate with their mentor teacher to include slowmation as part of the learning and teaching of a topic in science. This negotiation requires the pre-service teachers to explain their understanding of slowmation as a teaching strategy, explain why it is appropriate to use for the science concept they are teaching and consider how to use it appropriately as an assessment task. Issues of assessment are covered in another final-year subject, however, we do expect our pre-service teachers to address issues of assessment in our science course, as we view assessment as a significant part of the development of pedagogical knowledge, indicated by the RMPK model that we advocate.

Pre-service science teachers reporting on their experiences using slowmation in secondary school science classes

Pre-service teachers return to university after the semester 2 placement and give an oral presentation about their experiences using slowmation. They are expected to relate these experiences to facets of the model of pedagogical knowledge (RMPK). Pre-service teachers are asked to describe the context in which they used slowmation including the topic, class size, assessment and any issues that they faced. Pre-service teachers show their students' slowmations, identify any alternate conceptions that they recognised, and discuss how they dealt with these in their teaching. Each pre-service teacher fields questions from their peers, which generally turns into a discussion about issues related to learning and teaching science that expands their understanding of pedagogical reasoning. Issues range from using group work to effectively dealing with a variety of alternate conceptions as part of the learning process. The pre-service teachers are assessed on their oral presentation, which is the culmination of the entire slowmation task and is worth 50% of their final mark for semester 2.

Data comes from audio recordings of the pre-service teachers' oral presentations after they returned from practicum in semester 2 where they had their students create slowmations. Each pre-service teacher gave an oral presentation including an overview of their school, the students they were teaching and the teachers they were working with (context building). The discussion is organised so that pre-service teachers' presentations cover:

- the chosen topic for the slowmations the students would make;
- how slowmation was implemented with the class;
- when slowmation was used;
- how the pre-service teachers ran the class over several lessons;
- how they established groups;
- if and how they assessed and provided feedback; and,
- any other important information they want to share about their experience with slowmation.

Next, the pre-service teachers show their colleagues a small sample of their students' slowmations. We deliberately do not put a number on how many they show as we want them to make decisions about the importance of the slowmations they choose to show and discuss. Some pre-service teachers select the best examples, while others present the worst ones and some select the ones that have a story behind them.

We analysed the audio recordings of the pre-service teachers' presentations against the model in Figure 12.2 and the cycle of pedagogical reasoning shown in Figure 12.1. As we were looking to the oral presentation to elicit aspects of pedagogical reasoning and pedagogical knowledge, we coded the transcript from each presentation with the facets of pedagogical knowledge as outlined in RMPK. We also highlighted sections where pre-service teachers raised concerns about their teaching, including where they reflected on and seemed to come to new understandings about their own pedagogical knowledge.

For the purpose of this chapter, we present data that exemplifies how the use of slowmation helped pre-service teachers better recognise and articulate aspects of their developing pedagogical reasoning and knowledge. Pseudonyms are used throughout. Laura explains the teaching process she used to teach slowmation:

> I probably had about 18 kids maximum. We had one lesson talking about slowmation . . . I gave them a minimum to take 30 pictures because I think that makes about 30 seconds of film . . . all their lessons are doubles so we had another double with research and planning and we had a double to take the photos and then we had a double to put the movie together and then do some revision . . . they (students) did an oral presentation . . . Then they had to introduce their movie (slowmation), show their movie and then say . . . what they did well, what they could have done better and five interesting facts.

In terms of RMPK, Laura is explaining instructional models and teaching strategies (IMTS) for implementing slowmation. Here, Laura is sharing her personal practical experience (PPE). Since experience in a particular teaching situation is very personal, sharing aspects of PPE helps the pre-service teachers to contextualise the practicum for others. Later in her presentation, as a slowmation is playing, Laura articulates her new understanding of teaching and learning, as an indication of her pedagogical reasoning:

> This one was really surprising actually because it came from two girls, one indigenous girl who comes to school just for the kind of stability and who often refuses to do any work and doesn't even acknowledge you when you talk to her and requests to go the library and do her own project work and another girl who was being suspended for having a fist fight with another girl before we were doing these classes, so two really kind of troubled girls and they put together this and it was probably the best one out of the bunch.

Here, the pre-service teacher describes two students who find school difficult and rarely engage, yet by using slowmation they are not only interested in science but produce some of the best work from the class. Laura is also showing her understanding of students and her knowledge of how to engage students.

In developing understandings of teaching, pre-service teachers are often concerned with issues of classroom management and organisation (CMO) and Laura was no different. In the following excerpt, Laura describes a lesson where her students were peer reviewing each other's slowmations, which she reported during the presentation:

> And they really got into the peer reviewing . . . and I was getting really upset that they were so noisy because usually it had a really good feeling in the classroom and I was getting upset that they were all talking and then at the end . . . they were all talking about the movies, and so they were all on task.

In developing her pedagogical knowledge, this was a critical incident for Laura as she came to realise that for students to be engaged in discussions about their own work, they needed to be talking. Realising the difference between productive noise and disruptive noise in the classroom is something pre-service teachers learn from experience rather than just focusing on noise level or particulars of CMO. When asked what she learnt about teaching through slowmation, Laura responded, "not to jump on kids' backs when they're noisy and you know get upset but yeah, I was worried about it but they were talking about the movies [slowmations]". At the end of her presentation other pre-service teachers were encouraged to ask questions and to share their PPE. In this way pre-service teachers build on the different contexts and experiences of their peers and begin to develop a shared language for talking about teaching.

The following exchange is an example of how pre-service teachers explored ideas associated with instructional model and teaching strategies (IMTS):

> Colin: . . . what size groups did everyone specify cause I actually specified 3 or 4 but then you know the ones that were away when we began would join other groups and sometimes there was 5 and that was just too many.
>
> Jenny: I had groups of 4 and that worked really well.

Lecturer: So do you think this is about the right size? What do we think?

Caroline: I think 3 is a really good number, with 4 . . . there's somebody not doing something.

This brief exchange between the lecturer and pre-service teachers exemplifies that the pre-service teachers are thinking about how to effectively use group work. By sharing their experiences and exploring the possibilities and outcomes of varying group sizes the pre-service teachers came to an agreement about optimal group size for slowmation. In this way they are valuing each other as teachers with developing knowledge of science teaching rather than waiting for the lecturers to tell them the answer.

Pre-service teachers and student alternative conceptions

Eliciting students' alternate conceptions is difficult and can be even harder when the content is quite abstract. An example of this comes from Jenny who, in her presentation, felt that slowmation would be an ideal approach for an abstract topic such as DNA replication. From her students' storyboards, Jenny was able to identify several alternative conceptions about DNA replication that were displayed by some groups. Examples of the students' alternate conceptions included:

- replication beginning in the middle of the strand and not the ends;
- showing the acid-base pairs not matching so that the replicated DNA was in fact not a replica and;
- having acid-base pairs and the backbone seemingly fly in from nowhere.

Jenny provided feedback to students via sticky notes attached to the storyboards using leading questions, such as "Is this the way that DNA replication begins?" where, for example, the storyboard showed DNA replication beginning in the middle of the strand.

Jenny's supervising teacher was surprised to see some of the alternative conceptions displayed by students on the storyboards. The supervising teacher affirmed Jenny's comments, and thought the feedback was useful and effective while not explicitly giving answers to the students. Jenny reported that some of the alternative conceptions displayed on the storyboards re-emerged during model making and as a result, also made it into the final slowmation. The screenshots in Figure 12.3 show images from one of Jenny's groups.

The sequence in Figure 12.3a–f shows the DNA strands untwisting (a) and separating (b); the acid base pairs 'flying in' and matching up (c); the backbone then 'flying in' (d); the two now-replicated DNA sequences re-twisting together (e); and finally, the replicated DNA (f). Pre-service teachers were readily able to identify several alternative conceptions in the slowmation and ask why had they re-appeared

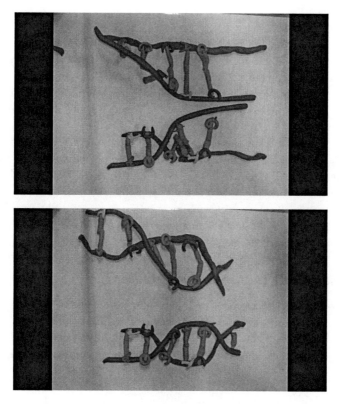

FIGURE 12.3 a–f Sequence of images as screen shots from Jenny's group

after Jenny identified them on the storyboard and while making the models. Even though pre-service teachers had researched an alternative conception and created lesson plans on how to teach this earlier in the course, they were surprised to see how strongly held such views were. This was a significant moment for the class, where the theory around alternative conceptions became 'real' for them. Often during the oral presentations pre-service teachers were drawing on the PPE of their peers and comparing it to their own:

Sarah: When you were talking about alternative conceptions earlier it made me think; when you find alternative conceptions that aren't related to the topic that they're supposed to be learning about, when do you address those? Do you address them as you see them or maybe when you go into that topic like when the moon was rising, where the sun was setting? Is that an alternative conception or are they just being lazy?

Jess: I would point it out at the time and you can ask them; 'Is that really what the moon would do?' Like there's no point ignoring and it doesn't have to be a big thing either you could just ask the question and see what their understanding is.

Lecturer: What would other people do? Liam?

Liam: Me? I'm not sure. I suppose it all depends on timing and what not. I think if it's something like that I'd probably address it at the time but I think it's all circumstance, like situation and whatnot because I mean if it's a big concept you think 'ok do I have the time to address it' or 'maybe you're learning about it next term'.

What this exchange demonstrates is that the students are developing ideas about how to deal with alternate conceptions in the classroom and that they are viewing each other as knowledgeable. The discussion moves from a hypothetical question about alternative conceptions to a tentative response and then encourages exploratory talk between pre-service teachers. While there is no right answer agreed upon here, with support and encouragement, the pre-service teachers explored possible situations and considered responses.

Pre-service science teachers and student learning

While most pre-service teachers used slowmation at the end of teaching as a revision tool, Monica began teaching the topic with slowmation. The alternative conceptions that were apparent in the slowmations created by her students were used as part of her teaching, referring to them to build students' understanding of levers:

> So it goes on for quite a while and pretty much the whole slowmation is just showing examples of Class 1 and Class 2 levers. So there's not really any alternative conceptions but they're not actually making the links between how low the fulcrum affects what's happening in the machine so what happens is ... doesn't mean you have to reduce the force ... And then while I was teaching that, we constantly referred back to the slowmation so they actually saw the value in doing them. So they were kind of like, 'Ah, yeah, that's what we did in our slowmation. And maybe next time if we were to do this again, we could do this, this, and this'. So, I thought that being able to link it back was a really beneficial experience for them because it gave them value for their own learning.

Monica wanted to build student ownership for the learning. Here Monica revealed the sort of teacher she wanted to be, sharing intellectual control with her students, with them at the centre of the learning and her facilitating it:

> They were kind of taking control over their own learning and at the end to be able to say 'This is what I produced and I kind of did this on my own with my friends as a group'. And as you went around you could hear all their discussions, talking about science. And it was just a good, good experience ... I got to be the teacher I wanted to be, but also still had that control over the students.

Monica was building on her pedagogical reasoning and her pedagogical knowledge, creating opportunities to explore being the type of teacher she wanted to be.

Discussion

From sharing experiences of implementing the same teaching strategy on professional experience, pre-service teachers recognised that how they organise a class is a major influence on student learning. Many pre-service teachers came to realise that student learning is more than just presenting science content – learning includes social learning, such as working together in a group, abilities to succeed in science, building students' confidence and nurturing self-esteem. Difficult students can and will engage when a teacher makes good decisions about what should happen in the classroom so that they are involved in thinking about activities. In some cases these difficult students even produced the best work, but only when the pre-service teachers made the science engaging and meaningful for them.

The model of pedagogical knowledge also assisted the pre-service teachers to recognise that there is more to teaching science than just presenting content. As the pre-service teachers present their experiences with slowmation to their peers, they unpack all of the aspects of teaching that they had to consider and, as a result, begin to articulate each facet of pedagogical knowledge. More importantly, they begin to see the overlaps and links between the facets of pedagogical knowledge that constitute the richness of quality teaching practice.

Again and again, using slowmation made clear to pre-service teachers the difference between teaching and learning, and the intricate connections between them. Much of their teaching and observation was about teaching but little was about the learning process. From this task they were more open to seeing the learning, and identifying student alternative conceptions, as compared to when things are learnt 'correctly'. That is because making a slowmation to represent a science concept means that students' ideas are exposed – in the model making, in the exchange of ideas with peers and in explaining the science of the slow-moving images. Another important aspect for the pre-service teachers was the opportunity to introduce something new to their supervising teachers and be able to justify to an experienced teacher the value of slowmation for student learning.

Why do we want pre-service teachers to do this?

We believe that this sequence of activities in tutorials and assessment related to slowmation is an important part of our students' development because it is an effective way of exemplifying the facets of the model of pedagogical knowledge that we promote as part of our course. RMPK plays a central role in our entire course and we have found that, by having our pre-service teachers use slowmation in the science classroom with secondary school students, the pre-service teachers are faced with most of the facets of pedagogical knowledge that make up the RMPK model. We have found that pre-service teachers respond well to this model because they are able to identify the facets in their mentor teachers' practice and can relate the facets to their own practice. We have also found that this model provides the basis for a common language for our pre-service teachers to use when they are discussing their teaching practice while on placement and, then, when back at university. By facing the aspects in a real environment, the pre-service teachers have an opportunity to put the theory into practice while they are still in the course. More importantly, because all of the pre-service teachers are compelled to use slowmation in their teaching while on placement, they have a shared, common experience on which to base their discussions about the facets of pedagogical knowledge. Even though their contexts and environments for teaching on practicum may be different, they have all used slowmation in a science classroom and have been asked to present their experiences in relation to the facets of pedagogical knowledge. For us, slowmation is the shared, common experience and, hence, is crucial to our teaching and our pre-service teachers' development.

A shared, common experience

Our notion of a shared, common experience is related to our desire for our teaching to promote discussion that is tentative, hypothetical and exploratory. Further, collaboration builds a shared language for learning and teaching science on two levels: academics with pre-service teachers and pre-service teachers with their students in schools. The value of a shared experience cannot be underestimated, as it allows pre-service teachers to share their PPE, which connects to that of their peers in ways that are fruitful, plausible and intelligible (Posner, Strike, Hewson & Gertzog, 1982). So, then why do we use slowmation? Because we believe it assists beginning teachers to understand and discuss their teaching in sophisticated ways. Using slowmation gives pre-service teachers something exciting to talk about because it is both a new practice and requires negotiation with a mentor teacher.

The pre-service teachers' presentations about their experiences with slowmation are a good indicator of being ready to teach. By considering what they highlight during their presentations in the methods subject, how they cope with and articulate CMO and IMTS and how they integrate these as part of their developing pedagogical knowledge, we can quickly see how our pre-service teachers are developing and what issues they have faced or are still grappling with.

Through our experiences with slowmation we have come to realise that there are multiple levels of learning around the slowmation-based task in the General Science Method subject. The secondary school students in schools are learning how to make slowmations and hopefully learning some science content. The pre-service teachers learn many other group work and ICT skills. Teachers in schools are learning about slowmation as a teaching strategy and the possibility offered for quality learning and teaching in science. Both pre-service teachers and classroom teachers are, perhaps, also learning something about their students, any alternate conceptions they may hold and how they like to learn. This requires that both pre-service teachers and classroom teachers take the time to observe their students and look at the work produced. Perhaps most importantly, the teachers can focus on how the experience of slowmation has helped their students develop science understanding.

Our pre-service teachers' learning could be summarised as learning about and how to use slowmation as a tool for learning and teaching science. Specifically, our pre-service teachers learn about identifying and dealing with alternate conceptions and just how difficult it can be to shift students' thinking. They learn about the different facets of pedagogical knowledge that are involved in quality teaching, but also that it is the smooth and seamless combination of these facets that makes for high-quality teaching. Finally, an exploration of pedagogical reasoning through well-scaffolded discussion offers our pre-service teachers the opportunity to reflect on their practice and to come to new understandings about the role they play in students' science learning. For us, the learning has been about the value of having a common experience and showing the many ways that slowmation can be used to support quality learning and teaching in science and science methods subjects. We have also learnt the power of peer-led discussions for exploring aspects of teaching slowmation but also for creating a supportive environment in which pre-service teachers can flourish.

References

Corrigan, D. & Gunstone, R. (2011). An approach to elaborating aspects of a knowledge base for expert science teaching. In D. Corrigan, J. Dillon & R. Gunstone (Eds.), *The professional knowledge base of science teaching* (pp. 83–106). Dordrecht, The Netherlands: Springer.

Hoban, G. (2005). From claymation to slowmation: A teaching procedure to develop science knowledge. *Teaching Science, 51*(2), 26–30.

Hoban, G., Loughran, J. & Nielsen, W. (2011). Slowmation: Preservice primary teachers representing science knowledge through creating multimodal digital animations. *Journal of Research in Science Teaching, 48*(9), 985–1009.

Morine-Dershimer, G. & Kent, T. (1999). The complex nature and sources of teachers' pedagogical knowledge. In J. Gess-Newsome & N. G. Lederman (Eds.), *Examining pedagogical content knowledge* (pp. 21–50). Dordrecht, The Netherlands: Kluwer Academic.

Nilsson, P. (2009). From lesson plan to new comprehension: Exploring student teachers' pedagogical reasoning in learning about teaching. *European Journal of Teacher Education, 32*(3), 239–258.

Peterson, R. F. & Treagust, D. F. (1992). Primary pre-service teachers' pedagogical reasoning skills. *Research in Science Education, 22*(1), 323–330.

Peterson, R. F. & Treagust, D. F. (1995). Developing pre-service teachers' pedagogical reasoning ability. *Research in Science Education, 25*(3), 291–305.

Peterson, R. F. & Treagust, D. F. (1998). Learning to teach primary science through problem-based learning. *Science Education, 82*(2), 215–237.

Posner, G. J., Strike, K. A., Hewson, P. W. & Gertzog, W. A. (1982). Accommodation of a scientific conception: Toward a theory of conceptual change. *Science Education, 66,* 211–227.

Shulman, L. (1987). Knowledge and teaching: Foundations of the new reform. *Harvard Educational Review, 57,* 1–22.

Wilson, S. M., Shulman, L. S. & Richert, A. E. (1987). '150 different ways of knowing': Representations of knowledge in teaching. In J. Calderhead (Ed.), *Exploring teachers' teaching* (pp. 104–124). London: Cassell.

Zeichner, K. M. (1995). Reflections of a teacher educator working for social change. In T. Russell & F. Korthagen (Eds.), *Teachers who teach teachers* (pp. 11–24). London: Falmer.

13

PRE-SERVICE TEACHERS' USE OF SLOWMATION

Developing transformative learning

Gillian Kidman

Context

In Chapter 12, Keast and Cooper described their use of slowmation (abbreviated from 'slow animation') with pre-service secondary science teachers in terms of promoting the development of pedagogical knowledge. In this chapter, I extend this pedagogic research to include the learning awareness of the pre-service teacher. Specifically, I explore how slowmation can lead to transformative learning experiences that result from the hidden affordances of an innovative learning environment.

There is a dearth of research pertaining to the metalearning resulting from the creation of an animation. Most research reports the procedural nature of slowmation (Hoban, 2005), the science learning (Hoban, Loughran & Nielsen, 2011) or the pedagogical approach for teaching science concepts in higher education classes (Kidman, 2011; Kidman, Keast & Cooper, 2012a, 2012b, 2013). Individually and collectively, the research of Kidman, Keast and Cooper has considered the creation of animations through the theoretical framework of conceptual change as well as the present account of transformational learning. This is responding to the call by Yore and Treagust (2006), who noted a need to investigate "the enhanced cognition that occurs during the transformation from one representation to another representation or one mode to another" (p. 308).

Keast, Cooper, Berry and Loughran (2008) described a three-step process they used in conjunction with slowmation:

1. *representation*: where the pre-service teacher recognises how the scientific concept can best be represented;
2. *deconstruction*: where the pre-service teacher identifies the major elements of the scientific process (chunking) through a storyboard; and
3. *reconstruction*: where the pre-service teacher re-chunks and synthesises the concept to create a model and movie creation.

Keast *et al.* describe slowmation as a translation task,

> ... in which learners translate information from one form into another. In this case, slowmation requires students to translate abstract scientific information into models to produce animated movies that demonstrate their understanding of the given concept, topic, or idea under consideration. (p. 3)

Viewing slowmation as a translation task is essential when considering the learning potential behind the creation of an animation.

Sterling (2010–11) writes of the assumption that learning is self-evidently a 'good thing' and that much learning discourse is directed toward "making learning effective, to learning to learn, learning methods and so on" (p. 18). There is scant discourse given to the notion of the *purpose* of learning. Through considering the process of learning, a qualitative shift in perception and meaning-making, as performed by the learner, can result in a reframing of assumptions and thinking customs – transformative learning. Sterling builds upon the earlier work of Bateson (1972), Mezirow (2000) and Morrell and O'Connor (2002) in defining and exploring this concept of transformative learning. This work describes three orders of learning and change.

1. *First-order learning* is the most common form of learning. It relates very much to the world external to the learner. The material is content led and often delivered through traditional transmissive pedagogies. This information transfer approach often leads to surface or shallow learning. Ideas already available to the masses are presented to the learner and regurgitated when required. Although this form of learning may be suited to some circumstances and material, it is an obstacle to deeper learning and change. Earlier work by Kidman, Keast and Cooper (2012b) describes a "model of learning and relearning through slowmation". In this model, the behaviours of pre-service teachers who work solely within this first-order learning level are described as surface learners. They create their animations through the use of non-original diagrams, usually copied directly from an existing text. They then assign characteristics to the elements of the diagram and accept the model as their animation. According to Gordon and Debus (2002), this may be viewed as an achievement approach to learning – the focus is upon achieving a product, in this case, the animation.

2. *Second-order learning* occurs when there is a change in thinking or personal awareness. Learning takes on an internal dimension whereby a critical examination of the self occurs in relation to the content matter – a form of metalearning. This learning is said to be deeper than the surface/shallow learning evident in first-order learning. Prior learning is challenged and questioned, and the purpose of an activity or the content is explored. Kelly and Cranton (2009) state that when learners question their assumptions, this can then lead to a shift in how the learners see themselves in relation to the world and

content. They can then be said to have engaged in transformative learning. In relation to the earlier-mentioned model of learning and relearning (Kidman et al., 2012b), the behaviours of pre-service teachers who work beyond the level of first-order learning are described as deeper learners. Surface learners consider non-original diagrams and assign characteristics to the elements of the diagram. However, deeper learners do not simply accept the model as their animation. Instead, they question the accuracy of the model, consider the model's imperfections, make modifications and reconsider the model. The deep learner undergoes this meaning-making cycle several times before accepting the model as their animation. Through successive iterations, deep learners undergo a process of metalearning and become self-aware of their learning processes. Consequently, deeper conceptual and pedagogical learning takes place. This may be viewed as an engagement in a quality learning approach, as the focus is upon the learning process and not on the animation product.

3. *Third-order learning* is epistemic learning. There is a further shift beyond seeing oneself in relation to the world and content (second-order learning), to that of seeing one's own worldview and then being able to draw upon other views and possibilities. It is seeing how learning can vary across contexts. O'Sullivan (2002) describes this as a shift in consciousness. Third-order learning was not considered by Kidman, Keast and Cooper (2012b) in their model of learning and relearning, however, it is described later in the current chapter in relation to the processes and functions of inquiry based pedagogical skill development for primary school pre-service teachers.

Sterling (2010–11) describes any learning shift from first order to second order or second order to third order as a sometimes 'painful process' for a learner. Resistance may occur as existing understandings, beliefs and values are challenged. The learner is required to reconstruct meanings, a process that may cause discomfort. However, a learner may also experience excitement and inspiration.

The aim of this chapter is to describe how slowmation leads to transformative learning through engaging pre-service teachers in representing science content. Just as it has been well-documented that teachers need to identify and build on their students' prior knowledge and ideas when teaching science, it is equally important for pre-service teachers to identify and build upon their own ideas of not only science subject matter, but of their own science pedagogical practices. Science subject matter knowledge alone is insufficient for teachers to teach well: they need the integration of pedagogical knowledge. Thus, the focus is very much upon learning *through* technology rather than learning *from* technology (Kidman et al., 2013).

Implementation

In my tertiary classrooms, the focus is on transformative learning and the exploration of the self as a learner (as well as exploring science pedagogies). As previously outlined, I am not interested in the creation of a slowmation as a final product. Rather, my emphasis is on the pre-service teacher developing self-awareness about their own cognitive processes, being able to engage in metacognitive activity and, more specifically, transformational learning. In the sciences, research by White and Frederikson (1998) showed that, by assisting physics students to explore their metacognitive strategies, the students experienced greatly improved understandings of the physics content as compared to those students who did not explore their metacognitive strategies. My work occurs in two contexts: that of the senior secondary methods course for potential biology, chemistry, earth science, physics and general science high school teachers; and that of the potential generalist primary school teachers.

Senior secondary science methods context

In pairs, pre-service teachers were required to conduct a 60-minute 'practical' lesson as part of their assessment. By combining two pairs and extending the time to 120 minutes, a tutorial class of approximately 25 pre-service teachers experienced a two-hour tutorial class that aimed to explore their learning styles through creating a slowmation (led by their four peers). In a lecture (60 minutes) prior to the tutorial, the process of creating an animation was explored through a short verbal and text description of the slowmation process. In the tutorial, the four pre-service teacher presenters facilitated the creation of animations. In small groups of four, pre-service teacher participants spent approximately 45 minutes (with access to the internet and an assortment of secondary school and tertiary science textbooks) familiarising themselves with their self-selected scientific concept, the plasticine materials and the slowmation processes.

Under the tutelage of their four pre-service teacher presenters, the small groups then created their animations. A digital recorder was placed in the centre of each group's workspace to record their on-task conversations. These on-task conversations as well as the group discussion at the end of the tutorial provided rich data relating to the pre-service teachers' understanding of learning, and an understanding of the science concepts represented in the animations. Both the pre-service teacher presenters and their peer participants discussed the various types and styles of learning that became evident during the creation of the animations. In a class discussion, the pre-service teachers' own learning preferences and the relevance of their new awareness to the classroom were explored. Much of the discussion centred around Ausubel's seminal work on rote and meaningful learning, which has been extended by Gordon and Debus (2002) into notions of surface, deep and achieving approaches to learning from the viewpoint of the teachers and that of the school student. The notion of conceptual change (Hewson, 1981) also featured in the discussions. The emphasis was very much upon understanding and learning in relation to pedagogy and science content, and not on the actual quality or output of the animation. In fact, the actual animations produced in the tutorial were not assessed at all. Examples of the pre-service teacher dialogue are provided in the discussion section later, as they are illustrative of the transformative learning aim of the work.

Primary science context

For the primary pre-service teachers, an integrated science and mathematics content knowledge unit was the context. There was a two-hour lecture and a two-hour practical tutorial timetabled each week. The delivery of science and mathematics pedagogies was not a formal component of the unit, however, previous cohorts had requested that pedagogies be incorporated in the unit, so the inclusion of inquiry-based learning was an investigation in itself for the academic staff. The learning experience for the primary pre-service teachers involved participation in inquiry-based teaching and learning tutorials where physics principles were explored *through* a biological context – the motion of an aquatic invertebrate was to be represented and described in an animation.

The learning experience was designed to occur at intervals over a four-week time period. Initially the pre-service teachers participated in a tutorial exploring freshwater invertebrates using the Digi-Blue digital microscope and working in groups of 3–4. The learning task was to save a JPEG file of their invertebrate (a photo to assist with later identification) and to record a short 10-second movie of their invertebrate, in motion, in their water sample (to assist with a subsequent ICT tutorial). They were to also produce anatomical sketches of a single invertebrate (to develop scientific and microscopic drawing skills, as well as to record their observations of their invertebrate in motion to aid in creating their slowmation). For example, during the 'chunking' stage of the slowmation process, one group focused their attention on the tail movement as a form of propulsion, and annotated the corresponding storyboard sketches. The group's slowmation then showed the tail movements as described by the annotations. During the presentation of the group's animation, one of the pre-service teachers explicitly referred to the difficulty she had in creating a representation of her knowledge.

The pre-service teachers were then given the out-of-class task to identify their group's invertebrate and determine its optimal environmental living conditions. The pre-service teachers were also informed that in their next tutorial they would be creating an animation that explained the motion and associated forces for their invertebrate. The pre-service teachers were free to investigate the concepts of motion and forces, in their own time, leading into this tutorial. In the subsequent lecture the pre-service teachers explored the development and use of a 'slowmation' for science teaching and learning. In the two-hour tutorial, the pre-service teachers accessed the Internet, their sketches, photo and 10-second movie, and used modelling clay and their own cameras or cell phones to create an animation that depicted their group's understandings of freshwater invertebrate motion and associated forces. To collect conversational data as the pre-service teachers created their animations, a digital recorder was placed in the centre of each group's workspace to record the conversation.

The participants were given a further two weeks of out-of-class time to work on their animations if they so chose. Each group then presented their animation to the class in a tutorial, discussing their learning and their creative intent. During all in-class sessions, the instructors modelled how to teach skills and content using an inquiry approach. The instructors were explicit in providing explanations for their pedagogical instructions to the pre-service teachers. As described by Whowell (2006), the instructors were there to guide rather than dictate – they explained the reasoning behind their guidance. The pre-service teachers participated in the lectures and tutorials from the perspective of learners and, in the final workshop, following the presentations, discussed how they envisaged enacting these ideas in an actual classroom. The on-task conversations as well as the group discussion in the presentation tutorial provided rich data relating to the pre-service teachers' understanding of learning, and an understanding of the science concepts represented in the animations. I have found the discussion and reflection time to be a better indication of science knowledge learning than that represented in the actual slowmation product.

Discussion

Over time, there have been multiple cohorts of senior secondary science pre-service teachers who have created slowmations and, more recently, a single cohort of primary pre-service teachers who used slowmation as a vehicle for exploring inquiry pedagogies. These multiple cohorts have resulted in numerous cycles of analysis of conversational and discussion data. Each cycle of analysis has included data from a previous cycle, which is updated by the inclusion of conversational and discussion data from each new cohort. Over time, I have used a variety of conceptual lenses to explore how slowmation can lead to deeper and transformative learning experiences as well as gauge the impact of the hidden affordances of an innovative learning environment.

In the initial cycle of analysis for a secondary cohort of pre-service science teachers, Hewson's (1981) notion of conceptual change was explored via the self-generated questions that emerged in the conversational data (see the method described in Kidman, 2011). This highlighted that the pre-service teachers were intellectually engaged with the science topic at hand. It was found that the process of socialisation (the creation of an animation in a small group rather than individually) was vital for the emergence of conceptual change as decisions for representation had to be justified to the other participants in the small group.

A second cycle of analysis, for an additional cohort of secondary pre-service science teachers further explored the socialisation process in terms of surface and deep learning along with the notion of meaning-making. This work, in conjunction with Keast and Cooper (see Kidman *et al.*, 2012a, 2012b) utilised Vygotsky's (1998) semiotic mediation, where groups of learners experience 'intermental thinking' and 'intramental learning'. Kidman, Keast and Cooper (2012a, 2012b) proposed two models that described the process of meaning-making. The first model is referred to as the 'Learning MMAEPER' (pronounced 'mapper'), which describes deep learning – when participants became deeply engaged with the science concept through the creation of a slowmation. The second model – the Model of Learning and Relearning – further explored the deep learner and meaning-making, but also considered the surface learner. In this model, meaning-making is shown to be a repetitive cycle where the animation creators research and re-research their topic, consider and reconsider the topic and their interpretation of the topic and finally adjust and re-adjust their representations until they are satisfied with their model and animation.

In the final analytical round, the conversational and class discussion data for the primary pre-service teacher cohort was considered along with another cohort of secondary pre-service science teachers. This data was analysed through the transformative learning framework outlined earlier in this chapter. Figure 13.1 is the resultant model. This model of transformative learning via slowmation has four clear pathways. The first pathway or starting point for all animation creators is their background knowledge and this includes testing the knowledge against published representations of the science concept. Should the existing representation be accepted as was previously published (first-order learning), the representation is copied and accepted (shown as 'A' in Figure 13.1), resulting in surface learning.

The second pathway (shown as 'B' in Figure 13.1) emerges once the animator engages with the science content. This is considered deeper learning – "I had this burning need for more information" (chemistry pre-service teacher) – and what Sterling (2010–11) calls second-order learning. Along this pathway, the animator mentally engages with prior knowledge, the new information provided in published sources and the information interpretation provided by group participants. The animator is required to make meaning of all this information, and then re-represent their new understandings in a slowmation. Pathway B is cyclical rather than linear as the representation is reworked several times, with scientific accuracy a key consideration. An animation that has a reasonable level of scientific accuracy would be a useful resource for pre-service teachers and having the ICT skills to create such resources could both be considered good outcomes for pre-service teacher methods courses. However, I consider it equally important for the pre-service teachers to be able to identify and build upon their science pedagogical practices. Hence, the pre-service teachers are prompted to consider what they are experiencing and why.

This consideration results in the third pathway (shown as 'C' in Figure 13.1) of the transformative learning model. This pathway occurs simultaneous to Pathway B. The majority of pre-service teachers do not take this pathway intuitively. Most require prompting and coaxing, however, they experience significant 'Aha moments' when they comprehend what it 'means' to understand a pedagogical strategy. This new understanding is referred to as metalearning. Again, this is a cyclical process where the pre-service teachers experience learning in such a way that they are aware of the meaning of this learning. They learn to learn, as articulated by one primary pre-service teacher "Is this what they call deep learning? Are we learning

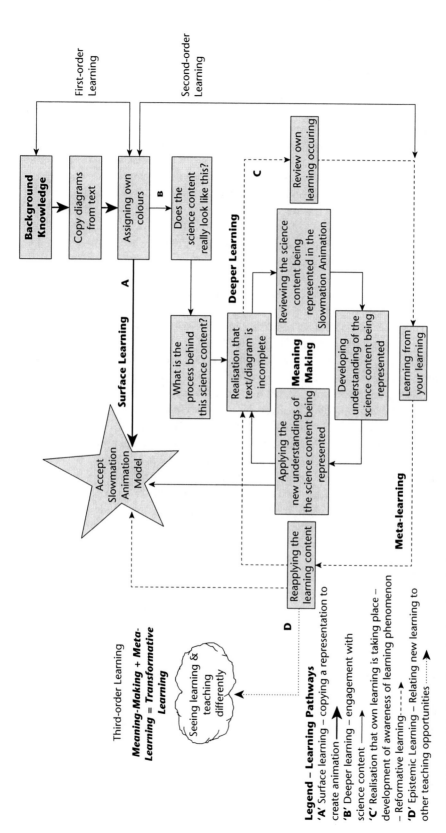

FIGURE 13.1 Model of transformative learning via slowmation

deeply about biol or physics? . . . No . . . it's that inquiry [pedagogy]" (Primary pre-service teacher 1).

In the time it takes to create a slowmation, there are many opportunities for metalearning to occur. These include the dynamics of group work, the art of questioning, the art of explanation and conceptual change. During the making of a slowmation, I have found that a majority of pre-service teachers intuitively take Pathway B into deeper learning. A small number of these pre-service teachers can intuitively take Pathway C simultaneously to Pathway B. However, I have observed that many pre-service teachers can be coaxed toward Pathway C during post-animation class discussion if not during the animation creation process.

The final pathway (shown as 'D' in Figure 13.1) results when pathways B and C are combined. As the pre-service teacher engages in meaning-making (Pathway B) as well as metalearning in relation to pedagogical practices (Pathway C), it is possible for a wider understanding to develop. This is what Sterling (2010–11) calls 'third-order learning', and O'Sullivan (2002) describes as 'transformative learning'. The teaching and learning of science is, thus, seen differently as the new learning is translated into other and new, more highly developed teaching opportunities.

It appears that transformative learning occurs when the metalearning opportunity is of a high quality. Consider the traditional use of slowmation – the pre-service teacher is given the simple task of creating an animation. The desired outcome may be the animation product itself, or the engagement in quality learning with the animation as a secondary minor focus. However, now consider the task given to the primary pre-service teachers described in this chapter: to participate in an inquiry based teaching and learning experience where physics principles are explored *through* a biological context – the motion of an aquatic invertebrate was represented and described in an animation. The few primary pre-service teachers who travelled down Pathway D did so as a result of an awareness of the inquiry learning process from the learners' and teachers' perspectives ("I think it is the benefit of knowing inquiry. I can see that a teacher might use this thinking in lots of subjects with different activities", Primary pre-service teacher 2).

There was also an awareness of learning physics through a biological context as described in a class discussion: "We just sort of created knowledge. I don't mean we invented theories, we just thought it up, the pushes and pulls 'n stuff. And it made sense from what we knew anyway from school, but didn't know we knew" (Primary pre-service teacher 3). The varied pedagogies were used to help the pre-service teachers experience and articulate a variety of forms of knowing. The pre-service teachers needed to be in a state of readiness to respond to the learning environment that was fostering metalearning. By being able to experience metalearning within diverse pedagogical contexts, the primary pre-service teachers could experience transformative learning. To facilitate transformative learning, the instructors must construct learning experiences through which the pre-service teachers can explore epistemic change as a collaborative enquiry. Slowmation is an approach that offers what Sterling (2010–11) refers to as a two-level learning process: "the new 'meaning making' of the designers/teachers facilitates the new 'meaning making' of others" (p. 27).

References

Bateson, G. (1972). *Steps to an ecology of mind*. San Francisco, CA: Chandler.

Gordon, G. & Debus, R. (2002). Developing deep learning approaches and personal teaching efficacy within a pre-service teacher education context. *British Journal of Educational Psychology*, 72(4), 483–511.

Hewson, P. W. (1981). A conceptual change approach to learning science. *European Journal of Science Education*, 3, 383–396.

Hoban, G. F. (2005). From claymation to slowmation: A teaching procedure to develop students' science understandings. *Teaching Science*, 51(2), 26–30.

Hoban, G., Loughran, J. & Nielsen, W. (2011). Slowmation: Pre-service elementary teachers representing science knowledge through creating multimodal digital animations. *Journal of Research in Science Teaching*, 48(9), 985–1009.

Keast, S., Cooper, R., Berry, A. & Loughran, J. (2008). *Slowmation as a pedagogical tool for improving science learning*. Paper presented at Australasian Science Education Research Association, Brisbane, Australia.

Kelly, R. & Cranton, P. (2009, January 19). *Transformative learning: Q&A with Patricia Cranton. Faculty Focus*. Retrieved from http://www.facultyfocus.com/articles/instructional-design/transformative-learning-qa-with-patricia-cranton (accessed 26 March, 2015).

Kidman, G. (2011). *Learning between representations: Slowmation and molecular biology dialogues of preservice teachers*. Paper presented at the National Association of Research in Science Teaching (NARST) Annual Conference, Orlando, Florida.

Kidman, G., Keast, S. & Cooper, R. (2012a). Responding to the 5Rs: An alternative perspective of slowmation. *Teaching Science*, 58(2), 24–30.

Kidman, G., Keast, S. & Cooper, R. (2012b). Understanding pre-service teacher conceptual change through slowmation animation. In S. Yu (Ed.), *Proceedings of 2nd International STEM in Education Conference*. Beijing: Beijing Normal University.

Kidman, G., Keast, S. & Cooper, R. (2013). Enhancing pre-service teacher learning through slowmation animation. *The International Journal of Engineering Education*, 29(4), 846–855.

Mezirow, J. (2000). *Learning as transformation: Critical perspectives on a theory in progress*. San Francisco, CA: Jossey-Bass.

Morrell, A. & O'Connor, M. (2002). Introduction. In E. O'Sullivan, A. Morrell & M. O'Connor (Eds.), *Expanding the boundaries of transformative learning: Essays on theory and praxis* (pp. xv–xx). New York: Palgrave Macmillan.

O'Sullivan, E. (2002). The project and vision of transformative learning. In E. O'Sullivan, A. Morrell & M. O'Connor (Eds.), *Expanding the boundaries of transformative learning: Essays on theory and praxis* (pp. 1–12). New York: Palgrave Macmillan.

Sterling, S. (2010–11). Transformative learning and sustainability: Sketching the conceptual ground. *Learning and Teaching in Higher Education*, 5, 17–33.

Vygotsky, L. S. (1998). *The collected works of L. S. Vygotsky, Vol. 5: Child psychology* (R. Rieber, trans.). New York: Plenum.

White, B. Y. & Frederikson, J. R. (1998). Inquiry, modelling, and metacognition: Making science accessible to all students. *Cognition and Instruction*, 16(1), 3–118.

Whowell, M. (2006). *A student guide to enquiry-based learning*. Retrieved from http://www.campus.manchester.ac.uk/ceebl/resources/guides/studentguide_july06.pdf (accessed 26 March, 2015).

Yore, L. & Treagust, D. (2006). Current realities and future possibilities: Language and science literacy – Empowering research and informing instruction. *International Journal of Science Education*, 28(2–3), 291–314.

14

LEARNER REFLECTIONS ON THE USE OF SLOWMATION AS A TOOL FOR CREATING EFFECTIVE EXPLANATIONS IN A SCIENCE TEACHER EDUCATION PROGRAM

Ruth Amos and Sandra Campbell

Context

Technology-enhanced teaching and learning has come increasingly to the forefront of educational practice in the twenty-first century (Laurillard, 2008). Evidence shows that the use of new technologies can play an important role in providing effective tools through which to construct new knowledge and skills (Webb, 2005). We work with graduate scientists training as pre-service science teachers on the Post Graduate Certificate in Education (PGCE) at the Institute of Education, University of London, UK. Using new technologies supports their pedagogical development (Amos, 2015). As the following sentiment from one of our pre-service teachers shows, they begin to gain an appreciation of the different aspects of creating effective explanations:

> David had a fantastic way for explaining how the shells are filled in an atom. He devised a (animated) model that was relatable, visual and simplistic in nature, which would allow pupils to grasp the concept. (Paulette)

Science teacher education in the UK attracts multidisciplinary graduate scientists, some of whom are career-changers. Trainees hold degrees in a variety of subjects, such as biomedical sciences and pharmacy, as well as classical biology, chemistry and physics (Royal Society, 2007). This presents challenges in supporting development of effective school subject knowledge and pedagogical content knowledge during the training period (Kind, 2014; Shulman, 1986). We model and encourage inspirational teaching, which pre-service teachers then develop in school alongside experienced teacher-mentors. Our goal is to foster a mutually supportive cohort of pre-service teachers, who are able to design creative learning opportunities underpinned by secure subject knowledge and pedagogical content knowledge.

Since its inception in 1989, the English National Curriculum (NC) has promoted the use of information and communication technologies (ICT) in teaching and learning (Department for Education, 2013). Koehler and Mishra (2008) argue that using technology is not simply part of 'normal' pedagogical content knowledge because it requires specialist understanding. Pre-service teachers recognise the potential for technology-supported learning and we encourage them to experiment with the use of data-logging, simple coding and programming, apps, simulations and animations in their teaching. The creation of slowmation (abbreviated from 'slow animation') as a learning tool has become increasingly popular, particularly in primary schools in the UK, in recent years. Garry Hoban created slowmation as a simplified way for school and university students to make stop-motion animations to explain science (Hoban, 2005; Hoban & Nielsen, 2010). A key feature is that digital still photos of objects that are moved manually are played at two frames per second to promote a slow-moving image that can be narrated. Hoban and Nielsen have developed the practice of slowmation as a mechanism for pre-service teachers to improve their own science subject knowledge (Hoban, Loughran & Nielsen, 2011; Hoban & Nielsen, 2010, 2013) and social interaction (Hoban & Nielsen, 2014).

Animations are frequently used in science classrooms as explanatory tools but mostly are expert-generated for students to observe. Yore and Hand (2010) suggest that teachers can introduce science content well by getting students to make their own stop-motion animations. Students' construction of representations that use more than one mode become multimodal (Jewitt, 2009). In designing and making multimodal representations, students make decisions about which modes to use that relate in complementary ways to enhance meaning-making. It is important developmentally for an early career science teacher to foster this deeper understanding of how signs and representations can make a significant difference to learners' progress because, in doing so, teachers learn what does and does not work to support meaning-making, especially in the construction of digital media that is now so prevalent.

Pre-service teachers face a number of challenges in becoming knowledgeable science teachers. Peer learning potentially provides support for development of subject knowledge outside their main subject specialty (Kind, 2014). By focusing on slowmation creation as part of technology-enhanced teaching and learning, we have explored its ability to support the following:

- learning and transforming science subject knowledge for school science;
- promoting the formation of a cohesive community of learners; and,
- developing the skills of the reflective practitioner.

As our slowmation project has evolved, we have seen its potential as a focus on reflective practice. Developing the ability to actively reflect upon one's learning and progress has long been considered a vital aspect of teacher development (Korthagen & Wubbels, 1995). Developing the skills of reflective practice is not straightforward, but underpins the success of a teacher and this chapter offers insights into pre-service teachers' initiation into such practice in the context of creating a slowmation.

The importance of reflective practice in teaching and learning

Schön (1983) maintains that reflection on action is a vital component of professional practice and his ideas have been readily adopted by the teaching profession. Pollard (2008) argues that reflective teaching supports good-quality learning and requires engagement with aims, means and technical efficiency. If pre-service teachers are to become reflective practitioners, they need to be open-minded and receptive toward critical feedback as well as be prepared to take responsibility for examining the progress students actually make as a result of the implemented learning strategies. Hence, the slowmation project provides pre-service teachers with their first active opportunity to experience 'reflection on action' in our program in a collaborative setting.

Reflecting on effective school science explanations: Conceptions and alternative ideas

Pre-service teachers' progress with deconstructing science explanations, and reconstructing those explanations appropriately for school science, paves the way to becoming a good science teacher. Osborne and Patterson (2011) define true science explanation as providing causal reasons for scientific phenomena, that is to say, explaining why things float or can be squashed and so forth. Reflection on how learners make meaning when exploring scientific ideas from a personal perspective as well as those of school students is also important (Mortimer & Scott, 2003). The collaborative creation of explanations in active ways through slowmation means that pre-service teachers can experiment with selecting appropriate imagery, dialogue, text, sound and symbols. A multimodal learning approach, which incorporates the use of new technologies as learning tools has been shown to enhance learners' understanding in science effectively (Jewitt & Kress, 2002; Jewitt, Kress, Ogborn & Tsatsarelis, 2001). Moreover, action and decision making in building a 'polished' explanation invokes several iterative cycles of reflective thinking. For example, pre-service teachers consider whether the slowmation is staged at the right level for specific learners (Hoban & Nielsen, 2013; Scott & Jewitt, 2003).

The definition of *science explanation* also needs exploring. Braaten and Windschitl (2011) contest notions of 'good explanation' in science, suggesting that many teachers tend to focus on *description* not *explanation*, despite clear guidance in curriculum documents. For example, when tasked with *explaining* what happens when a candle burns in the first session of their program, pre-service teachers focus primarily on *describing* observations. Science phenomena often have to be explained using unseen entities so pre-service teachers need to understand the nuances of supporting their students' progress here. The act of trying to explain abstract ideas such as the nature of the atom or forces during slowmation creation, gives pre-service teachers the opportunity to better understand scientific explanation (Osborne & Patterson, 2011).

As we interact with the world around us, we construct intuitive and alternative ideas about how things work from a young age (Duit & Treagust, 2003). Clement, Brown and Zietsman (1989) suggest strategies for building on naïve conceptions and at the heart of the constructivist approach is finding out what learners already know. Raising pre-service teachers' awareness of their own and their students' potentially deep-seated alternative ideas in science is an important aspect of their early training. If pre-service teachers research and tackle a typical misconception whilst making a slowmation, they actively engage in anticipating this phenomenon.

Analysis and interpretation of slowmation explanations

In this chapter, we focus on the affordances of slowmation creation in supporting pre-service teachers' initiation into reflective practice. Pre-service teachers make written journal reflections about their rationale for choosing explanatory modes, design decisions are made on using materials and artefacts and, finally, they evaluate outcomes. Turner and Simon (2013) suggest that written reflection is particularly successful in supporting teacher development, and this aligns well with Schön's (1983) active reflection-on-action. After watching pre-service teachers' slowmations, we analysed each two-minute recorded film for *descriptive* and *explanatory* elements, that is to say, sequences of image or text that only described phenomena, or went further in attempting to explain abstract ideas using multimodal signs and symbols (Hoban & Nielsen, 2013). This gives insights into pre-service teachers' understanding of *description* versus *explanation* of scientific phenomena. In this chapter, we highlight examples in which pre-service teachers designed *explanatory* signs for abstract ideas. We examine the intended explanatory ideas against construction of signs and symbols, which then may lead to successful meaning-making from the perspectives of peer learners (Hoban & Nielsen, 2013; Jamani, 2011).

Implementation

The slowmation project

The science pre-service teachers take part in a wide range of workshops and undertake different learning and teaching tasks at university and in school, designed to support their initial training over the first three months of the 36-week PGCE course. As part of a dual focus on technology-supported learning and crafting explanations, the pre-service teachers have two, two-hour preparatory sessions for creating the slowmation during the first few weeks. A colleague from our London Knowledge Lab (LKL) showcases some of the cutting-edge uses of emerging technologies in teaching and learning (e.g. Price, Davies & Farr, 2013). This is followed by a workshop on making short films, looking at use of voice tone, image, sound, emphasis and so forth (Hoban & Nielsen, 2013). The pre-service teachers then have to make a two-minute slowmation, which conveys an effective science explanation for 11–14-year-olds whilst tackling a typical misconception or alternative idea (Driver, Squires, Rushworth & Wood-Robinson, 1994). Pre-service teachers work in groups of three set by tutors, to ensure a mix of subject specialty. Over the following month, groups may spend time developing and finalising their slowmations before presenting them to peers in a subsequent class session.

In September and October 2012, 27 groups (82 pre-service teachers) created slowmations. The choice of topic was made independently by each group and drawn from the biology, chemistry and physics national curricula (NC). Groups named themselves distinctively. All data and artefacts from the project were stored on our virtual learning environment to allow for ease of sharing. These data consisted of pre-service teachers' chunking sheets (which contain staged explanation plans), storyboarding sheets (upon which design decisions and shot sequences are planned), recorded slowmations, individual pre-service teachers' written reflective journals, peer group reflective feedback and tutor observation field notes made during the slowmation presentation session.

The process of making a slowmation

We draw on Hoban and Nielsen's (2010, 2013) framework for slowmation creation in the making process. Pre-service teachers use chunking and storyboarding tools and, as they decide upon explanatory modes and have access to a wide range of commonly used craft materials (Plasticine, cardboard, paper glue, etc.). The slowmation-creation process is linked to a reflective cycle in which pre-service teachers note how ideas and decisions develop and then peers give written and dialogic feedback after watching the finished slowmations. Pre-service teachers follow the process summary in Figure 14.1 throughout phases 1–3. The process links reflective questions to each phase to guide progress in reflective thinking about what makes an explanation effective. In reality, steps in phases 1–3 are not linear but are set out as such for the sake of clarity.

The slowmations were presented in a three-hour microteaching session, during which written and dialogic peer feedback were given. During the session, one group had responsibility for giving reflective feedback to each presenting group using four questions provided in Phase 3. Additionally, after each slowmation was presented, wider discussions were facilitated by a tutor to explore specific explanatory features included in the slowmation. The presenting pre-service teachers were asked for points of clarification, decisions and thought processes. Each group was encouraged to reflect upon the critical feedback they received, and to use it to inform their own reflective thinking about the effectiveness of their explanations (Phase 3). Peer indication that signs and symbols led to secure understanding was considered a very-important attribute of an effective explanation. In order to illustrate design intention and enacted production, we present two slowmations in which pre-service teachers explained abstract ideas. The two groups chose to explain 'states of matter' and 'terminal velocity'.

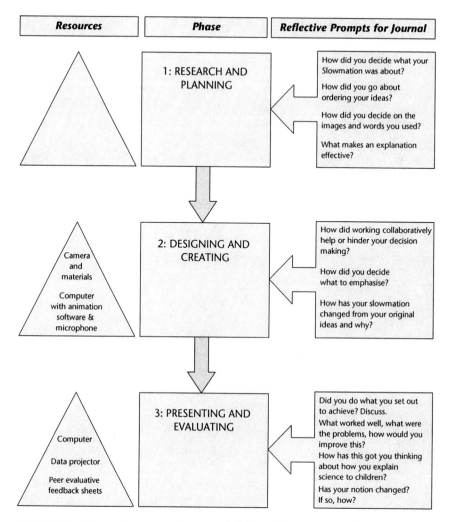

FIGURE 14.1 Slowmation process framework (adapted from Hoban & Nielsen, (2013). Reproduced with kind permission of Dr Paul Davies, IOE)

Phase 1: Reflections on research and planning decisions

In Phase 1 of slowmation-creation, pre-service teacher groups decide upon their topic. They carry out research into key ideas in the science curriculum and associated misconceptions that might be fruitfully tackled using slowmation creation. Pre-service teachers then use the chunking sheets to plan their explanation.

Team Fin (Melina – chemistry; Boris – physics with mathematics; James – physics) researched children's intuitive ideas about states of matter (Johnson & Papageorgiou, 2010). Chang, Quintana and Krajcik (2010) suggest that animation works well in supporting learners' understanding of the particulate nature of matter. Melina wrote:

> We researched common misconceptions KS3 [11–14-year-olds] . . . and found that pupils think that particles are lost and that mass changes as a material changes between states.

The three pre-service teachers brought different perspectives to this explanation in terms of their subject specialties. In planning discussions, Melina thought through overlapping image and textual modes:

> We wanted to make it explicit that particles are not lost by using a 'magnifying glass' to focus on a small area and verbally explain that the particles move out of view. We also wanted to show that gas can be invisible and decided to represent this in the slowmation [by something] 'disappearing'.

The pre-service teachers in this group reflected on the notion of an effective explanation during Phase 1. Melina elaborated on discussions between the members of Team Fin:

> We felt an effective explanation is a consistent one, where an idea is slowly built up in steps . . . Using this, we wanted to give our slowmation a narrative-like flow – so on our chunking sheet we grouped the explanation of properties of one state with one process where its state then changes – for example properties of a solid were grouped with melting (solid to liquid).

Whilst intentions are not explicit in this extract, the team was trying to sequence ideas purposefully. Melina went on:

> When compiling our chunking sheet we decided . . . how we could emphasise keywords during our slowmation. We decided that the key words to describe changes of state: melting, evaporation, condensation and freezing, were all to be of the same colour and style (as they are all processes) and to completely fill the screen – to strongly emphasise them.

So Team Fin was carefully designing visual cues as textual representations to link ideas together throughout, which can be done very effectively using slowmation.

In our second example, Team Free Fall (Rhiannon – chemistry; Sakina – biology; John – physics) began with a broad search of typical misconceptions, and Rhiannon noted that they were drawn to those in physics as their focus narrowed:

> After a brainstorming session . . . we decided on 'how skydivers fall to the ground safely using air resistance'. As we began to plan out our ideas, we realised that we would be able to deal with several misconceptions.

Explaining abstract physics concepts for younger learners can be challenging for pre-service teachers regardless of their subject specialty (Geelan, 2013). Team Free

Fall decided to use a plastic skydiver falling and opening his plastic parachute, to explain the forces acting as the diver reaches terminal velocity. John explained that this allowed for exploration of multiple ideas:

> [jumping from an aeroplane] would lend itself well to a sequenced approach. The topic of free fall also has a few misconceptions, which we thought that we could address (falling faster and faster forever, unbalanced forces, going upwards when the parachute is released).

After the research and planning phase, the pre-service teachers set about designing and creating their slowmations.

Phase 2: Reflections on designing and creating

In Phase 2, pre-service teachers construct their slowmations. They make decisions about which objects and materials to use to transform their ideas from chunking sheet and storyboard into actual signs and representations, script the narrated commentary and take still photographs of each storyboard shot. The slowmation is then created using a software program, which allows still photographs to be sequenced in a two-minute video and synchronised narration to be recorded. The majority of pre-service teachers used the free Windows Movie Maker for PCs to create their films in 2012. Some pre-service teachers come to the PGCE course with experience of making short films so use their own preferred software. In design and creation Phase 2, Team Fin tackled ideas about conservation of matter by purposeful use of a Play-doh cube (Figure 14.2). The cube 'melted' when energy was transferred in but the same amount of material was still clearly visible in the 'puddle' afterwards:

FIGURE 14.2 a, b *(continued)*

FIGURE 14.2 a, b Conservation of matter during melting using Play-doh

Melina noted:

> We decided to use a cube of Play-doh as a visual representation. We decided in the cube form it could be used to represent a solid. We would squash it into a puddle shape to represent a liquid and make it disappear completely [from view] to represent a gas.

Melina offered insights into Team Fin's design strategy. They decided to overlay the images of Play-doh changing shape with clear enunciation of key words, using exaggerated voice intonation. She explained the reinforcing strategy to their slow-mation as well:

> We decided to loop our explanation – we started and ended with the same image. Also to reinforce how particles move and behave in the different states, we had originally decided to assign a different piece of music to each state, for example, solid – very mellow, boring 'elevator' type music to represent the restrictive nature of the particles only being able to vibrate. We felt this would make it very memorable for young pupils as it was a fun idea.

Therefore, Team Fin's design approach shows attention to the impacts of sound and emphasis, rather than only basic narration in an attempt to gain viewer attention and to reinforce learning. Several groups used exaggerated intonation, for example, to emphasise key words and phrases or to add humour to their slowmations. Teachers often use humour to ease younger students into tackling difficult ideas – in our second example Team Free Fall did so in their explanations about forces. Toward the end of their slowmation, the skydiver (who turns out to be a soldier) is confronted by the enemy upon landing and meets a sticky end:

John: He has landed safely using air resistance.

Rhiannon: Uh, oh . . . or maybe he hasn't . . . [he is captured by the enemy].

Team Free Fall planned how to explain free fall visually in a convincing manner. They set a series of narrated questions against a backdrop of the falling skydiver and then attached a developing sequence of force arrows to the diver. The use of force arrows represents a conventional depiction of the action of forces (Wendel, 2012), and this is one example of the many strategies for modelling abstract ideas that have been developed over the years, particularly for concepts in physics. Images from their slowmation are shown in Figure 14.3.

Some of the overlaid narration was as follows:

John: How can a skydiver land safely?

Rhiannon: On Earth, all moving objects experience air resistance. Air resistance is the force acting in the opposite direction to the object's movement.

Sakina: This is caused by the friction between the air particles and the skydiver.

Team Free Fall used a small, upward arrow as a sign representing low air resistance before the parachute opens, then at the moment of opening the upward arrow suddenly increases in size. Upward and downward arrows then begin to equalise as terminal velocity is reached. The intention was to reinforce the notion of balanced forces for 13-year-olds through the use of image overlaid with narrated dialogue. Rhiannon gave insights into how their design choices had developed during Phase 2:

We had originally wanted key words to come up on the screen, however, after taking the stills we couldn't work out how to go back and do this. Also, we were originally going to move some cloud wallpaper around a table, but then realised it would be more effective to move the clouds (scrunched up tissues), to show the speed that the skydiver is falling.

Team Free Fall showcased the potential for slowmation to use images and narrated modes of representation effectively when building an animated explanatory tool in science. In the final stage of the project, each group reflected on how well their slowmation had supported peers in understanding intended ideas. Peers also predicted how younger learners would respond to the explanations.

Phase 3: Reflections on slowmation presentation and evaluation

The third phase of the project is a microteaching session. Pre-service teachers present their slowmations to a large group of peers. Pre-service teachers self-reflect

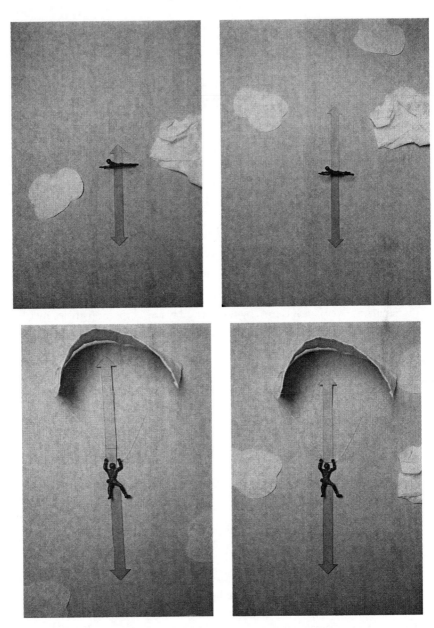

FIGURE 14.3 a–d Sequence of shots showing image mode arrows for: free fall, reaching terminal velocity, parachute opening and re-establishment of terminal velocity

on the overall effectiveness of their slowmations and receive evaluative feedback from peers and tutors. The peer group demonstrates how they understand the concepts as a result of watching the slowmation. Tutors and other pre-service teachers also give discursive feedback during discussion. Peer feedback was recorded via the following questions:

1. What did you learn from this slowmation?
2. Were the misconceptions clearly addressed? What were they?
3. Comment on the quality of the explanation and clarity of communication, speed, emphasis on key words.
4. How could this slowmation have been improved? Were there any distractions?

Frequently, pre-service teachers highlighted technical problems rather than explanatory issues in self-reflections. Melina and James (Team Fin) both commented on challenges they had with first filming the visual sequence and then trying to record the narration over the top. They felt that composing the script first would have been a better way to do this. However, they were proud of the matched colour links in their explanations for the changing states of matter throughout. However, the colour themes were not mentioned by the evaluating group, so this intended impact did not necessarily make its mark. Team Fin also realised that the slowmation did not show the arrangement of particles in a liquid particularly well, an issue that was highlighted by the peer group:

> ... particles are lost as state changes – not super clear.

The 'disappearance' of particles in the vapour state was also raised by peers as problematic, and despite planning to describe particles disappearing *from view* in the narration, Melina confirmed that Team Fin actually forgot to do this as they had intended in the final version. Indeed, at key points, all groups inadvertently introduced or reinforced misconceptions. This shows that care is needed when transforming ideas in the planning phase into accurate signs and symbols in the design phase. It may also be an indication of challenges to pre-service teachers' subject knowledge, revealing their own misconceptions. It is easy for pre-service teachers to lose focus on some of the transformations, which can then influence the learners' understanding. However, it is also difficult to anticipate which partially explained signs will have greatest impact on learners. The peer group feeding back to Team Free Fall suggested labelling force arrows because the arrows themselves were not an accurate enough representation in the explanation. Team Free Fall did receive positive feedback about the moving clouds indicating downward motion of the skydiver, and for the use of changing size of arrows as signs for varying forces during free fall. Their peer group felt clear that young learners would see that the parachute slows the skydiver down and in fact he does not go back up (as the moving clouds slowed down), which is a frequently-held misconception. In movies, when falling skydivers are filmed by a static camera, the diver appears to go up when a parachute slows their fall. Therefore, Team Free Fall was judged to have created a successful explanation. Rhiannon gave some pertinent reflections on crafting a good science explanation in general, which has relevance for her own teaching:

The most important lesson I have learnt in doing this task is that you have to think very carefully about the words you use to explain, how slowly you talk, using the repetition of key words. When you have time to think about your explanations, they are much more successful than when you are put on the spot in the classroom.

Rhiannon was aware of the need for carefully pre-planned science explanations before going 'live' into the classroom, as well as issues about the vocal and visual quality of the components of a good explanation, whether animated or non-animated. Pre-service teachers can understandably underestimate the important aspects of explanation in the science classroom, which perhaps contributes to defaulting to more *description* rather than *explanation*. Table 14.1 summarises the main impacts of signs and modes of representation as identified by the evaluating peer groups for all 27 slowmations, which capture simple yet important outcomes when working with pre-service teachers and slowmation. Three of the slowmations in Table 14.1 were entirely *descriptive* in nature, showing that some pre-service teachers had not used the task well to craft a good explanation.

TABLE 14.1 Salient features of signs and modes of representations from peer perspectives

Sign or Mode	Positive Feature	Negative Feature
Image	Quirky 'memorable' cues for representations were helpful. Appropriate speed of image display and transition on the screen.	Three 'non-animated' slowmations just relied on photo backgrounds (to 'save time'). Transitions too fast.
Voice	Voice used very deliberately to convey the importance of words; to attract attention to an idea; to inject humour; for example, with a dramatic voice or imitation of a well-known personality such as David Attenborough. Appropriate speed of narrated dialogue. Shouting keywords altogether.	Voice was too quiet; monotone. Dialogue was too fast.
Text	Moving words and letters made impact as keywords entered, or built up, for emphasis. The time of text on screen was appropriate.	Lack of text was unhelpful. Text on screen too fleeting.
Background	Colour, size and materials for background and emphasised images were well considered.	Background too static; not engaging; not relevant.
Multimodal	Image, voice and text matched well.	Image, voice or text not matched well.

All the other 24 groups combined *description* followed by *explanation* of abstract ideas with varying degrees of success. The examples we have highlighted in this chapter contained the greatest emphasis on *explanation*.

Outcomes for students

Using slowmation creation with pre-service teachers in the early stages of their training provides several important opportunities for promoting developmental skills. We recognise a number of benefits, as well as limitations, of the use of slowmation creation with pre-service teachers, having worked on the project over three years.

Benefits of slowmation creation with pre-service teachers

Slowmation creation and subsequent peer presentation gives pre-service teachers opportunities to explore science explanations in depth over an extended period of time. As a result, pre-service teachers understand the need to think very carefully about the effectiveness and use of the different modes of image, voice, sound and text in both animated and non-animated explanatory tools. Rather than simply reading about children's misconceptions in science, pre-service teachers benefit from researching children's alternative ideas, then actively tackling them and testing explanatory power, as judged by peer learners. The extracts from our sample groups show that pre-service teachers begin to act as reflective learners (Roychoudhury & Rice, 2013) during a slowmation project and put skills into practice that under-pin progress in understanding school science subject knowledge, pedagogical content knowledge and technological pedagogical content knowledge (TPCK). Some, like Jason (in a different group), demonstrated detailed attention to design features and technical issues in their reflections:

> We located the key words in the timed script and decided that many of the images we wanted to use could be triggered by these words (e.g. as opposed to explaining what ionisation was verbally, we decided to use a schematic image); in some cases we wanted an image to support the voice-over (e.g. we wanted to demonstrate the penetrative ability of each type of radiation with a diagram, as well as describe it).

Situating peer presentations of slowmations in a 'live' microteaching session, rather than watching them online provided a productive forum for developing reflective practice. Self-evaluation and peer feedback enabled pre-service teachers to recog-nise the importance of breaking science concepts down into manageable steps for learners during explanation, as well as the explanatory potential for using specific signs in a slowmation that can have differing impacts on learners' understanding.

Jonassen, Myers and McKillop (1996) suggest the value of using approaches like slowmation lies in learners becoming designers, so they think like teachers. In thinking like teachers, the slowmation creators have to first understand a concept, break it down into coherent and sequential 'chunks' and consider the most-suitable language for the audience. This is similar to the process of preparing a lesson for teaching. Hence, learners, in this case pre-service teachers, consider multiple ways of making meaning and the process of articulating their knowledge to a specific audience invites reflection on that knowledge in new and meaningful ways. Slowmation, therefore, is an ideal creative task for science pre-service teachers in training. Phase 3 of the process, in which pre-service teachers receive feedback from peers, gives pre-service teachers important reflective insights into creating effective science explanatory tools. However, there are some pitfalls and limitations associated with the project as well.

Limitations of slowmation with pre-service teachers

Our slowmation-creation task requires pre-service teachers to tackle a commonly held intuitive idea or misconception, which they generally handle well. However, some pre-service teachers inadvertently reinforced other misconceptions in their slowmations, because they created or chose representations that did not convey ideas accurately. Pre-service teachers usually noted these issues or were prompted to note them through peer feedback. This highlights the importance of following through from chunking ideas to storyboarding signs in Phase 1, as correct representations were often planned at the chunking stage. It would be interesting to include a second, revised slowmation where the pre-service teachers incorporate the feedback. However, in a time-constrained program, this is not possible.

A limitation, as noted by Hoban and Nielsen (2014), was that whilst making a slowmation is seen as useful and enjoyable by pre-service teachers, the process was perceived to be time-consuming. Several of our pre-service teachers saw taking the slowmations into school as a way to make time well spent. However, some younger students who were used to seeing contemporary animated film found slowmation 'so lame' (a comment made by a 12-year-old). Hoban now advocates the use of 'blended media' for crafting explanations that incorporates a combination of slowmation, video and still images to complement a narration, which is a positive future approach (Hoban, Nielsen & Shepherd, 2013). This is particularly useful if students understand the affordances of when to use video, slowmation or still photos to complement a voiceover in the media product. O'Toole (2011) notes that stop motion 'old cartoons' lack fluidity within the shot. He asserts that a much-greater range of movement, intertextuality, verbal trickery and so forth are now possible through computer-generated imagery, and while this may improve the visual appeal, we acknowledge that the learning is in the making rather than in the technical quality of the product.

Future directions for using slowmation creation with pre-service teachers

In our particular training context, 2012 was the start of a new PGCE course in England – physics with mathematics. The pre-service teachers in this course train alongside their science peers, and have a small number of sessions looking at subject knowledge and pedagogical content knowledge for mathematics. We are looking for synergies between science and mathematics pedagogical content knowledge that support pre-service teachers, as they tend to experience rather different teaching and learning approaches within science and mathematics departments. Moreover, groups in our 2012 project (for example, Team Free Fall) did not include even simple quantitative explanations in their slowmations, which could have been helpful for some of the concepts. We see value in encouraging future cohorts, particularly the physics with mathematics pre-service teachers, to use slowmation as a tool for exploring abstract mathematical learning and teaching in science. Many learners report mathematical concepts as being problematic in studying the sciences and Niess (2005) puts forward a framework for TPCK in science and mathematics to promote useful links. Here we see great potential for helping pre-service teachers develop their mathematical pedagogical content knowledge and TPCK for improved science teaching.

We are currently looking at ways to support early career science teachers over a period of five years and beyond and suggest that, once teachers become more experienced, reintroducing the use of explanatory tools like slowmation creation has the potential to enhance their teaching. An opportunity exists, therefore, in teacher development courses aimed at supporting such teachers in incorporating slowmation creation in a range of pedagogical strategies, such as improving technology-enhanced science explanations.

References

Amos, R. (2015). Using technologies to support learning science. In R. Toplis (Ed.), *Learning to teach science in the secondary school* (pp. 204–219). 4th ed. Abingdon, UK: Routledge.

Braaten, M. & Windschitl, M. (2011). Working toward a stronger conceptualization of scientific explanation for science education. *Science Education, 95*(4), 639–669.

Chang, H., Quintana, C. & Krajcik, J. (2010). The impact of designing and evaluating molecular animations on how well middle school students understand the particulate nature of matter. *Science Education, 94*(1), 73–94.

Clement, J., Brown, D. & Zietsman, A. (1989). Not all preconceptions are misconceptions: Finding 'anchoring conceptions' for grounding instruction on student intuitions. *International Journal of Science Education, 11*(5), 554–565.

Department for Education (2013). *National curriculum in England: Science programmes of study.* Retrieved from https://www.gov.uk/government/publications/national-curriculum-in-england-science-programmes-of-study/national-curriculum-in-england-science-programmes-of-study (accessed 26 March, 2015).

Driver, R., Squires, A., Rushworth, P. & Wood-Robinson, V. (1994). *Making sense of secondary science: Research into children's ideas.* Abingdon, UK: Routledge.

Duit, R. & Treagust, D. (2003). Conceptual change: A powerful framework for improving science teaching and learning. *International Journal of Science Education, 25*(6), 671–688.

Geelan, D. (2013). Teacher explanation of physics concepts: A video study. *Research in Science Education, 43*(5), 1751–1762.

Hoban, G. F. (2005). From claymation to slowmation: A teaching procedure to develop students' science understandings. *Teaching Science, 51*(2), 26–30.

Hoban, G., Loughran, J. & Nielsen, W. (2011). Slowmation: Pre-service elementary teachers representing science knowledge through creating multimodal digital animations. *Journal of Research in Science Teaching, 48*(9), 985–1009.

Hoban, G. & Nielsen, W. (2010). The 5 Rs: A new teaching approach to encourage student generated animations (slowmations) of science concepts. *Teaching Science, 56*(3), 33–38.

Hoban, G. & Nielsen, W. (2013). Learning science through creating a 'slowmation': A case study of preservice primary teachers. *International Journal of Science Education, 35*(1), 119–146.

Hoban G. & Nielsen, W. (2014). Creating a narrated stop-motion animation to explain science: The affordances of 'slowmation' for generating discussion. *Teaching and Teacher Education, 42*, 68–78.

Hoban, G., Nielsen, W. & Shepherd, A. (2013). Explaining and communicating science through student-created blended media. *Teaching Science, 59*(1), 32–35.

Jamani, K. (2011). A semiotics discourse analysis framework: Understanding meaning making in science education contexts. In S. C. Hamel (Ed.), *Semiotics theory and applications* (pp. 192–208). Hauppauge, NY: Nova Science.

Jewitt, C. (Ed.) (2009). *The Routledge handbook of multimodal analysis.* Abingdon, UK: Routledge.

Jewitt, C. & Kress, G. (2002). More than words: The construction of scientific entities through image, gesture and movement in the science classroom. In J. Koppen, I. Lunt, & C. Wulf (Eds.), *Education in Europe: Cultures, values, institutions in transition* (pp. 225–245). Münster, New York: Waxmann.

Jewitt, C., Kress, G., Ogborn, J. & Tsatsarelis, C. (2001). *Multimodal teaching and learning: The rhetorics of the science classroom.* London: Continuum.

Johnson, P. & Papageorgiou, G. (2010). Rethinking the introduction of particle theory: A substance-based framework. *Journal of Research in Science Teaching, 47*(2), 130–150.

Jonassen, D., Myers, J. & McKillop, A. (1996). From constructivism to constructionism: Learning with hypermedia/multimedia rather than from it. In B. Wilson (Ed.), *Constructivist learning environments* (pp. 93–106). Englewood Cliffs, NJ: Educational Technology.

Kind, V. (2014). Science teachers' content knowledge. In H. Venkat, M. Rollnick, J. Loughran & M. Askew (Eds.), *Exploring mathematics and science teachers' knowledge: Windows into teacher thinking* (pp. 15–28). London: Routledge.

Koehler, M. & Mishra, P. (2008). Introducing TPCK. In M. Koehler & P. Mishra (Eds.), *Handbook of technological pedagogical content knowledge (TPCK) for educators, American Association of Colleges for Teacher Education* (pp. 3–30). New York, NY: Routledge.

Korthagen, F. & Wubbels, T. (1995). Characteristics of reflective practitioners: Towards an operationalization of the concept of reflection. *Teachers and Teaching: Theory and practice, 1*(1), 51–72.

Laurillard, D. (2008). Technology enhanced learning as a tool for pedagogical innovation. *Journal of Philosophy of Education, 42*(3–4), 521–533.

Mortimer, E. & Scott, P. (2003). *Meaning making in secondary science classrooms.* Maidenhead, UK: Open University Press.

Niess, M. L. (2005). Preparing teachers to teach science and mathematics with technology: Developing a technology pedagogical content knowledge. *Teaching and Teacher Education, 21*(5), 509–523.

Osborne, J. & Patterson, A. (2011). Scientific argument and explanation: A necessary distinction? *Science Education, 95*(4), 627–638.

O'Toole, M. (2011). Art vs. computer animation: Integrity and technology in *South Park.* In K. O'Halloran & B. Smith (Eds.), *Multimodal studies: Exploring issues and domains* (pp. 239–252). New York: Routledge.

Pollard, A. (2008). *Reflective teaching: Reflective and evidence informed practice.* London: Continuum.

Price, S., Davies, P. & Farr, W. (2013). Teachers' tools: Designing customizable applications for mlearning activities. In Z. Berge & L. Muilenburg (Eds.), *Routledge handbook of mobile learning* (pp. 307–311). London: Routledge.

Royal Society (2007). *The UK's science and mathematics teaching workforce: A state of the nation report.* The Royal Society: London. Retrieved from https://royalsociety.org/education/policy/state-of-nation/teaching-workforce/ (accessed 26 March, 2015).

Roychoudhury, A. & Rice, D. (2013). Preservice secondary science teachers' teaching and reflections during a teacher education programme. *International Journal of Science Education, 35*(13), 2198–2225.

Schön, D. (1983). *The reflective practitioner: How professionals think in action.* London: Temple Smith.

Scott, P. & Jewitt, C. (2003). Talk, action and visual communication in teaching and learning science. *School Science Review, 84*(308), 117–124.

Shulman, L. (1986). Those who understand: Knowledge growth in teaching. *Educational Researcher, 15*(2), 4–14.

Turner, K. & Simon, S. (2013). In what ways does studying at M-level contribute to teachers' professional learning? Research set in an English university. *Professional Development in Education, 39*(1), 6–22.

Webb, M. (2005). Affordances of ICT in science learning: Implications for an integrated pedagogy. *International Journal of Science Education, 27*(6), 705–735.

Wendel, P. (2012). Adding value to force diagrams: Representing relative force magnitudes. *Physics Teacher, 49*(5), 308–311.

Yore, L. & Hand, B. (2010). Epilogue: Plotting a research agenda for multiple representations, multiple modality, and multimodal representational competency. *Research in Science Education, 40*(1), 93–101.

BLENDED MEDIA OVERVIEW

Blended media is any combination of visual media such as animation, still photos or video that students can mix and match to complement a narration like an 'educational mash up' or 'media collage' to explain a science concept to a specific audience. It fosters creativity with content, as students can mix and match their own media with the media of others from YouTube or Google Image as long as it has a Creative Commons License or they have permission from the original creators. Blended media was created by the lead author, Garry Hoban, two years ago, assisted by Wendy Nielsen and Alyce Shepherd, to provide students with more-creative ways to engage with and explain science (Hoban, Hyland & Nielsen, 2014; Hoban & Nielsen, 2013; Hoban, Nielsen & Shepherd, 2013).

In Chapter 15, Dennis Jablonski from Southern Oregon University in the USA shows how he used blended media as one of the many technological strategies that he employs in his technology course for pre-service teachers. In particular, the chapter shows the planning process that students experience when creating a blended media. In Chapter 16, Karma Pearce from the University of South Australia in Adelaide shows how her pharmacology students improved their communication skills by designing and making different forms of digital media. The process of her implementation is like a 'Russian doll' assignment, whereby one aspect feeds into the next. For example, the students conduct a literature review and then develop a community-based survey about a pertinent topic. The students then develop a storyboard as a plan for a blended media product to explain a health issue and then test its communicative ability to a community audience. In Chapter 17, Jessica Vanderlelie from Griffith University in Australia shows how she gets her students in biochemistry, a notoriously challenging subject, to make up animated songs about biochemical pathways and put them to the music of popular tunes that resembles a form of academic karaoke. Whilst time consuming for students, they say it is the most-creative assignment of their degree and they always score top marks in the exam question that is the focus of their musical explanation.

References

Hoban, G., Hyland, C. & Nielsen, W. (2014). *Engaging students in explaining and representing pharmacology by creating blended media.* Paper presented at the Australian Conference for Science and Mathematics Education, University of Sydney.

Hoban, G. & Nielsen, W. (2013). Learning, explaining and communicating science with student-created blended media. In M. Sharma & A. Yeung (Eds.), *Proceedings of Australian Conference for Science and Mathematics Education* (pp. 148–153). Canberra: Australian National University.

Hoban, G., Nielsen, W. & Shepherd, A. (2013). Explaining and communicating science using student-created blended media. *Teaching Science, 59*(1), 32–35.

15

USING BLENDED MEDIA AS A PEDAGOGICAL TOOL FOR SCIENCE LEARNING IN THE USA

Dennis Jablonski

Context

Over the last two decades, researchers have documented that using digital devices in the classroom motivates and engages students in numerous subjects and levels (Anastopoulou, Sharples & Baber, 2010; Jarvinen, Jarvinen & Sheehan, 2012; Lehrer, 1993; Yu, Lai, Tsai & Chang, 2010). But with recent reports indicating that the United States performs poorly among industrialised nations in science, the Department of Education is pressing for an improvement in STEM (Science, Technology, Engineering and Mathematics) education. Among the 65 countries that administered the Program for International Student Assessment (PISA) in 2012, 26 countries outperformed the United States in science literacy when comparing the percentages of 15-year-olds in the top proficiency levels and 27 countries outperformed the United States when the average scores of all students were compared (National Center for Education Statistics, 2012).

At the same time, educational standards in the United States are undergoing intense scrutiny and revision with expectations that schools develop the capacity for students to generate digital literacies. Three significant policy documents regarding educational standards have been created since 2011. The first of these is the Common Core State Standards, originally adopted by 45 states in an effort to raise the performance levels of school students while promoting singular national benchmarks (National Governors Association Center, 2010). Within the Common Core, there are over 90 references to using digital sources, multimedia or the Internet for reading, writing, speaking and listening in grades K–12. Two anchor standards that are incorporated into science and the technical subjects are:

> Anchor Standard 7 for Reading: "Integrate and evaluate content presented in diverse media and formats, including visually and quantitatively, as well as in words".

Anchor Standard 8 for Writing: "Gather relevant information from multiple print and digital sources, assess the credibility and accuracy of each source, and integrate the information while avoiding plagiarism". (National Governors Association Center, 2010)

A second standards initiative was the development of the Next Generation Science Standards that complemented the Common Core. The grade-level performance expectations in physical science, life science, earth/space sciences, engineering and technology are supported by science and engineering practices and crosscutting concepts. With the recommendation at nearly all grade levels "to use digital tools where possible and feasible" or "gather information from print and digital sources" (Next Generation Science Standards, 2014), designers of the Next Generation Science Standards expect students to be digitally literate, that is, to learn from various media and formats and be able to explain, communicate and create their ideas within a digital environment. The Next Generation Science Standards designers also recognised the critical need to attract and support diverse and under-served student populations in science and have identified using "multiple representation and multimodal experiences" (National Research Council, 2013, p. 5), as being among the effective instructional strategies promoted.

The third significant initiative is the recently designed Technology and Engineering Literacy Assessment, which is a part of a battery of tests called National Assessment of Educational Progress (NAEP). Known as the 'nation's report card', NAEP is the only standardised national assessment that can compare students across regions, types of schools and grades. The area of the assessment most pertinent to the concerns of digital literacy addresses information and communication technology. For the first time in 2014, eighth graders will demonstrate their knowledge and skill in communicating and exchanging ideas, and in using appropriate digital tools for various purposes. For example, a problem assessing a student's 'selection and use of digital tools' might present the following scenario: "Using articles and simulated websites, create a media-rich presentation designed to persuade people to move to your city" (National Assessment Governing Board, 2013, p. 28).

These three national movements emphasise the importance of students interacting with multiple digital formats in science education. Students' digital literacy skills involve more than just viewing media and require a more-active role for students as designers and creators of media and texts broadly defined. Identified in the Next Generation Science Standards, "Reading, interpreting, and producing text are fundamental practices of science", with the understanding that the term 'text' refers to all types of communication, from "printed text to video productions" (National Research Council, 2012, p. 74). In particular, getting school students to create 'science texts' using different modes of communication is one way for them to develop multimodal awareness to inform the design of student-created media products. This has implications for science teacher education in terms of how pre-service teachers learn to develop their future students' multimodal literacies and awareness.

Multimodalities and multimedia

Previous chapters in this book have described how engaging with digital content develops multimodal literacies when students make decisions about what and how to combine different modes of communication. *Modes* represent information in various ways, for instance, using words, pictures or sounds, even animation or gesture (Lauer, 2009). Teachers may appreciate Selfe, Owen-Fleischer and Wright's (2007) definition, in their edited manuscript on multimodal composition: multimodal texts are those that "exceed the alphabetic and may include still and moving images, animations, color, words, music and sound" (p. 1). In contrast, media are the "tools and material resources" used to create texts (Kress & van Leeuwen, 2001, p. 22). Examples of media tools include our voices, cameras, an instrument, ink, paint or a computer. Media choices in the digital age have become more accessible because, with digitisation, all modes can be converted into one binary code, and "operated by one multi-skilled person, using one interface, one mode of physical manipulation, so that he or she can ask, at every point: 'Shall I express this with sound or music? Shall I say this visually or verbally?'" (Kress & van Leeuwen, 2001, p. 2).

Multimedia has become more accessible and diverse over the last several decades as technology has evolved. For Briand (1970), using multimedia in an English composition class involved projectors and film. Predating all-digital media, Baggett (1987) divided multimedia stimuli into "visual, verbal/auditory, verbal/written, and motoric (actual practice)" (p. 183). Jonassen, Myers and McKillop's (1996) use of multimedia included the term 'hypermedia', for example, the collection of text, audio, video, images and hyperlinks to take advantage of a computer's evolving capabilities. For Mayer (2001) a concise but comprehensive view of multimedia was "the presentation of material using both words and pictures" (p. 2), with the possibility that *words* can be spoken or printed, and that *pictures* included such examples as photos, graphics, maps, illustrations, animations, video and other pictorial forms.

The aforementioned descriptions of multimodal and multimedia may appear similar, a point with which Lauer (2009) agrees. Lauer considers the term 'multimodal' to be the preferred term by academics, while multimedia is more familiar to the public and companies: "Multimodal is a term valued by instructors because of its emphasis on design and process, whereas multimedia is valued in the public sphere because of its emphasis on the production of a deliverable text" (p. 225).

With over two decades of research on the topic, Mayer (2001) developed the cognitive theory of multimedia learning, based on empirical research. His framework of seven principles outlined what designers of multimedia should consider so that learners can effectively process and retain information. For example, according to his Principle of Multimedia, a digital presentation promotes greater learning if words are used with pictures than if words are used alone. Further, the Principle of Modality suggests that students learn better from an animation accompanied by spoken text (a narration) than from an animation accompanied by printed text. Fundamentally, Mayer's work validated the use of multimedia for learning, but positioned the learner as a *processor* of information, specifically, processing previously created media. In contrast, the constructivists of the 1990s using multimedia promoted the learner as a *producer* of knowledge (Jonassen *et al.*, 1996; Lehrer, Erickson & Connell, 1994).

The current study presents learners as producers of knowledge, evidenced by students planning, deciding and communicating with one another, all characteristics of constructivism, and social constructivism in particular. Social constructivism emphasises the social, cultural and contextual influences on learning (Anderson, Reder & Simon, 1998; Bredo, 2000; Brown, Murcia & Hackling, 2013). Instead of merely viewing and interpreting a pre-made multimedia product, that is, a text, image, audio or video presentation, students might *plan*, *design* and *construct* multiple modes of communication to fit their newly constructed explanation, add an original narration and create an artefact. A media form whereby students mix and match different media forms such as animation, video and still images to provide a coherent explanation to a specific audience is called 'blended media' (Hoban & Nielsen, 2012). This is like a 'mash-up' but for educational purposes.

Implementation

Blended media is a multimedia form in which pre-service teachers make choices in combining multiple modes of communication to explain a concept or tell a story. The key mode of communication is usually a narration (voice) that explains a science concept and is complemented by any combination of other modes of communication such as still images, slow-moving images, fast-moving images, music or sound effects. In a blended media project, the learner starts with a science concept that he or she wishes to explain or represent. In order to represent ideas of a concept, it is necessary to do some preliminary research, in most cases, using resources found on the Internet or in books. The collection of resources might include science facts, such as background information on the concept, along with digital images, audio and video clips. A storyboard format is used to organise the resources, and a script is written to provide for a narration by the authors to explain the concept. One unique feature of constructing blended media is the option of using slowmation (Hoban, 2005). Slowmation has the unique affordance of showing objects in motion at a slow speed (typically two frames per second) that allows a sequence or process to be more-easily seen and understood by the viewer during the narration. Another mode rarely used in typical student projects is video clips that can be downloaded from the Internet via Creative Commons and edited with relative ease. Video clips provide the affordance of showing a real-life example. This editing capability has been technically difficult until only recently and, in consideration of copyright, students are encouraged to use only media that is copyright free. Taken as a whole, it is the multimodal nature of a blended media movie that makes the process unique.

In this example, students from the graduate-level teacher education program at Southern Oregon University were assigned the task of creating a blended media movie to explain a science concept. The process was described in a 20-minute introduction at the beginning of a 3-hour class, which included slowmation and blended media examples. Students were provided with supporting articles (Hoban & Nielsen, 2012; Hoban, Nielsen & Shepherd, 2013) and step-by-step instructions for using Windows Movie Maker and iMovie to create and compress the finished product and upload to YouTube. Students had the choice of working alone or with a partner, and each individual or pair arrived in class prepared with their story idea and their 'props' for the slowmation part of their project. The students were given the following instruction:

> Create a blended media movie 3–5 minutes in length, explaining a scientific concept that you don't know much about, that contains the following modes: text, digital images, slowmation, video from the Internet and narration. Music or sound effects are optional, and you must make an effort to use copyright-free material.

Script writing in a storyboard format was needed to plan and organise the sequence of digital images and video clips as well as facilitate the narration. Students could use their own materials and digital equipment if desired, but items such as poster paper, coloured construction paper, Play-doh, markers, crayons, scissors, glue and tape were provided, in addition to digital cameras, laptops and movie-editing software for PCs and Macs. In order to learn more about the participants' thinking and decisions, pre-service teachers volunteered to wear audiorecorders to record their conversations while constructing their movies. In addition, post-activity interviews were conducted to capture reflective comments about their decision making throughout the process. The next section outlines the steps explaining how two pre-service teachers, Meghan (M) and Bekkah (B), created their blended media to explain the scientific phenomenon of what bears do in winter to survive the extreme conditions. The data was collected during the construction process as well as after construction during a follow-up interview.

Selecting a topic

When creating blended media in a classroom, the selection of a topic typically depends on the teacher's curricular objectives. For example, after a unit on Newton's laws of motion, the task might be for students to represent their understanding of how those laws are applied. Or, in a more open-ended assignment, students would choose their topic based on what they are curious about in science, perhaps forming a question, for example, 'What's happening when lightning flashes in the sky?' In the post-activity interview, Meghan reflected on how they chose their topic:

> We initially wanted to do something just with animals and we were kind of throwing out ideas about things that everyone knows – the life of a butterfly and we got to bears and hibernation and another girl in the class who's going

to be a science teacher, she let us know that bears don't actually hibernate; they go into torpor. So it was something we didn't know about and we thought it was something most other people wouldn't know about so we decided to go with that and explain the difference between hibernation and torpor.

Identifying Internet resources

To prepare their explanation, students need skills in information literacy to locate factual information, images, audio and video clips, which primarily involves Internet research. The students are interpreting and 'reconstructing' their knowledge as well, because their limited prior knowledge about a topic is bolstered by new information from credible sources. Note the shift in the students' thinking in the following exchange:

> B: So one of the main differences that I found in doing my research is that bears can go up to a hundred days without eating or getting rid of waste or drinking water or anything. But they can wake up really easily; their body temperature doesn't drop as low, and their metabolic rate doesn't slow down as much.

> M: Mm-hmm.

> B: On the other hand if you look at say a chipmunk, who is a true hibernator, its body temperature drops to near-freezing, but it has to wake up periodically – like say every 10 to 15 days to eat food, and then it goes back to sleep.

> M: Wait, that seems like the opposite of what hibernation would be?

> B: Isn't it weird? See we learned something new, [laughter] we didn't really know that much about hibernation.

Using a storyboard

A storyboard is essentially a graphic organiser that shows the sequence of a story from start to finish, using sketches and notes to help students organise their information. When students plan in pairs or groups, this tool helps to narrow opinions and becomes a form of 'agreement'. In a K–12 setting, one simple method is to distribute an A4 sheet of paper with a grid of eight large cells drawn on it to help the students get started. Each cell would represent a 'chunk' of the story and contain drawings and notes about images or videos. Meghan and Bekkah decided to start with a storyboard.

> B: So, should we type up a narration first or do you want to start with a storyboard?

> M: Probably storyboard, and . . . like, exact info we want to say.

B: Okay, like a really general idea of the arc of our 'story'. Okay. Hmm. All right – so I think that we should start out with some text, maybe.

M: Okay.

B: I was thinking something along the lines of ... um ... obviously 'torpor in bears'. Or I like the idea of it being like 'Do you know that bears don't actually hibernate?'

This preparatory stage can also be assigned as homework and, by using a shared digital document, students can collaborate from home on their computers during the planning phase. In the preparatory phase, simple notations of the intended digital content suffices.

Writing a script

The script is the explanation of the science topic in a story-like form that will be narrated over the final compilation of digital images and clips. Typical storytelling devices are used such as having a beginning, middle and end of a story, perhaps using an attention-grabbing opener, and incorporating appropriate tone, grammar, meaning and so on for the intended audiences. Meghan and Bekkah used a shared Google document to set up their opening premise with a compare/contrast strategy:

B: [Reading script] – When people think of hibernation, they often think of bears. But what they don't know is that bears are not true hibernators. They actually go into a state called torpor, or winter lethargy.

The script can drive what images need to be located, and the reverse is also true, the images can determine what is written. For Meghan and Bekkah, the iconic image of a bear fishing for salmon became their first scene.

M: I want to find the classic 'bear eating a salmon' video.

B: Yeah. Yeah ... So we would talk about a bear in a river ... And a fish ...

Making media choices

In making decisions about different media forms, students need to carefully consider what they are trying to explain and then the affordances of the different media forms to complement the narration. To use slowmation scenes, students create 3D models out of Play-doh or 2D cutouts from construction paper, or use any real-life objects (plants, toys, etc.) to represent parts of the story. The previous stages of doing research, making a storyboard and writing a script identify what types of models need to be prepared. Meghan and Bekkah clearly understood the affordances of slowmation, which has the special capability to demonstrate a process that is not easily seen or to compress a lengthy process. Bekkah's interview showed how the slowmation was 'blended' with still shots of smaller animals for a compare/contrast:

> We decided to use the slowmation process to show the process of the bear getting ready to go into hibernation, which in reality takes place over a long period of time. So we figured that it would be the best thing to animate because we could show a lot of different things – the bear eating food and sort of nesting in its den and then waking up during the winter; things that we couldn't really find images or videos of. Then we blended that with still shots to illustrate maybe what a woodchuck looks like or what the size comparisons were between a small animal that goes into hibernation and a bear that goes into torpor.

Shooting digital images

When making the slowmation component, a digital camera on a tripod is pointed vertically toward the background scene (made with construction paper) on a table or on the floor, and the models are manipulated within the background 'environment'. Each placement of the moveable objects gets photographed, and when the sequence of photographs is played back in the movie-editing software, an animation is revealed. In this process the representations follow the script. Meghan and Bekkah were cognisant of how their design choices correlated with the script.

> M: Okay, so what we're going to do is make the bear out of felt. And because we have a limited amount of felt and the bear needs to get fatter, we are gonna shoot the scenes where the bear is fat first, and then trim the fat off, so we have to actually think about how we're going to work this backwards. So are we going to do the den scenes first? The den will be full and complete, and then we'll have to show it dragging things in . . .

> B: Hey that looks great! Nice. We can do it here and then we can just slide it (the bear) forward. This is going to be awesome. I see things coming together with the narration sort of developing this arc, and seeing our scene develop, I'm feeling really excited and I feel like this is going to turn out really well.

Movie editing process

In the movie-editing stage, the pre-service teachers import the photographs of the models to create the slowmation and add other images and video from their research on the Internet to correspond with their script. The slowmation images are typically played back at two frames per second, and timings for the remaining still shots can be adjusted during the narration stage. Videos from the Internet are easily downloaded and edited to create short clips to blend into the movie. We recommend that students save all their images and videos in one folder in order to be easily imported into movie-editing software, which typically are the free versions of Windows Movie Maker and iMovie. The success of video editing is dependent on the time allotted for the task and the experience and motivation of the editor – it may even become 'homework' for the editor. In the post-activity interview, Meghan explained her decision to edit the final movie at home:

> M: [editing] . . . took about 4 hours because I was getting really picky and had to shrink the pictures down so that you weren't looking at the same picture for 5 seconds. But it was totally worth it. I had a lot of fun, I'm glad I laid over a nature-y track that was built into the program so there's kind of nature-y music in the background. It was worth it to me to go home and put that extra time into it.

Adding narration

The last, but most important stage, of the movie creation is adding a narration that explains the scientific topic. Using a combination headset–microphone provides the best audio quality. If the script has been well written, the challenge is to match the timing of the words to the corresponding images. Most movie-editing software allows a narration track to be added with a simple 'add narration' command or 'import' of an audio file. If extensive audio editing with multiple tracks is desired (e.g. sound effects, music, voice), a free audio-editing software (e.g. Audacity) can be used to record an enhanced narration that can be imported into the movie project.

A well-crafted narration is essentially a recorded presentation that synthesises the research conducted throughout the project. This stage connects directly to the Common Core Anchor Standard 5 for Speaking and Listening: "Make strategic use of digital media [e.g., textual, graphical, audio, video and interactive elements] and visual displays of data to express information and enhance understanding of presentations" (National Governors Association Center, 2010). In practice, some students are uncomfortable with the sound of their own voices, but others discover a hidden talent that blossoms during this process. In addition, repetition of the narration and replaying it should aid retention of the information presented. See Table 15.1 for the final script and the accompanying figures for examples of images presented in the blended media.

Finalising

The final step after adding the narration is to export the movie by compressing the 3–5-minute movie into a smaller file size. The finalised formats, for Windows Movie Maker (.wmv) and iMovie (.mov) are compatible with most playback systems and can be uploaded directly to YouTube in a matter of minutes. Display on a class website or blog is an easy process of copying YouTube's embed code and

TABLE 15.1 Digital composition of final blended media movie (length: 2:25)

When people think of hibernation, they often think of bears, but what they don't know is that bears are not true hibernators; they actually go into a state called 'torpor' or 'winter lethargy'. The fact of the matter is, no animal larger than a woodchuck can truly hibernate. During the fall, bears begin preparing for the winter by building up large stores of fat. They consume berries, fish, roots, grass and sometimes carcasses. During this time, bears can gain up to 30 pounds per week. They also begin to look for a den that will be small enough that their body heat will warm it but large enough to move around and stretch. They will prepare the den by dragging dead leaves and branches to sleep on.

Sometimes a den will include a sow with up to four cubs. When a bear goes into torpor, its body temperature drops by only a few degrees. Compare that to smaller animals whose body temperature drops to near freezing. A bear's body mass and fur help it to retain heat. A bear's heart rate also drops by approximately 75% from 40 beats per minute to about 8 whereas a smaller animal that hibernates will drop its heart rate by 98%. A bear's breathing rate will also decrease from 6 to 10 breaths in a minute to one breath every 45 seconds.

When smaller animals hibernate they need to wake up every week or so to eat stored food and pass waste before returning to hibernation. Bears, on the other hand, can go up to 100 days without eating food, drinking water or passing waste. Bears can also wake up relatively quickly during torpor compared to smaller animals that wake up slowly from hibernation. This process helps to allow sows to care for their young that may be born during the winter months, usually late January or early February. A bear may also be awakened by a loud noise such as a tree falling or a sound of a gun.

Unlike hibernators that require a few hours to wake up, bears can be on the move in a matter of seconds. Always be cautious if you're out in the woods during the winter or early spring; a bear's body uses its fat stores and can regenerate muscle while in torpor. However, it will be hungry when it wakes up.

Digital Composition of Final Blended Media Movie (Length: 2:25)

Figure 15.1	Figure 15.2	Figure 15.3
Video clips – 5	Slowmation segments – 3	Still images – 14
Average length: 6.5 seconds	Average length: 16 seconds	Average length: 3 seconds

FIGURE 15.1 Video clips – 5, Average length: 6.5 seconds

FIGURE 15.2 Slowmation segments – 3, Average length: 16 seconds

FIGURE 15.3 Still images – 14, Average length: 3 seconds

pasting it into a webpage's HTML editor. The technical aspects involved in editing and finalising a project challenges most computer users, but can be managed with persistence, collaboration and support.

Discussion

In an era of new and more-rigorous standards, students are expected to think critically and synthesise, not just regurgitate science facts. Using blended media offers teachers a creative and open-ended method to engage students in science content. It also gives students an opportunity to be knowledge producers by creating their own 'science explanation'. In the previous example, Meghan and Bekkah were clearly co-authors of their presentation – planning, designing and constructing the content, form and message of their movie. Their script was based on their research of scientific facts, but the mixture of hands-on model making and use of digital devices engaged them in a multimodal, dynamic experience – much different from a unidimensional and somewhat predictable experience of simply reading from a science textbook. Acquisition, processing and presentation of information were facilitated by the high level of engagement when using a variety of digital tools. Using new media has been shown to enhance authentic learning (Shaffer & Resnick, 1999), and these students were making choices to communicate the information to an audience other than the teacher. Given the fact that the blended media product becomes a classroom or public artefact, it could be argued that such a presentation is viewed by a broader and more-discerning audience than a typical live classroom presentation, with considerable potential for high replay value.

Given the ubiquity of everyday digital devices and readily available software, blended media has broad applications to any content area because it is process driven and not limited within a specific subject. Research-oriented digital explanations can be created for any content area, whether language arts, social studies or physical education. A blended media could also be generated by students to represent other genres, such as narratives and reports. In terms of outcomes, although it is quite common to find that classroom technology use spurs student engagement and motivation (Brown *et al.*, 2013; Chen & McGrath, 2003; Harmer & Cates, 2007; Lehrer, 1993; O'Neill & Barton, 2005; Wu & Huang, 2007), documentation of achievement or retention gains based on students *creating* media have been limited to date, which suggests an agenda for future studies.

One example from the early days of multimedia experimentation illustrates the promise of measuring learning through creation of media. Lehrer (1993) found that learning differences between two groups of eighth graders creating projects on Civil War events were not observed when they were tested immediately after the curriculum unit. But a year later, when researchers asked the same students what they learned in the unit, the group of students who created hypertexts about Civil War events demonstrated "knowledge that was richer, better connected, and more applicable to subsequent learning and events", while the control group of students, who studied in the traditional textbook fashion, "could recall almost nothing about the historical content" (Lehrer, 1993, p. 221).

The difficulty in measuring multimodal learning in a natural setting lies in the complexity of variables that are difficult to control, for example, knowledge and experience of the user, types of hardware and software or pedagogical approaches. The challenge for educators going forward is deciding what is important to measure – for example, acquisition of information (i.e. retention) or something else, such as problem solving; effectiveness of communication styles or development of multiliteracies through collaborative authorship. Research studies must attempt to keep pace with rapidly changing technologies, so we can assure teachers that employing complicated multimedia projects in the classroom helps students learn science content in a multimodal world.

References

Anastopoulou, S., Sharples, M. & Baber, C. (2010). An evaluation of multimodal interactions with technology while learning science concepts. *Written Communication, 27*(4), 441–468. doi: 10.1111/j.1467-8535.2009.01017.x

Anderson, J. R., Reder, L. M. & Simon, H. A. (1998). Radical constructivism and cognitive psychology. In D. Ravitch (Ed.), *Brookings papers on education policy* (pp. 255–278). Washington, DC: Brookings Institution.

Baggett, P. (1987). Learning a procedure from multimedia instructions: The effects of film and practice. *Applied Cognitive Psychology, 1*, 183–195.

Bredo, E. (2000). Reconsidering social constructivism: The relevance of George Herbert Mead's interactionism. In D. C. Phillips & M. Early (Eds.), *Constructivism in education: Opinions and second opinions on controversial issues: Vol. 1. Ninety-ninth yearbook of the National Society for the Study of Education* (pp. 127–157). Chicago, IL: University of Chicago.

Briand, P. (1970). Multimedia and advanced composition. *College Composition and Communication, 21*(3), 267–269.

Brown, J., Murcia, K. & Hackling, M. (2013). A multimodal strategy for engaging children with primary science. *Teaching Science, 59*(4), 14–20.

Chen, P. & McGrath, D. (2003). Moments of joy: Student engagement and conceptual learning in the design of hypermedia documents. *Journal of Research on Technology in Education, 35*(3), 402–422.

Harmer, A. J. & Cates, W. M. (2007). Designing for learner engagement in middle school science: Technology, inquiry, and the hierarchies of engagement. *Computers in Schools, 24*(1/2), 105–124.

Hoban, G. (2005). From claymation to slowmation: A teaching procedure to develop science knowledge. *Teaching Science, 51*(2), 26–30.

Hoban G. & Nielsen, W. (2012). Using 'slowmation' to enable preservice primary teachers to create multimodal representations of science concepts. *Research in Science Education, 42*(6), 1101–1119. doi: 10.1007/s11165-011-9236-3

Hoban G., Nielsen, W. & Shepherd, A. (2013). Explaining and communicating science using student-created blended media. *Teaching Science, 59*(1), 32–35.

Jarvinen, M. K., Jarvinen, L. Z. & Sheehan, D. N. (2012). Application of core science concepts using digital video: A 'hands-on' laptop approach. *Journal of College Science Teaching, 41*(6), 16–24.

Jonassen, D. H., Myers, J. M. & McKillop, A. M. (1996). From constructivism to constructionism: Learning *with* hypermedia/multimedia rather than *from* it. In B. Wilson (Ed.), *Constructivist learning environments: Case studies in instructional design* (pp. 93–106). Englewood Cliffs, NJ: Educational Technology.

Kress, G. & van Leeuwen, T. (2001). *Multimodal discourse: The modes and media of contemporary communication.* New York: Oxford University Press.

Lauer, C. (2009). Contending with terms: 'Multimodal' and 'multimedia' in the academic and public spheres. *Computers and Composition, 29*, 225–239.

Lehrer, R. (1993). Authors of knowledge: Patterns of hypermedia design. In S. P. Lajoie & S. J. Derry (Eds.), *Computers as cognitive tools* (pp. 197–227). Hillsdale, NJ: Lawrence Erlbaum.

Lehrer, R., Erickson, J. & Connell, T. (1994). Learning by designing hypermedia documents. *Computers in Schools, 10*(1–2), 227–254.

Mayer, R. E. (2001). *Multimedia learning.* New York: Cambridge University Press.

National Assessment Governing Board (2013). *Technology and engineering literacy framework for the 2014 National Assessment of Educational Progress.* Retrieved from http://www.nagb.

org/content/nagb/assets/documents/publications/frameworks/naep_tel_framework_
2014.pdf (accessed 26 March, 2015).

National Center for Education Statistics, Program for International Student Assessment
(2012). *Science literacy performance of 15-year-olds*. Available: http://nces.ed.gov/surveys/
pisa/pisa2012/index.asp (accessed 26 March, 2015).

National Governors Association Center (2010). *English language arts standards*. Retrieved
from http://www.corestandards.org/ELA-Literacy/ (accessed 26 March, 2015).

National Research Council (2012). *A framework for K–12 science education: Practices, crosscutting
concepts, and core ideas*. Retrieved from http://www.nextgenscience.org/framework-k–
12-science-education (accessed 26 March, 2015).

National Research Council (2013). *Next generation science standards: For states, by states,
Appendix D 'All standards, all students': Making next generation science standards accessible to all
students'*. Retrieved from http://www.nextgenscience.org/sites/ngss/files/Appendix%
20D%20Diversity%20and%20Equity%206-14-13.pdf (accessed 26 March, 2015).

Next Generation Science Standards (2014). *Next Generation Science Standards: For states, by
states (homepage)*. Washington, DC: Achieve. Retrieved from http://www.nextgenscience.
org (accessed 26 March, 2015).

O'Neill, T. & Barton, A. C. (2005). Uncovering student ownership in science learning: The
making of a student created mini-documentary. *School Science and Mathematics*, *105*(6),
292–301.

Selfe, C. L., Owen-Fleischer, S. & Wright, S. (2007). Words, audio and video: Composing and
the processes of production. In C. L. Selfe (Ed.), *Multimodal composition: Resources for
teachers* (pp. 13–28). New York: Hampton Press.

Shaffer, D. W. & Resnick, M. (1999). 'Thick authenticity': New media and authentic learning.
Journal of Interactive Learning Research, *10*(2), 195–215.

Wu, H. K. & Huang, Y. L. (2007). Ninth grade student engagement in teacher-centered and
student-centered technology-enhanced learning environments. *Science Education*, *9*(5),
727–749. doi: 10.1002/sce.20216

Yu, P. T., Lai, Y. S., Tsai, H. S. & Chang, Y. H. (2010). Using a multimodal learning system to
support music instruction. *Educational Technology & Society*, *13*(3), 151–162.

16

MULTIMEDIA PRODUCTION TO PROMOTE AN UNDERSTANDING OF HEALTH LITERACY AND COMMUNICATE HEALTH MESSAGES

Karma Pearce

Context

Communication between healthcare professionals and patients is central to quality healthcare. However, patients commonly report having difficulty understanding and comprehending instructions from healthcare professionals (Howard, Gazmararian & Parker, 2005; Williams, Davis, Parker & Weiss, 2002). Health professionals often have a poor understanding of health literacy (Macabasco-O'Connell & Fry-Bowers, 2011), commonly over-estimate health-literacy levels (Bass, Wilson, Griffith & Barnett, 2002) and even when provided with information on a patient's health-literacy level often fail to communicate effectively (Seligman *et al.*, 2005). In addition, healthcare professionals often use terminology not familiar to the patient and deliver too much information without checking the level of under-standing (Ong, De Haes, Hoos & Lammes, 1995). Moreover, communication techniques rarely integrate issues of culture, language, literacy and learning. Consequently, patients often report remembering less than half of the information conveyed during a consultation and are unclear how to manage their medical condition(s) (Makaryus & Friedman, 2005).

However, healthcare professionals are a key source of health information for patients and significantly impact the health-literacy demands placed on their patients through the communication techniques employed (Commonwealth of Australia, 2013). It is, thus, important that healthcare professionals acknowledge the inadequacy of a 'one-size-fits-all' approach when communicating with patients, particularly those with low health literacy, and tailor communication styles to meet the needs of the patient (Australian Commission on Safety and Quality in Health Care, 2014). It is also necessary to check that the information conveyed to patients has been fully understood. Similarly, the Institute of Medicine of the National

Academies (US), an independent, non-profit organisation, recommended that "professional schools and professional continuing education programs in health and related fields . . . should incorporate health literacy into their curricula and areas of competence" (Nielsen-Bohlman, Panzer & Kindig, 2004, p. 161). While there is an emergence of health-literacy curricula in some allied health areas (Cotugna & Vickery, 2003), there is a paucity of such curricula that emphasise different forms of communication. It could be that getting students to design and create digital media forms to convey health messages could be useful to inform them about the importance of communicating clearly to a specific audience for a specific purpose.

Media forms

A contemporary approach to teaching with multimedia is to have learners make an explanatory resource such as slowmation (Hoban, 2005, 2009) or a digital story (Lambert, 2013; McKnight, Hoban & Nielsen, 2011). Digital stories are narratives or instructional multimodal products created using computer-based programs and images, music, animations or video clips and narration. Typically, a digital story involves 10–12 still images that are played in sequence and narrated over 2–3 minutes. In the context of health literacy, storytelling with digital technologies facilitates the critical evaluation of complex key concepts, while distilling them into succinct thoughts to create appropriate health messages delivered to the public using lay language and displaying dynamic rather than static images. This is an important opportunity to learn about health literacy for emerging health professionals, as digital storytelling employs multiple literacies, such as information processing, communication and multimedia literacy, which are pertinent in health promotion. Attending to principles of media design is also important, so that the intended messages are effectively communicated.

Effective multimedia design draws on Mayer's (2001) Cognitive Theory of Multimedia Learning, which is based on dual-channel coding theory (cited in Mayer, 2005) and Sweller's (1999) cognitive load theory, to overcome limitations of memory and promote deep learning. There are three key principles underpinning Mayer's dual coding theory: (i) humans process multimedia information using dual channels (visual or pictorial processing and audio or verbal processing); (ii) each channel has a limited capacity for processing; and (iii) active learning requires performing a systematic set of cognitive processes. Cognitive load theory describes the amount of mental effort required to process information: selecting relevant words from the narrative; organising these words into meaningful representations; selecting relevant images or pictures for the visual representations; organising these images into meaningful representations; and, finally, integrating the images and words into meaningful integrated representations. Thus, when the multimedia presentations are constructed so as to minimise cognitive load and engage dual-channel processing, the viewer is not confused or overwhelmed and can learn the intended message.

Use of multimedia in addressing low health literacy

Multimedia presentations have been shown to help bridge learning gaps and improve comprehension amongst individuals with low health literacy (Kandula et al., 2009). Specifically, in low-literacy populations multimedia presentations have been effective in communicating health messages about diabetes (Carbone, Lennon, Torres & Rosal, 2005), cardiopulmonary resuscitation decision making in advanced cancer (Volandes et al., 2013), tuberculosis (Wieland et al., 2013) and HIV (Aronson, Rajan, Marsch & Bania, 2013).

Students as multimedia composers

As emerging healthcare professionals, undergraduate students with limited information-technology skills can easily generate multimedia presentations (Hay, Guzdal, Jackson, Boyle & Soloway, 1994). This is due to recent advances in digital technologies. Software to generate animations and edit videos is standard with Windows and Macintosh packages and freeware music and pictures are accessible through the web.

Traditionally, multimedia construction has not formed part of tertiary health education curricula. Furthermore, multimedia production is emerging as a platform to promote critical thinking, problem solving and deep learning (Meeks & Ilyasova, 2003) through purposeful student engagement with 'real-life' scenarios (Kearsley & Schneiderman, 1998), particularly when grounded in educational theory.

As multimedia technology continues to evolve, opportunities arise for advancing new pedagogical models to keep pace with the emerging digital culture in the undergraduate classroom (Clark, 2010). Clark suggests that the digital classroom is progressing toward a judiciously employed pedagogy focused on promoting students' digital literacy. Kearsley and Schneiderman's (1998) framework for technology-based teaching and learning via engagement theory, conceptualised as 'Relate–Create–Donate', encapsulates three key themes: "learning occurs in a social context (Relate), coursework should be hands-on and project-based (Create) and the project must have an authentic 'real world' focus (Donate)" (Kearsley & Schneiderman, 1998, p. 20). Relate–Create–Donate is an example of pedagogy applicable to multimedia production, particularly when coupled with cognitive load theory. The digital product acknowledges the amount of mental effort required to process information (Mayer, 2005). In the context of health literacy, we also argue that students need to ensure that the message communicated through the multimedia product has been fully 'heard', and propose a fourth component 'Clarify', to advance the framework to Relate–Create–Clarify–Donate.

This pedagogical framework was used in a fourth-year Nutrition and Therapeutics undergraduate pharmacy four-week intensive course at an Australian university in 2012 and 2013. The intensive course equates to 180 hours of study, both inside and outside the classroom. Embedded within the course was a health-literacy module that included a series of small-group discovery activities. The principle objective of the health-literacy module was to create an awareness of all the issues encompassing 'health literacy' and the impact of these issues for those with low health literacy to access quality care and positive health outcomes. The module involved community interviews and the production of a multimedia product to convey health messages to minority groups. Through multimedia production, it was envisaged that students would learn a range of communication skills when dealing with the public including the use of multimedia to convey scientific messages and the 'teach-back technique'. Used in the current context, healthcare professionals should ask members of the public (who consume the information or message) to repeat (i.e. 'teach back') the information conveyed, so that understanding can be verified (Davis, Williams, Marin, Parker & Glass, 2002; Devereux, 2004).

Implementation

How students make the media

The concept of health literacy was introduced to students during the first tutorial of the module along with a range of effective communication techniques for individuals with low levels of health literacy. Students were also introduced to cognitive load theory and principles of media design (Mayer, 2005; Mayer, Heiser & Lonn, 2001) and, in groups of 4–5, were invited to choose a scenario to promote a health message that they would develop through the health-literacy module in this course.

The health-literacy module

The health-literacy module consisted of four key elements:

- an initial community-based questionnaire developed by students based on a literature review they conducted;
- creation of a storyboard and audio script;
- creation of a three-minute multimedia production. Students could use any form of media, ranging from slowmation to video or any other form of blended media; and
- community evaluation (follow-up questionnaire) of the multimedia production and student self-assessment of the module.

The multimedia product was composed in class, while the remaining elements were conducted outside of the classroom. In this section, one example of a health message created by a student group is presented. The health message involves vitamin D deficiency and bone health in young Muslim women.

The primary goal of the initial student-designed questionnaire was to enable students to gain an authentic understanding of the topic, in this case, knowledge and beliefs of vitamin D deficiency on bone health held by young Muslim women.

The students also designed questions for the chosen population group, in order to explore the effects of other determinates on low health-literacy levels, such as self-efficacy, response efficacy, motivation to change, gender, age, educational background, languages other than English frequently spoken in the home, and cultural and socio-economic factors. This allowed students to identify misconceptions and knowledge gaps that may result in low health-literacy levels. The questionnaire findings formed the basis of a literature review and, together with academic feedback, were used to formulate a storyboard and audio script for a three-minute slowmation to inform young Muslim women of the possible impact on their bone health from vitamin D deficiency.

Students used the movie-making software of their choosing and produced any form of (blended) multimedia. The multimedia product was constructed during a two-hour tutorial session using a smartphone camera, Windows Movie Maker software and standard Microsoft headphones. Students proficient in the use of other media software were encouraged to bring their own laptop computers to class. Students were reminded of copyright legislation and encouraged to select freeware music, props and any pictures that they wanted to use and bring them to the tutorial class. Numerous craft supplies were also provided. Students producing slowmations were provided with the methodology described elsewhere (Hoban, 2005; University of Wollongong, 2009). Groups that chose to produce movies usually had a member proficient in video editing.

Finally, students were required to determine the effectiveness of their multimedia product in communicating the health message to young Muslim women and were assessed on the appropriateness of the multimedia product in communicating scientific health messages. Students drew from a range of communication techniques introduced during the first tutorial, with the majority using both a follow-up questionnaire and the teach-back technique. Students then evaluated their own learning. Comprehensive marking rubrics are available elsewhere (Pearce, 2013).

The multimedia product

This section presents excerpts from the group's narration to illustrate material that the students needed to learn and how it was portrayed in the multimedia presentation:

> We need essential nutrients from food, water and sunlight to live healthy … when we wear a hijab we do not absorb enough sunlight. We absorb sunlight through skin to produce vitamin D, which improves calcium absorption for stronger bones. We can also absorb vitamin D from the food we eat.

The group used lay language to relate key nutritional information and, further, described diagnosis and treatment in culturally appropriate terms:

Low levels of vitamin D decrease calcium absorption leading to increased risk of osteoporosis, which means weaker bones that can fracture easily. As Muslim women you are able to practice freely in Australia to wear a hijab, but do you have enough vitamin D? Studies show that in Australia most veiled Muslim women have lower vitamin D levels. In fact, our risk is double compared to other Australian women ... A diet rich in fatty fish like salmon, mackerel or tuna will help. Vitamin D is also added to milk, margarine and olive oil. However, food alone is not enough to provide sufficient vitamin D. If your vitamin D levels are low, don't worry, there are a few things you can do to help get your vitamin D levels back to normal. Firstly, in your backyard where no one can see you, get sunlight of 5–7 minutes in summer and 30 minutes throughout winter without wearing a hijab. While you are in your backyard, why not do some exercise?

The video goes on to invite women to do other sorts of activities if uncovering in the backyard is not possible and advises the use of halal vitamin D and calcium supplements (and where to find them) to prevent possible health consequences if dietary intake and sun exposure are inadequate. It also explains that the only way to know if levels are low is through a blood test. An image from their three-minute slowmation is shown in Figure 16.1.

Evaluation

After creating their multimedia presentations, in addition to the assessment of all four parts of the health-literacy module (including the student-generated questionnaire, follow-up questionnaire and self-evaluation), all students were surveyed

FIGURE 16.1 An image from the 3-minute slowmation

anonymously about their experiences in the health literacy module. The survey included demographic information, feedback on the tasks, use of multimedia and perspectives on assessment, using open and closed questions. Construction and validation of the survey through group-wise paired t-test is reported elsewhere (Pearce, Birbeck & May, 2014). Data reported in this chapter include students' perspectives from the initial and follow-up questionnaires and the student survey of the activity.

Preparing a multimedia presentation: Feedback from the community

Students constructed an initial questionnaire to ascertain baseline knowledge of a health message within the community. Through these questionnaires, students identified misconceptions, such as elderly men and women believed "orange juice contained calcium and was also good for strong bones . . . but you don't hear it publicized as much as milk". When the student interrogated this comment, she realised that the respondents had mistaken vitamin C for calcium and, further, that since both nutrients start with the letter 'C' the respondents assumed that they had the same function in the body. Such misconceptions were then addressed in the multimedia products to ensure effective communication of all aspects of the health message.

Generally, data from the student-generated follow-up questionnaires were gathered through interviewing members of the public. Data show that the multimedia products were very effective tools in conveying health messages, although there were still a very small number of incongruities. For example, one group chose to ignore feedback from the initial questionnaire and from academics, which included a suggestion to use familiar imperial units of measure for reporting healthy body weight. This group's animation ignored this and described healthy weight using the term 'kilograms'. The follow-up questionnaire showed community members did not understand the modern metric term. In reflecting on their multimedia product, one student commented on the self-evaluation:

> This activity has taught me not to be so arrogant! Our group thought we knew best. We lose marks at Uni for not using the correct units, which are always metric units. It never crossed our minds that not everyone else used these units and bathroom scales still exist in imperial units.

By not relating the weight measures in terms familiar to those who would view the message, the follow-up questionnaire helped these students realise the missed opportunity and, thus, have a new appreciation for the need to carefully design messages.

Students used a range of methodologies to appraise the effectiveness of the multimedia products to communicate health messages to members of the community and the students saw the product as a chance to engage with the community and offer benefit in terms of the health message. Students generally chose to develop a follow-up questionnaire specific to their own health message, coupled with the teach-back technique. As students designed their surveys to elicit feedback from community members specific to their multimedia product, differences in survey design makes comparison of the results difficult. However, members of the community were very accepting of the multimedia products, describing them as 'fun', 'informative', 'educational', 'held their attention' and 'entertaining'. Further, students also reported success, such as this comment from a self-evaluation:

> Our participants loved the slowmation and the simple language used. A number of them had poor eyesight so really appreciated not having to read pages of information. I originally thought our product would have to be a lot longer to convey all the necessary health information. I was wrong! I now know participants lose interest quickly, so you really need to be selective about the 'chestnuts' of essential information to include.

Such comments reflect the students' growing awareness of the importance of how health information is presented, especially if health consumers struggle to read and understand written information (Berkman *et al.*, 2004) that is too wordy, technical or rich in jargon (Ong *et al.*, 1995).

Process of preparing a multimedia presentation: Student feedback

At the completion of the unit, students were invited to provide feedback through a survey comprised of demographic information, general comments on the unit, assessment and the use of multimedia in conveying health messages, with the use of open and closed questions. The close-ended questions employed a seven-point Likert scale, ranging from 'completely disagree' to 'completely agree'. An example of a close-ended question is: 'Did you feel that the task increased your critical thinking, ... problem solving and ... teamwork skills?' The survey also included several open-ended questions designed to seek student feedback on the series of tasks. An example of such a question is: 'What aspect of the health literacy task did you enjoy most, or had the most impact on your learning?'

A total of 215 (out of 221) students undertaking the unit in 2012 and 2013 provided feedback on the unit: 33% were international students; 73% were female; almost all were aged 21–25 years; and just over half indicated that English was not their first language. Similar patterns were observed in both of the year cohorts (2012, 2013). These students previously demonstrated a slightly lower-than-average level of nutrition knowledge compared to the Australian public, using the Australian General Nutrition Knowledge Questionnaire (Pearce & Cross, 2013).

Survey item responses (shown in Table 16.1) indicated that almost all the students believed that the initial questionnaire they conducted in the community helped them to understand nutritional beliefs and cultural nuances in their chosen population. They also strongly believed this questionnaire, along with instructor

TABLE 16.1 Survey of nutrition and therapeutics students' perceptions of the series of tasks after completing the health literacy module

Student Survey Item	% Agree or Strongly Agree
My understanding of health literacy issues has improved	91
The initial questionnaire conducted in community helped me to understand nutritional beliefs and cultural nuances of the chosen population	94
Conducting the initial questionnaire along with instructor feedback helped in developing the storyboard and audio script	94
Checking consumer understanding of health messages is a key component of effective communication	94
Enjoyed using their creative talents	90
Creation of a multimedia product enabled us to connect with and engage the audience more so than print material to convey a health message	74%
The task helped me develop graduate attributes of:	
Critical thinking	69
Problem solving	70
Team work	77

feedback, helped in developing the storyboard and audio script. Similarly, almost all of the students believed that checking consumer understanding of health messages through a follow-up questionnaire and the teach-back technique was an essential component of the communication strategy. The uptake rate of the teach-back technique was much higher in this study than rates reported by Coleman (2011) in a 12-month health-literacy course (31%). This is an important result because, irrespective of the mode in which the message is delivered, health professionals need to ensure the health message has been fully understood (Makaryus & Friedman, 2005; Ong et al., 1995; Schillinger, Bindman, Wang, Stewart & Piette, 2004), particularly as individuals with low levels of health literacy often report recalling less than half of what was discussed after meeting with health professionals (Calkins et al., 1997; Makaryus & Friedman, 2005; Ong et al., 1995).

Most importantly, the majority of students believed that the series of activities provided iterative ways of learning through deconstructing complex health messages, 'bouncing ideas between group members', reconstructing health messages to convey ideas and confirm understanding. In addition, students either agreed or strongly agreed that the creation of a multimedia product enabled them to connect with and engage their audience more so than print material to convey a health message (74%) and that the activity helped them develop the graduate attributes of critical thinking (69%), problem solving (70%) and team work (77%).

Open-ended questions invited students to provide feedback on the aspects of the health literacy task they enjoyed most or had the most impact on their learning. Typical comments included: "hearing misconceptions from the community members themselves was one of the most powerful aspects of the course" and:

> I was initially sceptical – making a video didn't seem like an appropriate assessment task for final-year pharmacy students, who are months away from joining the workforce and forging a career . . . however, as the process evolved I began to see what a great tool it was for demonstrating that sections of the community need to have information conveyed to them in varying formats to maximise everyone's understanding. It also highlights the flexibility that a community pharmacy can use more than pamphlets to convey health information.

This student's initial apprehension of this type of assessment task was not uncommon, but, as she notes, the task was overwhelmingly embraced as the groups produced a multimedia product of a high standard. The students revealed that they generally valued the opportunity to use their creative talents. The following is an example of a comment from a self-evaluation:

> I really appreciated the opportunity to use my creative talents and do something really different. I spent a disproportionate amount of time on this assignment very willingly as I was just having so much fun and everyone in the community loved it.

Overall, the scaffolded series of activities in the unit increased the students' knowledge of the aspects underpinning health literacy and overall knowledge of health literacy while providing an alternative digital medium to communicate health messages.

Discussion

Benefits and limitations

Overall, there were three main benefits of the study: (i) the majority of students advanced understanding of the importance of effective communications through the scaffolded series of activities; (ii) the students developed their own health-literacy understandings; and (iii) the students were able to successfully dissect complex physiological concepts and present them in lay language, which is an important skill for health professionals (Seligman *et al.*, 2005).

Perhaps the most convincing support for the health-literacy module and multimedia production comes from the students' self-evaluations, with many describing how they intend to incorporate their new-found understanding of health literacy into both their personal and professional lives. The majority of students stated that as a direct result of this activity they will alter the way they approach and counsel customers in the community pharmacy setting, as reflected by these students:

> I now recognise that stereotypes and biases have influenced the way I communicate with segments of the community and therefore in future [I] will try to extract information from them directly and address the knowledge gaps when communicating health messages or designing health promotional material.

Reflecting on the process, making the video has definitely opened my eyes to how little the average person typically knows about their health. I feel that this information will change the way I interact with people when discussing health topics and will help me to enter into a situation without making assumptions about others' health knowledge base.

While many students felt their multimedia communication was highly effective, unfortunately, 38% of students experienced difficulties in using the Windows software. These students reported a lack of confidence in using the software, difficulties in editing audio voiceovers and problems with software freezing. Students also acknowledged some limitations with their multimedia products:

Our short video could have been improved by being more fluid rather than constantly pausing the voices. In terms of the content, the key issues could have had a stronger emphasis on them, and the use of a quick summary would have been beneficial.

Some of the content could have been delivered in a more succinct and simplified form to ensure that the viewer remains engaged and doesn't become overwhelmed with all the newly acquired information.

Given that students had no formal training in multimedia production and a four-week time frame to complete all tasks, the overall quality of the multimedia presentations was very high. However, only students with at least one team member proficient in video editing chose to produce videos. The majority of student teams opted to prepare a slowmation, as noted by this student in her self-evaluation:

We wanted to make something we would be proud to show people, would be visually captivating and appropriately educational. We chose to make a slowmation as it looks visually appealing, [is] simple to make and can be made using simple and inexpensive props. Also none of us really like acting.

Reflections from the academic

Traditionally, written and oral communication has been the main form of communication between health practitioners and healthcare consumers. This subject used a scaffolded approach, where undergraduate students created blended-media presentations. The approach was successful in creating awareness of health-literacy levels within an Australian community group and enabled effective communication of health messages to individuals with low health literacy within the community.

Creating community health messages can be an effective learning tool to help students develop health-literacy competency, particularly when accompanied by instructions that incorporated training in communication skills and multimedia techniques. The series of activities were well received by the students who, despite the volume of work required over a very short time period, remained engaged and enthusiastic. The tutorial in which the multimedia presentations were constructed was chaotic, busy and noisy but, at the same time, very productive. Students were generally very happy and many of the shy students demonstrated significantly improved levels of confidence upon completion of the task. The scaffolded 'active learning' small-group discovery approach, with academic feedback at each step in the process, directly contributed to the success of the overall product and the students' learning. However, there was a significant increase in the workload for the academics, as the course was delivered as a four-week intensive course. These time pressures would be ameliorated if the course were delivered over 12 or 13 weeks. This, however, is offset by deep learning by the students and 'light bulb moments' with respect to preventative health and communication with low health-literate clients.

Future directions

Health literacy is a national health problem and should be incorporated into the curriculum for all healthcare professionals. Preparing health professionals for the workforce includes equipping them with the necessary skills and techniques to effectively communicate with members of the community, who have varying levels of health literacy. This series of activities could be employed to teach any health professional about the issues surrounding health literacy. In addition, the module format that included community-based surveys and a literature review in addition to the multimedia product could be embedded in any education curriculum where the use of lay language and communication of technical concepts is required. Future directions include a more-detailed assessment of the impact of the multimedia presentation for individuals with low health literacy. It seems appropriate to conclude with the voice of a student:

> I offer our most sincere appreciation and gratitude for the opportunity to run the Health Literacy project. As Muslims ourselves, it wasn't until this project that we are fully aware of the issue of vitamin D deficiency in our community (young Muslim women). This project has also brought a great impact in delivering and communicating this issue to young Muslim women as the message was delivered from one Muslim woman to another Muslim woman ... We highly hope that this project will continue in future years to benefit the juniors and most importantly, to the community. We are very proud to report approximately 80 women at the mosque have now had blood tests to determine their vitamin D levels and where necessary are taking action to correct low levels.

Acknowledgements

I would like to acknowledge the help of Dr David Birbeck and Professor Esther May in constructing the small-group discovery activities.

References

Aronson, I. D., Rajan, S., Marsch, L. A. & Bania, T. C. (2013). How patient interactions with a computer-based video intervention affect decisions to test for HIV. *Health Education & Behavior, 41*(3), 259–266.

Australian Commission on Safety and Quality in Health Care (2014). *Goal 3: Partnering with consumers action guide*. Retrieved from http://www.safetyandquality.gov.au/publications/goal-3-partnering-with-consumers-action-guide/ (accessed 26 March, 2015).

Bass, P. F., III, Wilson, J. F, Griffith, C. H. & Barnett, D. R. (2002). Residents' ability to identify patients with poor literacy skills. *Academic Medicine, 77*(10), 1039–1041.

Berkman, N. D., DeWalt, D. A., Pignone, M. P., Sheridan, S. L., Lohr, K. N. & Lux, L. (2004). *AHRQ Evidence Report Summaries. Literacy and health outcomes: Summary*. Rockville, MD: Agency for Healthcare Research and Quality. Retrieved from http://www.ncbi.nlm.nih.gov/books/NBK11942/ (accessed 26 March, 2015).

Calkins, D. R., Davis, R. B., Reiley, P., Phillips, R. S., Pineo, K. L. C. & Delbanco, T. L. (1997). Patient–physician communication at hospital discharge and patients' understanding of the postdischarge treatment plan. *Archives of Internal Medicine, 157*(9), 1026–1030.

Carbone, E. T., Lennon, K. M., Torres, M. I. & Rosal, M. C. (2005). Testing the feasibility of an interactive learning styles measure for US Latino adults with type 2 diabetes and low literacy. *International Quarterly of Community Health Education, 25*(4), 315–335.

Clark, J. E. (2010). The digital imperative: Making the case for a 21st century pedagogy. *Computers and Composition, 27*(1), 27–35.

Coleman, C. (2011). Teaching health care professionals about health literacy: A review of the literature. *Nursing Outlook, 59*(2), 70–78. doi: dx.doi.org/10.1016/j.outlook.2010.12.004

Commonwealth of Australia (2013). *Consumers, the health system and health literacy: Taking action to improve safety and quality. Consultation paper*. Retrieved from http://www.safetyandquality.gov.au/wp-content/uploads/2012/01/Consumers-the-health-system-and-health-literacy-Taking-action-to-improve-safety-and-quality3.pdf (accessed 26 March, 2015).

Cotugna, N. & Vickery, C. E. (2003). Health literacy education and training: A student–professional collaboration. *Journal of the American Dietetic Association, 103*(7), 878–880.

Davis, T. C., Williams, M. V., Marin, E., Parker, R. M. & Glass, J. (2002). Health literacy and cancer communication. *C.A.: A Cancer Journal for Clinicians, 52*(3), 134–149.

Devereux, J. (2004). Nursing: Low health literacy: A covert barrier to patient self-management. *HIV Clinician, 16*(1), 12–14.

Hay, K. E., Guzdal, M., Jackson, S., Boyle, R. A. & Soloway, E. (1994). Students as multimedia composers. *Computers & Education, 23*(4), 301–317.

Hoban, G. (2005). From claymation to slowmation. *Teaching Science, 51*(2), 26–30.

Hoban, G. (2009). Facilitating learner-generated animations with slowmation. In L. Lockyer, S. Bennett, S. Agostino & B. Harper (Eds.), *Handbook of research on learning design and learning objects: Issues, applications, and technologies* (pp. 313–330). Hershey, PA: IGI Global.

Howard, D. H., Gazmararian, J. & Parker, R. M. (2005). The impact of low health literacy on the medical costs of Medicare managed care enrollees. *The American Journal of Medicine, 118*(4), 371–377.

Kandula, N. R., Nsiah-Kumi, P. A., Makoul, G., Sager, J., Zei, C. P., Glass, S., . . . Baker, D. W. (2009). The relationship between health literacy and knowledge improvement after a multimedia type 2 diabetes education program. *Patient Education and Counseling, 75*(3), 321–327.

Kearsley, G. & Schneiderman, B. (1998). Engagement theory: A framework for technology-based teaching and learning. *Educational Technology, 38*(5), 20–23.

Lambert, J. (2013). *Digital storytelling: Capturing lives, creating community*. London: Routledge.

Macabasco-O'Connell, A. & Fry-Bowers, E. K. (2011). Knowledge and perceptions of health literacy among nursing professionals. *Journal of Health Communication, 16*(supp. 3), 295–307. doi: 10.1080/10810730.2011.604389

Makaryus, A. N. & Friedman, E. A. (2005). Patients' understanding of their treatment plans and diagnosis at discharge. Paper presented at the Mayo Clinic Proceedings.

Mayer, R. E. (2005). Cognitive theory of multimedia learning. In R. E. Mayer (Ed.), *Cambridge handbook of multimedia learning* (pp. 31–48). London: Cambridge University Press.

Mayer, R. E., Heiser, J. & Lonn, S. (2001). Cognitive constraints on multimedia learning: When presenting more material results in less understanding. *Journal of Educational Psychology, 93*(1), 187–198.

McKnight, A., Hoban, G. & Nielsen, W. (2011). Using slowmation for animated storytelling to represent non-Aboriginal preservice teachers' awareness of 'relatedness to country'. *Australasian Journal of Educational Technology, 27*(1), 41–54.

Meeks, M. & Ilyasova, A. (2003). A review of digital video production in postsecondary English classrooms at three universities. *Kairos: A Journal of Rhetoric, Technology, and Pedagogy, 8*(2). Retrieved from http://kairos.technorhetoric.net (accessed 26 March, 2015).

Nielsen-Bohlman, L., Panzer, A. M. & Kindig, D. A. (2004). *Health literacy: Prescription to end confusion*. Washington, DC: National Academies Press.

Ong, L. M. L., De Haes, J. C. J. M., Hoos, A. M. & Lammes, F. B. (1995). Doctor–patient communication: A review of the literature. *Social Science & Medicine, 40*(7), 903–918.

Pearce, K. L. (2013). *Marking rubrics: Health literacy and blended media*. Retrieved from http://www.digiexplanations.com/resources/blended_1.docx (accessed 26 March, 2015).

Pearce, K. L., Birbeck, D. & May, E. (2014). The use of animations and the 'teach-back' technique to facilitate an understanding of health literacy levels within the general community. *ERGO: The Journal of the Higher Education Research Group of Adelaide, 3*(2), 39–45.

Pearce, K. L. & Cross, G. (2013). A 4-week nutrition and therapeutics course in an undergraduate pharmacy program. *American Journal of Pharmaceutical Education, 77*(7), article 154. doi: 10.5688/ajpe777154

Schillinger, D., Bindman, A., Wang, F., Stewart, A. & Piette, J. (2004). Functional health literacy and the quality of physician–patient communication among diabetes patients. *Patient Education and Counseling, 52*(3), 315–323.

Seligman, H. K., Wang, F. F., Palacios, J. L., Wilson, C. C., Daher, C., Piette, J. D. & Schillinger, D. (2005). Physician notification of their diabetes patients' limited health literacy: A randomized controlled trial. *Journal of General Internal Medicine, 20*(11), 1001–1007.

Sweller, J. (1999). *Instructional design in a technical area*. Camberwell, Australia: ACER.

University of Wollongong (2009). *Slowmation*. Retrieved from http://slowmation.com/ (accessed 26 March, 2015).

Volandes, A. E., Paasche-Orlow, M. K., Mitchell, S. L., El-Jawahri, A., Davis, A. D. & Barry, M. J. (2013). Randomized controlled trial of a video decision support tool for cardiopulmonary resuscitation decision making in advanced cancer. *Journal of Clinical Oncology, 31*(3), 380–386.

Wieland, M. L., Nelson, J., Palmer, T., O'Hara, C., Weis, J. A. & Nigon, J. A. (2013). Evaluation of a tuberculosis education video among immigrants and refugees at an adult education center: A community-based participatory approach. *Journal of Health Communication, 18*(3), 343–353.

Williams, M., Davis, T., Parker, R. M. & Weiss, B. (2002). The role of health literacy in patient–physician communication. *Family Medicine, 34*(5), 383–389.

17

MUSICAL EXPLANATIONS

Using blended media for learning biochemistry

Jessica Vanderlelie

Context

As a discipline, biochemistry is considered by students to be a notoriously difficult strand of science (Vella, 1990; Wood, 1990). Accordingly, a didactic method is frequently used by academics for the teaching of biochemistry, in combination with a significant number of expert-generated complex resources (Meyer & Land, 2003). These antiquated pedagogies are often decontexualised from students' everyday life and perpetuate epistemological beliefs that the content is impersonal, objective and difficult to learn (Palmer 1986; Vella, 1990). As a result, it is common that students of biochemistry lack enthusiasm for the subject matter and struggle to acquire the skills necessary to apply knowledge obtained from one area of the discipline in order to gain insight into another (Meyer & Land, 2003). Common approaches to biochemistry education have been suggested to nurture shallow learning, especially the rote learning of biochemical pathways, and so it is of little surprise that students treat biochemical knowledge as non-overlapping sets of information (Palmer, 1986). As a result, students struggle to engage in deep learning and have difficulty finding enduring relevance and maintaining long-term learning outcomes (Wood, 1990).

There is a body of literature describing the benefits of alternate educational approaches that supplement the didactic lecture and improve retention of knowledge and engagement (e.g. Taylor & Parsons, 2011). In an attempt to increase engagement and facilitate a shared experience of learning in a second-year undergraduate metabolic biochemistry course, a student-generated, multimedia-based group assignment was developed and implemented. This task was first implemented in 2011 as part of a diversification of the assessment strategy, aimed at improving student engagement and performance. The task itself was designed to facilitate exploration of fundamental biochemical content, help students to make decisions about how to present their explanations utilising a variety of modalities and generate multiple representations for their own study and collaborative sharing.

Background literature

Motivating students to take an interest in science and develop deeper approaches to learning has long been identified as a challenge in science education. The abstract nature of science is, at times, challenging to students, and visualisations used in teaching play an important role in bridging the gap between theoretical constructs, helping students to form a mental picture and develop deeper understanding. Within the biochemistry discipline, it is increasingly recognised that resources utilising multiple representations (Ainsworth, 2008) that encourage visualisation of biochemical content are important for improving understanding and learning outcomes (Herraez & Costa, 2013; Schonborn & Anderson, 2006). The increased availability of expert-generated, animated and other visual representations provided through the Internet and other published forms means that today, more than ever before, tertiary students can seek alternative explanations of theoretical concepts to assist their learning (Lee, Paik & Joo, 2012). With this in mind, a number of authors have raised concerns about students' capacity to correctly interpret the visualisations presented to them and consequently encourage the active support of improved visual literacy through constructivist pedagogy (e.g. Hegarty, 2004; Reed, 2010). Such pedagogical considerations help to ensure students benefit from the array of visualisation tools available to them (Christopherson, 1996; Herraez & Costa, 2013; Reed, 2010; Schonborn & Anderson, 2006) and correctly interpret such tools to build understanding (Eilam, 2012, 2013).

For close to 30 years, the importance of a constructivist approach in science education has been emphasised (Trumper, 1997; Yore & Treagust, 2006). This approach encourages students to overcome misconceptions and build upon prior knowledge to construct new understanding (Trumper, 1997; Yore & Treagust, 2006). By taking a constructivist approach to developing visualisations in an assessment task, students may show increased gains in visual literacy from the catalytic learning effect of assessment (Herraez & Costa, 2013; Norcini et al., 2011). In addition to the power of assessment to drive student learning, the use of accessible technology to enable students to create their own multimedia representations of scientific information has been suggested as a powerful means of engaging students in the content and improving learning outcomes (Hand, Gunel & Ulu, 2009; Hoban, Loughran & Nielsen, 2011; Prain & Waldrip, 2006).

The increased familiarity that modern students have with digital technology in the form of access to free software on their computers and media-capturing devices in phones enables them to create visualisations that take on a multimodal nature (Prain & Waldrip, 2006). No longer are students confined to the development of static images and text to explain scientific concepts. Today, students have the capacity to generate their own multimodal representations incorporating modes such as voice, music, fast and slow-moving images, 2D and 3D models in order to facilitate their learning.

The theoretical framework previously applied to the process of constructing understanding and building such representations is semiotics (Hoban *et al.*, 2011;

Lemke, 1998; Peirce, 1931/1955). Semiotics explains how meaning is constructed as students interpret available information and subsequently design a representation of that information. This interplay by students between interpreting the information and designing the representation facilitates meaning-making and in the process of combining different modes of communication results in the production of a multimodal representation. The benefit of these external representations is that they may be shared, have the capacity to make abstract scientific concepts visible (Rapp & Kurby, 2008; Traver, Kalsher, Diwan & Warden, 2001) and help to foster deeper understanding (Hoban et al., 2011). In the case of student-generated media, these visual representations often take a format that engages particular demographics by utilising modes of communication that students relate to, for example, popular music and lyrics.

Despite the common use of singing and music to catalyse learning for young children in early childhood (Paquette & Rieg, 2008; Standley, 2008; Wiggins, 2007), little has been written in the literature about the benefit of students utilising music for learning in higher education (Tinari & Khandke, 2000; Whitmer, 2005). Moreover, literature regarding the use of music to educate scientists is almost non-existent. However, the notion of using song to brighten our theoretical perspectives is not new to the science discipline of biochemistry. In 1982, British biochemistry Professor Harold Baum (1989) published *The Biochemists' Song Book*, a collection of biochemical explanations written in the context of familiar tunes. This publication made Professor Baum famous as the world's leading biochemical song writer, however, the publication was produced more as a comedic collection of songs written for the yearly Biochemistry Departmental Christmas party at the University of London than for any educational value to supplement student learning. In spite of this, there is recent research into the power of singing and music for university students learning biochemistry (Vanderlelie, 2013).

Music has the power to evoke sensorial and emotional responses (Lacher & Mizerski, 1994) and to increase spatial reasoning and cognitive processing that, in turn, may increase engagement with scientific content, understanding and academic achievement (Morrongiello & Roes, 1990; Rauscher, 1995). When considering the importance of music in our lives and the prevalence of song in the early education of children and in the lives of our students (Paquette & Rieg, 2008; Standley, 2008; Wiggins, 2007), why is it that, for tertiary educators, the power of song appears to be forgotten as a pedagogical approach?

Implementation

The task

The assignment was designed as a semester-long, group-based (five students) project worth 10% of the final grade for the course. Students had flexibility to choose their topic from any of the fundamental content areas and to decide which modes of communication and media form would best suit their description. The only caveat placed on the project was that presentations were required to be less than five minutes long and take a multimedia format. The most common media forms chosen by the students were podcast (song), slowmation, digital story and video. The majority of groups decided to adapt a popular song to demonstrate their biochemical pathway in video format over any other type of modality (Table 17.1). For example, pathways such as glycolysis, the citric acid cycle and the electron transport chain were explained using adaptations of songs by One Direction, the Spice Girls and Queen, respectively (see the case study that follows for further detail).

Assessment is widely acknowledged as a key component of learning and teaching, with a strong capacity to drive learning (Miller, 1990) as well as catalyse learning (Norcini *et al.*, 2011). The task was considered an integral part of the course pedagogy and was introduced to students in the first week of the semester, where exemplars were presented to help build conceptual understanding of the task. The assessment strategy for the task drew upon a constructivist framework (Hodgson, 1996) and multimodal learning. Students were encouraged to construct their own understanding of a chosen topic and receive feedback about their understanding and from this foundation make decisions about how best to convey the information. The project was designed in two stages with a combination of examiner, peer and group assessment that consisted of:

- Part 1 (40%): Theoretical overview and project plan including storyboard;
- Part 2 (50%): Final presentation, a five-minute multimedia production, assessed on the basis of technical accuracy, entertainment value and usefulness as a learning tool;
- Peer assessment (10%): Class evaluation of individual group projects; and,
- Intragroup assessment: Grade moderation based upon participation within groups. Participation percentages of 25, 50, 75 or 100% available for each member with average percentages applied to final grade.

The first stage of the project was submitted midway through the semester and this facilitated exploration of the content through the preparation of a brief literature review of the topic. The teaching team assessed understanding and provided feedback to correct misunderstandings/misconceptions. At this stage of the project, an overview of the proposed presentation was also submitted that included a storyboard/script and details of the chosen modality. Final project submissions were made in the penultimate week of the semester and were reviewed by all members of the class and teaching team. This review component fostered a collaborative exploration of the content within the cohort, helping to make students aware of the presentations of their peers that they could then draw upon for future study. After final assessment of the media projects, the teaching team held a two-hour revision session that showcased high-quality presentations to the entire class and linked student presentations to the learning objectives and revision of the course.

When creating multimodal representations, students engage in a stepwise process. Through a series of group discussions, students identify their topics by considering prior understanding of the theory, lecture content, considering a pathway they are most interested in or perhaps feel they will have the most difficulty understanding. There is no limit to the number of groups that can choose a particular topic and, although there is a greater proportion of projects that cover topics presented early in the semester (prior to submission of Part 1 of the task), a number of groups (40%) show interest in topics that are presented much later in the semester.

After identifying a topic, groups spend time brainstorming and clarifying their ideas. Students collate multiple sources of information from their chosen topics, including lecture notes, textbook summaries, static images of pathways and expert-generated representations. After assessing and synthesising the information, students choose the most-effective media form through which to convey their message. Key themes arise when designing project representations including: familiarity with technology associated with particular media; preference for a modality by group members; types of media that are considered more engaging/fun to the group; types of media that would help to most clearly explain the concept; and the complexity of the content. Often groups choose different blended media approaches to create their representation.

To create their final presentations, students utilise a wide variety of commonly available technology, such as video cameras, iPhone applications, PowerPoint, slow-mation software and video production software (iMovie and Windows Movie Maker). Students are not encouraged to utilise one form of technology over another, instead, they are able to draw upon the technological experience of group members. With this in mind, technological quality is not a component of the assessment, rather, it is the quality of the explanation and suitability of the approach that is graded.

Case study: A musical representation of glycolysis

Of the 40 representations produced in 2013, greater than 60% of those identified as high quality by the cohort utilised voice (singing) as the primary mode of communication. The use of voice was often supported by other modes of communication such as gesture (dancing), writing, still images and moving images to produce a type of biochemical karaoke. A representation of glycolysis with lyrics adapted as a parody of the well-known pop song 'That's What Makes You Beautiful' by One Direction was considered the most-popular representation by the cohort. The lyrics have multiple benefits for student learning. Not only are they scientifically accurate, covering the individual reactions of glycolysis and points of regulation, the application of them in the context of a well-known pop song makes this a very catchy song that easily gets 'stuck in your head'.

'That's What Makes Glycolysis' by One G
(Alternate lyrics for One Direction's 'That's What Makes You Beautiful')

Reaction 1, using glucose, convert it to G-6-P with some ATP.
Hexokinase, is what we need, it is just one of the enzymes you'll see.
Regulation with the ATP, inhibition is what you will see.

[Chorus]

Baby you light up our world with your ATP.
The way that you get broke down gets us on our feet,
And when you finish the job you make pyruvate.
You should know . . . oh oh, that's what makes glycolysis!

Using the cofactor NAD,
Plus some enzymes that catalyse all we need.
Regulation of reactions 1, 10, 3.
You should know . . . oh oh, this is called glycolysis . . .
oh oh that's what make glycolysis!

Reaction 2, makes F-6-P, with help of Phosphoglucoisomerase.
Reaction 3, add ATP, Fructose-1, 6-Bisphos come with me.
Regulation with PFK-1, AMP gives it activation.

[Chorus]

Reaction 4 uses Aldolase, to produce DHAP and some G-3-P.
And when coupled with reaction 5 you end, the investment phase
We produce 2 G-3-P . . . ee ee, and we use 2 ATP.
Reaction 6, use NAD, used G-3-P, now we have 1,3-BPG.
Catalyse with the enzyme, G-3-P dehydrogenase now it's time.
Reduction of NAD let's see, NADH inside you and me.

[Chorus]

Reaction 7 gives ATP,
Substrate phosphorylation of ADP.
We use the enzyme Phosphoglycerate Kinase
3-Phosphoglycerate comes from 1,3-BPG.. oh oh
That's what makes glycolysis!

Reaction 8, is really great! 3-PG goes to 2-phosphoglycerate.
PG Mutase then Enoylase, takes 2-PG and converts it to PEP.
Gives us some water to maintain order, need to hydrate it's essential for us.

[Chorus]

Reaction 10 is the final step.
Using Phosphoenoylpyruvate we make.

2 Pyruvate and ATP, you know it's great.
Pyruvate Kinase.
You know it's irreversible . . . oh oh.
That's what makes glycolysis!

Na, na, na, na, na, na, na, na, na, na
Na, na, na, na, na, na, na, na, na..

[Chorus – slow]

Baby you light up our world with your ATP.
The way that you get broke down gets us on our feet.
And when you finish your job you make pyruvate.
You should know . . . oh oh, this is called glycolysis!

Using the cofactor NAD,
Plus some enzymes that catalyse all we need.
Regulation of reactions 1, 10, 3.
You should know . . . oh oh, this is called glycolysis . . .
oh oh, this is called glycolysis . . .
oh oh, that's what makes glycolysis!

In addition to catchy lyrics, the group chose to incorporate additional modes of text and static and fast-moving images to demonstrate the pathway, by drawing the pathway in the sand (Figure 17.1a) and incorporating subtitles (Figure 17.1b) to help the viewer understand the lyrics. Finally the group added a comedic dimension to their representation by dancing (Figure 17.1c, d) in a manner similar to the original One Direction band members during their video.

FIGURE 17.1   (a) Title slide with sand diagram of pathway (static image); (b) sand diagram (static images) and subtitles; (c) dancing; (d) parody of original film clip *(continued overleaf)*

FIGURE 17.1 *(continued)*

Evaluation and outcomes

To evaluate the effectiveness of the assessment task on student satisfaction and performance in the 2011–2013 cohorts, a number of evaluation measures were employed. Detailed methodology for the evaluation of this task has been previously described (Vanderlelie, 2013). Qualitative and quantitative data were gathered in relation to the creative assessment task and then overall for the subject. Evaluation assessed the usefulness of the assessment task in the students' learning process, the likelihood that students would utilise student-generated representations for their study and overall engagement in, and enjoyment of, the subject. Student performance data was collected for the creative assessment task and overall for the course, in addition to access data for each group presentation from the course Blackboard site, including the total number of views for each representation and number of views per student.

For all three years, performance was consistently high, with a mean grade of 8.9 ± 0.95 out of a possible 10, and a range of 2.94–10 achieved by the cohorts (Table 17.1). For all iterations the failure rate for the task was less than 2% and Cronbach's Alpha analysis generated reliability scores of >0.72 and an average of 0.85 for the entire course-assessment strategy over the three years (Table 17.1). Despite the relatively low reliability scores for the task itself, these data may prove to be a reflection of engagement with the task. Indeed qualitative comments from students support this hypothesis with students reporting:

> Finally an assessment item I actually enjoyed doing.

> It was fun and it reinforced the topic that we chose it also made it relevant to everyday life.

Quantitative evaluation of the project from 2011–2013 further supported the value of the task from an educational standpoint, with 88.2% of students responding positively to the statement "the creative group project helped me understand the theory of our project" and 83.1% finding the project useful as a tool for their learning.

> It was great to get to do something creative, and engage with the content in a deeper way.

> Helped me understand difficult concepts. I now at least know one topic for the final exam inside out.

> We chose the electron transport chain and oxidative phosphorylation. It really helped me to learn it; I find it pretty easy to understand now.

Further information regarding student engagement and benefit from the task may be ascertained through the consideration of the high levels of student access to the individual projects loaded onto the course site (Table 17.1). A total of 12,349 (2011), 16,790 (2012) and 27,570 (2013) student views were recorded for all projects submitted, with students on average spending 10 hours each watching the student-generated representations in the three weeks from submission to the end of the examination period. Quantitative evaluation revealed that 81% of students found the presentations of other groups useful for their study with comments such as:

> I think all of the group presentations are amazing! I'm finding them to be so useful in preparation for the end of semester exam. Love them!!

> Alternate revision method, fun and easy way to procrastinate and actually learn something when studying for the exams.

The projects identified by the teaching team as the highest quality and presented in the final revision lecture were viewed over 500 times each (Table 17.1). The fact that all presentations were available for download from the course site and a number were also loaded on YouTube may mean that these figures are an underestimate for the actual number of views.

When the multimodal nature of the projects is considered, students were very flexible in their choice of modality. Presentations with musicality varied in their multimodal approaches, with combinations of fast and slow-moving images, voice and text (subtitles) utilised to supplement their musical explanations. In addition to the popularity of utilising music in explanations within these cohorts, greater than 50% of all the musical explanations produced by students appeared in the top 10 rated productions when assessed by both the teaching team and students. On average, musical explanations rated 35% higher in terms of the number of student views than any other choice of modality, regardless of quality. Students qualitatively reported that they enjoyed musical representations and said:

TABLE 17.1 Record of student access to creative group projects from the 2011MSC Metabolism Blackboard site for years 2011–2013.

	2011	2012	2013
Total number of projects	31	35	38
Mean student grade	8.81 ± 1.10	8.85 ± 1.17	8.81 ± 0.97
Reliability (Cronbach's Alpha)	0.72	0.73	0.75
Total number of views	12,349	16,790	27,570
Number of views per student	79.6	95.9	149.0
Average number of projects viewed by each student	24.0 ± 6.36	26.5 ± 7.38	30.78 ± 5.75
Average number of views for top 10 projects	531.5 ± 63.86	566.8 ± 62.21	556.3 ± 40.62
Average hours spent watching videos per student	6.63	7.99	12.41
Number of presentations incorporating songs with biochemical lyrics	11	12	14

So much fun, I can't get the songs out of my head.

Prefer these lyrics over the real song.

The songs are really catchy and help heaps in remembering the pathways.

Although it was not possible to elucidate the exact effect of the creative task on student performance and engagement, both significantly improved as a result of the diversified assessment strategy for this course. A significant improvement in student performance (p <0.0001) in the course was noted for all years studied, when compared with results prior to the course redesign (Vanderlelie, 2013).

Discussion

As educators, scientists have utilised a variety of means to make our disciplines more engaging. Expert-generated animations, videos, computer simulations, 2D and 3D imagery have all been utilised with increasing frequency and are widely considered beneficial to the construction of knowledge (Lightfoot & Steffen, 1977; Lowe, 2003; McClean *et al.*, 2005; Wood, 1992). However, the use of such representations has raised concerns about students' capacity to correctly interpret them and, as a result, call for more-structured pedagogy designed to teach skills in visual literacy (Christopherson, 1996; Eilam, 2013). The power of assessment to drive student learning and provide opportunities for students to construct their own media as an explanatory resource has been suggested as a possible opportunity to develop such skills (Herraez & Costa, 2013).

The creative student-created multimedia task of musical explanations outlined in this chapter is a response to this suggestion, in that it requires students to generate their own multimedia representation of a biochemical pathway with the power to collaboratively engage the class, which is a strategy known to improve scientific visual literacy (Gobert & Clement, 1999). The task itself draws upon the inherent media literacy and technological proficiency of modern students and requires groups to synthesise the wide range of available theoretical information from multiple modalities and form a coherent representation that is detailed, technically accurate and entertaining.

In completing the assessment task, students gained a deeper understanding of their chosen biochemical pathway and significantly utilised their peers' visualisation products for study purposes. Exposure of students to multiple productions of similar content fostered a multiple representation approach to visualisation similar to Ainsworth (2008), which has been proposed as one of the 10 guidelines for teaching visual literacy (Piez & Voxman, 1997; Schonborn & Anderson, 2006). Further, the approach allowed students flexibility in choice of presentation that fit best with their learning-style modality preferences.

For students carrying out this creative task, the utilisation of music and adaptation of lyrics to explore biochemical content through popular music resulted in some of the most-popular and engaging projects produced by the cohorts. The combination of music and voice into a multimodal representation of science content is an important facet unique to this assessment task and one that was born out of the organic preference of students toward musical explanations, rather than any 'coaching' from the teaching team. Regardless of the quality of the recording, singing and other representations, the cohort viewed presentations that utilised music in the multimodal approach as fun and entertaining. The learning benefit of musical representation compared to other forms of representation was not examined in this study; however, this is a particularly interesting area of focus for future research.

A series of limitations and considerations need to be reflected upon when embarking on a project such as this. Qualitative feedback from students suggested that, for the input of time, this assessment task should have been ascribed a higher weighting for the overall subject. 10% is a relatively small percentage to attribute to a task that students so actively engaged with and clearly invested significant time to complete. Additionally, support for students around the logistics of group work in the crowded academic timetable has also been considered after feedback from students. Finally, as with most innovative assessment ideas, this task is labour intensive in terms of time for marking and provision of detailed feedback, particularly at the early stages of the project where checking of understanding is an important component.

On the whole, students found this assessment task to be a useful learning and study tool that added a fun dimension to the course. By developing multimedia-based representations of complex biochemical pathways, students were able to improve their understanding of their chosen topics and generate a repository of clips that could be utilised for study purposes. The importance of developing skills in the interpretation of multiple representations is not limited to students of biochemistry, as noted by Christopherson (1996) in a report that determined visual literacy was important to students across a range of science and non-science disciplines. As such, an assessment task that builds skills in visualisation while utilising a collaborative framework may be of benefit for any discipline that requires students to synthesise information in order to develop understanding. This assessment task takes one step in the right direction and lays the foundation for further work to quantify the changes in visual literacy that may be achieved through such an approach and, more specifically, the benefits of student-generated musical explanations in the learning of biochemistry.

References

Ainsworth, S. (2008). The educational value of multiple-representations when learning complex scientific concepts. In J. K. Gilbert, M. Reimer & M. Nakhleh (Eds.), *Visualisation: Theory and practice in science education* (pp. 191–208). Dordrecht, The Netherlands: Springer.

Baum, H. (1989). *The biochemists' song book*. Oxford: Pergamon.

Christopherson, J. T. (1996). The growing need for visual literacy at the university. In R. E. Griffin, J. M. Hunter, C. B. Schiffman & W. J. Gibbs (Eds.), *VisionQuest: Journeys toward visual literacy*. Retrieved from http://www.ivla.org/selected_readings/bor96.htm (accessed 26 March, 2015).

Eilam, B. (2012). *Teaching, learning and visual literacy: The dual role of visual representation in the teaching profession.* New York: Cambridge University Press.

Eilam, B. (2013). Possible constraints of visualisation in biology: Challenges in learning with multiple representations. In D. F Treagust & C.-Y. Tsui (Eds.), *Multiple representations in biological education. Models and Modeling in Science Education Vol. 7* (pp. 55–72). doi:10.1007/978-94-007-4192-8_1.

Gobert, J. D. & Clement, J. J. (1999). Effects of student-generated diagrams versus student-generated summaries on conceptual understanding of causal and dynamic knowledge in plate tectonics. *Journal of Research in Science Teaching, 36,* 39–53.

Hand, B., Gunel, M. & Ulu, C. (2009). Sequencing embedded multimodal representations in a writing to learn approach to the teaching of electricity. *Journal of Research in Science Teaching, 46*(3), 225–247.

Hegarty, M. (2004). Diagrams in the mind and in the world: Relations between internal and external visualisations. In A. Blackwell, K. Mariott & A. Shimojima (Eds.), *Diagrammatic representation and inferences: Lecture notes in artificial intelligence* (pp. 88–102) Berlin: Springer.

Herraez, A. & Costa, M. J. (2013). Biochemical visual literacy with constructive alignment: Outcomes, assessment and activities. *Biochemistry and Molecular Biology Education, 41*(2), 67–69.

Hoban, G., Loughran, J. & Nielsen, W. (2011). Slowmation: Preservice elementary teachers representing science knowledge through creating multimodal digital animations. *Journal of Research in Science Teaching, 48*(9), 985–1009.

Hodgson, D. (1996). Laboratory work as scientific method: Three decades of confusion and distortion. *Journal of Curriculum Studies, 28,* 115–135.

Lacher, K. T. & Mizerski, R. (1994). An exploratory study of the responses and relationships involved in the evaluation of, and in the intention to purchase new rock music. *Journal of Consumer Research, 21,* 366–380.

Lee, J. Y., Paik, W. & Joo, S. (2012). Information resource selection of undergraduate students in academic search tasks. *Information Research, 17*(1). Retrieved from http://informationr.net/ir/17-1/paper511.html (accessed 26 March, 2015).

Lemke, J. (1998). Multiplying meaning: Visual and verbal semiotics in scientific text. In J. R. Martin & R. Veel (Eds.), *Reading science: Critical and functional perspectives on discourses of science* (pp. 87–113). New York: Routledge.

Lightfoot, D. R. & Steffen, R. F. (1977). Simplified production of videotape programs for the biochemical laboratory. *Biochemical Education, 5*(3), 47–48. doi: 0.1016/0307-4412(77)90033-4.

Lowe, R. K. (2003). Animation and learning: Selective processing of information in dynamic graphics. *Learning and Instruction, 13,* 157–176.

McClean, P., Johnson, C., Rogers, R., Daniels, L., Reber, J., Slator, B. M., . . . White, A. (2005). Molecular and cellular biology animations: Development and impact on student learning. *Cell Biology Education, 4*(2), 169–179.

Meyer, J. & Land, R. (2003). Threshold concepts and troublesome knowledge: Linkages to ways of thinking and practicing within the disciplines. *Enhancing Teaching-Learning Environments in Undergraduate Courses.* Occasional Report. 4. Edinburgh, UK: School of Education, University of Edinburgh.

Miller, G. (1990). The assessment of clinical skills/competence/performance. *Academic Medicine, 65,* S63–S67.

Morrongiello, B. A. & Roes, C. L. (1990). Children's memory for new songs: Integration or independent storage of words and tunes? *Journal of Experimental Child Psychology, 50*(1), 25–38.

Norcini, J., Anderson, B., Bollela, V., Burch, V., Costa, M. J., Duvivier, R., . . . Roberts, T. (2011). Criteria for good assessment: Consensus statement and recommendations from the Ottawa 2010 conference. *Medical Teaching, 33*(3), 206–214.

Palmer, R. E. (1986). A strategy and approach for teaching the metabolic pathways. *Biochemical Education, 14*(1), 11–12.

Paquette, K. R. & Reig, S. A. (2008). Using music to support the literacy development of young English language learners. *Early Childhood Education Journal, 36*(3), 227–232.

Peirce, C. (1955). Logic as semiotic: The theory of signs. In B. Justus (Ed.), *Philosophical writings of Peirce (1893–1910)* (pp. 98–119). New York: Dover. (Original work published 1931.)

Piez, C. N. & Voxman, M. H. (1997). Multiple representations: Using different perspectives to form a clearer picture. *Mathematics Teaching, 90*, 164–166.

Prain, V. & Waldrip, B. (2006). An exploratory study of teachers' and students' use of multi-modal representations of concepts in primary science. *International Journal of Science Education, 28*(15), 1843–1866.

Rapp, D. N. & Kurby, C. A. (2008). The 'ins' and 'outs' of learning: Internal representations and external visualisations. In J. K. Gilbert, M. Reiner & M. Nakhleh (Eds.), *Visualisation: Theory and practice in science education* (pp. 29–52). Dordrecht, The Netherlands: Springer.

Rauscher, F. (1995). Does music make you smarter? *PTA Today, 20*(5), 8–9.

Reed, S. K. (2010). *Thinking visually.* New York: Psychology Press.

Schonborn, K. J. & Anderson, T. R. (2006). The importance of visual literacy in the education of biochemists. *Biochemistry and Molecular Biology Education, 34*(2), 94–102.

Standley, J. M. (2008). Does music instruction help children to learn to read? Evidence of a meta-analysis. *Applications of Research in Music Education, 27*(1), 17–32.

Taylor, L. & Parsons, J. (2011). Improving student engagement. *Current Issues in Education, 14*(1). Retrieved from http://cie.asu.edu/ojs/index.php/cieatasu/issue/view/12 (accessed 26 March, 2015).

Tinari, F. D. & Khandke, K. (2000). From rhythm and blues to Broadway: Using music to teach economics. *Journal of Economic Education, 31*(3), 253–270.

Traver, H. A., Kalsher, M. J., Diwan, J. J. & Warden, J. (2001). Student reactions and learning: Evaluation of a biochemistry course that uses web technology and student collaboration. *Biochemistry and Molecular Biology Education, 29*, 50–53.

Trumper, R. (1997). Applying conceptual conflict strategies in the learning of the energy concept. *Research in Science and Technology Education, 5*, 1–19.

Vanderlelie, J. (2013). Improving the student experience of learning and teaching in second year biochemistry: Assessment to foster a creative application of biochemical concepts. *International Journal of Innovation in Science and Mathematics Education, 21*(4), 46–57.

Vella, S. (1990). Difficulties in learning and teaching of biochemistry. *Biochemical Education, 18*(1), 6–8.

Whitmer, M. (2005). Using music to teach American history. *OAH Magazine of History, 19*(4), 4–5.

Wiggins, D. G (2007). Pre-K music and the emergent reader: Promoting literacy in a music-enhanced environment. *Early Childhood Education Journal, 35*(1), 55–64.

Wood, E. J. (1990). Biochemistry is a difficult subject for both student and teacher. *Biochemical Education, 18*(4), 170–172.

Wood, E. J. (1992). Videotapes in biochemistry teaching. *Biochemical Education, 20*(1), 19–20.

Yore, L. D. & Treagust, D. F. (2006). Current realities and future possibilities: Language and science literacy-empowering research and informing instruction. *International Journal of Science Education, 28*, 291–314.

PART III

Predictions for student-generated digital media

18

FUTURE TRENDS FOR STUDENT-GENERATED DIGITAL MEDIA IN SCIENCE EDUCATION

Alyce Shepherd

The 2014 *Horizon Report* is an international predictor of key trends that examines "emerging technologies for their potential impact on and use in teaching, learning, and creative inquiry within the environment of higher education" (Johnson, Adams Becker, Estrada & Freeman, 2014, p. 3). The 2014 report identified six key trends that will have a major impact on the higher education sector over the next 3–5 years. These are: (i) the growing ubiquity of social media; (ii) the integration of online, hybrid and collaborative learning; (iii) the rise of data-driven learning and assessment; (iv) a shift from students as consumers to students as creators; (v) an agile approach to change; and (vi) the evolution of online learning. Of these six trends, the two most likely are students as content creators rather than being consumers and the use of social media. Creating content can take many forms such as creating products or artefacts when talking about 'makerspaces' but media is certainly one form. This trend suggests that promoting student-generated media in university assignments in all courses may increase exponentially as academics become aware that students are calling out for new ways to engage with content.

This book will therefore help bring the *Horizon Report* trends to fruition. Whilst some of the media-making ideas in this book have been in development by chapter authors over the last 10 years, this is the first time to our knowledge that the key ideas for students' media making are pulled together in one place for science education. In short, there are many creative ideas in the previous chapters to complement the key themes of the *Horizon Report*, especially students as content creators. Accordingly, the ideas in the preceding chapters will support science academics and science teacher educators in designing assignments that encourage students to generate media to engage with, learn about, explain and communicate science content and experiences. The key ideas in the chapters are summarised in Table 18.1.

TABLE 18.1 Summary of key examples in book

Ch.	Science Discipline or Science Teacher Education	Course Context	Media Making Idea
4	Science Discipline	Chemistry	Podcast as analogy
5	Science Discipline	Science Communication	Digital story of personal experiences
6	Science Discipline	Science Principles	Digital story of science concept
7	Science Discipline	Food Science	Video of interviews with career mentors
8	Science Discipline	Chemistry	Video blogs explaining properties of molecules
9	Science Discipline	Biology	Video explaining environmental issues
10	Science Discipline	Electronics	Videos of students explaining circuits
11	Science Teacher Education	Science and Technology	Video for two purposes, explaining and capturing processes
12	Science Teacher Education	Secondary Science Methods	Slowmation to develop pedagogical knowledge
13	Science Teacher Education	Secondary and primary science	Slowmation to explain concepts with insights into learning approaches
14	Science Teacher Education	Secondary Science methods	Slowmation to explain science and reveal misconceptions
15	Science Teacher Education	Technology course	Blended media about science concepts
16	Science Discipline	Communication in Pharmacology	Blended media to communicate pharmacology to general community
17	Science Discipline	Biochemistry	Musical explanations to popular songs

We will now offer predictions for what we think are seven trends in relation to students' media making over the next 5 years.

Trend 1: Students as creative generators of content

As emphasised in the 2014 *Horizon Report*, there is an ever-present "shift from students as consumers to students as creators" (Johnson, Adams Becker, Estrada et al., 2014, p. 14) that will drive change in higher education within 3–5 years. Whilst we agree with the aim, we disagree with the timing – it is already happening. This shifting of responsibility to students for creative representation of content can occur at a broad program level, but it can occur most simply at a course level with visionary course coordinators designing assignments that encourage students to engage with content by creating various forms of media. As such, media making in assignments is one way to address the three principles of student engagement discussed in Chapter 1 – encouraging students to use cognitive, metacognitive and volitional strategies.

Complementing the trend of students as generators of content is student creativity. Ironically, as academics put fewer constraints on representational forms in assignments, students become more creative. Many of the chapter authors have stated that the less-constrained guidelines they give students in assignments, the more creative they become. Again, the 2014 *Horizon Report* encourages students to devise new ways to represent content because "creativity, as illustrated by the growth of user-generated videos, maker communities, and crowd funded projects ... is increasingly the means for active, hands-on learning" (Johnson, Adams Becker, Estrada *et al.*, 2014, p. 14). A consequence of students representing content in different ways is that many like to be creative with content, especially with their increasing digital skills. Whilst computers can be used by students to write essays and prepare PowerPoint slides, they can also be used to create more innovative assignments that incorporate the use of podcasts, videos, animations and blends or combinations of media. If students are enrolled in a 3-year degree and do eight subjects a year with three assignments each, they complete 72 assignments in their program, most of which involve writing to summarise reports, producing essays, e-lab reports or PowerPoint slides for presentations. It is important not to deny the value of these traditional forms of assignments, but our argument is that there could be more diversity in assignments in terms of representational forms and use of technology. See the website www.digiexplanations.com for more information about diverse media forms and instructions for students that can be used in any discipline. The website identifies and describes five media forms that students can create (podcast, digital story, slowmation, video and blended media) to explain content using free movie-making software – iMovie on a Mac or Windows Movie Maker on a PC. Traditionally, university assignments have been commonly presented using the communication mode of writing but are now being presented using additional modes such as still images, moving images, music, gesture and voice in a combination of digital multimodal forms. The chapters in this book provide many examples of ways in which this can occur, such as putting science ideas to popular songs (Chapter 18), engaging students in communicating social issues with animation (Chapter 16), using personal experiences to make digital stories (Chapter 5) and using analogies when making podcasts (Chapter 4).

Trend 2: Assessment and collaboration

The 'elephant in the room' associated with students as content creators with digital media is the validity of students' representations. In other words, our role as university educators is not just to foster students to generate content, but to foster *appropriate* and *accurate* student-generated content. This can take many forms. In most cases this has to do with accuracy of content representation in the sciences but it also has other forms, such as appropriate representation of experiences, points of view and communication to an appropriate audience. In designing any form of digital media, as is the case with written assignments, students need to take into account the purpose, audience and context of their communication. Similarly, academics need to consider this when writing and framing an assignment so as to avoid the 'anything goes' process. This raises the age-old chestnut of assessment and the role of the academic in marking assignments. This role has not changed, but because students can distribute their work more widely via the affordances of the

Internet, there are many more people who can contribute to and comment on student work.

An important consideration, therefore, for academics is how to assess the various media forms that students create. With the possibilities for widespread sharing of media through the Internet, more possibilities are created for peer review of students' media making and even peer creation with students in different courses and countries. With the increasing ease of uploading to media-sharing websites such as YouTube, Vimeo and Facebook, what counts as a correct representation of science knowledge can be considered from multiple perspectives. It is important, however, to keep in mind that any representation of content is an approximation and so can always be improved. What is important for science learning is how students represent the content accurately and the discussion that the media generates in both construction and feedback. Students will no doubt play a stronger role in helping to contribute to assessment criteria and making judgements about the appropriateness of various science media for particular purposes, contexts and audiences.

Trend 3: Mobility

Again, highlighted by the 2014 *Horizon Report*, "we are in the midst of a complete shift of the devices we use" (Johnson, Adams Becker, Estrada *et al.*, 2014, p. 7). Mobile devices (including smartphones and tablets) have completely transformed the way we utilise technology and we predict that they will continue to act as central vehicles for capturing rich digital content and driving student-generated media making. Today's mobile devices are more intuitive and capable than previous computing tools and, unlike desktop computers, they are not place-bound. This has many benefits when it comes to gathering digital content for students' media making. For example, many mobile devices capture multiple media forms, including image, video and audio. This means that we no longer have to rely on three separate devices to capture sound, photographs and video footage because of the convergence of technologies into hand-held devices, and we no longer have to be tied by a power cord. Further, mobile devices enable individuals to upload and blend different media forms from the one device. Today we see a growth in mobile applications, social networks and programs that support individuals creating and blending media from their personal digital devices. It is our prediction that these programs will extend to support the creation of digital content for educational purposes and, as mobile devices become more advanced, so too will the ease of media creation, manipulation and sharing.

Mobile devices are becoming increasingly more compact and lightweight, encouraging individuals to carry their devices with them everywhere. This means that we are able to digitally capture specific experiences and environments that previously would have gone unrecorded, or in some instances may have only been captured by professional photographers using specialist equipment. For example, today it is common practice for news programs on television and online news websites to showcase footage of specific events captured from the mobile devices of everyday individuals, rather than solely relying on footage from journalists. This implication is particularly interesting, as it is changing the role and face of those perceived as responsible for generating and sharing news. There appears to be a shift toward entrusting the public with input in terms of generating digital content to be broadcast by media channels that would previously only accept content gathered in partnership with professional news reporters, photographers and video production staff. Perhaps such a trend is a cost-saving measure, as it enables the cutting of camera crews and staff. The implication that such a trend has for students as digital media makers is that the environments and experiences that can now be captured as a result of having a mobile device with media capabilities on hand are limitless. Further, by capturing and sharing digital media content using a mobile device, individuals are able to gain recognition for their media and share digital content with a larger audience, as the platforms for showcasing digital media are ever expanding and more widely accessible to the public.

The advent of mobile devices has had a significant impact on the ways in which we create, interact with and share content. Moreover, the shift toward using mobile technologies has transformed where learning takes place and has redefined what is meant by the term 'learning space' (Keppell, Souter & Riddle, 2012). It is now possible to listen to lecture recordings while walking the dog and to participate in work conferences over Skype from a coffee shop overseas. We can collaborate with peers from different locations to write a paper in the cloud from a smartphone, and we can email and post to forums whilst simultaneously streaming online music from our iPods. Further, mobile devices enable individuals to capture rich data from outside a classroom context (e.g. images/interviews from field trips) and, because many of these devices have Internet connectivity, it is becoming easier and faster for individuals to share their digital media with others online. Disappearing are the days of having to connect clunky cameras, video cameras and voice recorders to desktop computers via a USB connection so as to upload content from a device to a computer, and then a computer to the Internet. In line with the 2014 *Horizon Report*'s mention of the 'Bring Your Own Device' trend, it is our prediction that the number of students who use their own mobile devices to create and upload media will continue to expand.

We are more connected than we have ever been, with Internet access continually expanding. Never before have we been able to access such a wealth of information so quickly and from the convenience of our fingertips, wherever we are in the world. Perhaps an expectation is that students use the most up to date scientific findings in their assignments with new knowledge being so accessible. Individuals are increasingly accessing the Internet from their smart devices (e.g. smartphones, mp3 players, tablets) – in many ways, this can be attributed to their portability and, increasingly, their economic accessibility. Many mobile devices are even more accessible than computers as they are less expensive than laptops and desktop computers. Moreover, the user is not tied down to a desk within an office when using a mobile device, and with a mobile device often comes access to a myriad of apps (many of which are free and have educational value). We anticipate the affordability of such devices will improve their popularity and use, thus enhancing the possibilities for media making anywhere and anytime using mobile devices.

Trend 4: Transforming online learning environments

Online learning has evolved significantly over the last decade and is increasingly viewed as a valid alternative to the physical face-to-face learning environment. In some instances the online learning environment is considered to be more favourable than the physical learning environment, as a result of the many unique benefits it affords, such as increased flexibility and accessibility, and opportunities for enhanced engagement and collaboration while "equipping students with stronger digital skills" (Johnson, Adams Becker, Estrada *et al.*, 2014, p. 10). In light of these affordances, an increasing number of educational institutions are adopting more online, blended and hybrid learning models for science learning. It is anticipated that even though currently face-to-face interaction is still the primary means of science learning in Australia, the delivery of content online will inevitably continue to rapidly increase as educational institutions continue to make Internet access available for students to interact using online tools and resources. As universities begin to go paperless, we anticipate that an increasing amount of information will be communicated to students using various types of digital media. Perhaps this change in teaching may cause changes to occur to student assessment. To make links to the real worlds of students and to support the online learning environment and shift toward student input in assessments, we predict that more assessments will call for student-generated media to feature as a means of output.

The advent of audio and video tools (e.g. Audacity, Movie Maker, iMovie, Skype, Adobe Connect) have considerably enhanced online communication and bridged gaps so that it is now possible for teachers and students to communicate one-on-one as was previously only made possible in a physical learning environment. This has had far-reaching implications for the online teaching and learning environment, as it is now possible to have real-time meetings with individuals from all over the world and to communicate using voice, image, eye contact and body language. Further, teachers are still able to provide a presence in an online learning environment and foster collaboration in ways that are not possible in the physical learning environment. Online learning allows for engagement with a far broader range of asynchronous communication (e.g. forums, chatrooms, blogs and emails) and synchronous communication (e.g. live classes, Skype and live chatrooms). As has been demonstrated in this book, it is possible for the use of these audio and video tools to similarly support students in generating and blending digital media for learning. It is possible for students to share their media online with peers and to include students in the generation of digital support resources for online science courses, rather than relying on the teacher to create and provide these. When students create science resources to teach others, students are more engaged and likely to understand concepts on a deeper level when they have been actively involved in creating a digital product to represent and explain specific content to peers.

The ever-changing landscape of online learning has many implications for teaching and learning in the twenty-first century. One consideration should be the significance of a science teacher's presence in enabling learning online. Research has shown that the greater the presence of an online instructor, the greater the engagement and performance of students (Johnson, Adams Becker, Estrada *et al.*, 2014). There are many ways that an online science instructor can engage students in meaningful learning, especially with regard to media making. The 2014 *Horizon Report* points to the need for teachers to purposefully integrate "sophisticated multimedia and technologies" (Johnson, Adams Becker, Estrada *et al.*, 2014, p. 18) into their teaching, encompass interactivity and to effectively utilise digital media to communicate and engage students in learning. Many online courses feature the presentation of text complemented by online discussion spaces, but students can make media at home using their own devices to contribute to the discussion of the science course content. The use of voice and video tools can support both the quantity and quality of interaction that can take place online. There is also an expectation placed upon teachers to "create top-quality resources" (Johnson, Adams Becker, Estrada *et al.*, 2014, p. 19) for online learning, drawing on digital tools and training afforded by educational institutions.

Trend 5: Digital citizenship

Once upon a time, literacy referred to a person's ability to read books and write with pencils and pens, but today, e-books have replaced many books and the stylus and keyboard challenge the traditional pen and pencil as tools for creating and shaping text. Moreover, uses of video and audio tools have made it possible to receive and communicate science meaning using image (still, slow moving and fast moving), voice, music and gesture. Our contemporary means of engaging with and creating content have evolved to incorporate consideration of an array of digital and touch screens that demand our attention and connection to the digital and online world. As a result of this transformation, navigating our way through the constantly evolving digital landscape as learners and communicators of science requires very different approaches and literacies than those to which we have been traditionally accustomed.

As students continue to create and upload digital content online, there is a need for them to engage with a toolkit of digital literacies. In doing so, today's students, as digital content creators, are faced with the challenge of upholding digital citizenship – the norms of responsible and appropriate technology use (O'Brien, 2010). To be digital citizens, students need to develop social networking and online communication skills, multimodal and transliteracy skills, and an understanding of the digital law with regards to copyright, privacy, identity and the notion of a digital footprint (Lea & Jones, 2011). Also integral to digital citizenship is the maintenance of digital health and wellbeing in relation to digital media/technology use. It is our prediction that more of a focus on these skills will emerge among educational institutions in the coming years, as there continues to be an increase in both the amount of digital content used to support teaching and learning and strict policies and laws governing acceptable technology, digital content and Internet use.

We are fortunate to have access to more digital information than ever before and, with the advent of catch-up TV, browsing filters and customised device settings, it is now possible to view the media we want to view whenever we want to view it. We now have more control of what we watch, when we watch it, how we watch it and the ways that we spend our time engaging with digital content. The wealth of available video content and images online has significant educational implications for students as media makers. There is a wealth of digital content available online that can be used as stimuli to learn from but, more important to learning, much of this content can be downloaded, clipped, remixed and reused in student-generated media products created for educational purposes. While the educational value of blending pre-existing media is significant, it is important to note that as students create media drawing on pre-existing content (e.g. YouTube clips) and images sourced online, there is a need for them to be aware about copyright laws (especially when sharing pre-existing digital media online). Students are able to access content that is free to use, share and modify if it is licenced and they need to be made aware of how to do this by using sites such as Creative Commons that filter content for fair use (visit http://creativecommons.org.au/). Creative Commons Licencing will become more common but attribution is essential. Whilst providing appropriate referencing is standard for a written assignment, so too will digital referencing or attribution become essential parts of students' assignments as they incorporate more digital content.

Multimodal literacy is also an important facet of digital citizenship in that students need to be aware of how specific modes such as images can produce affordances for communicating specific content and achieving specific purposes. While students need to learn skills to use specific technologies, equipping them with multimodal understandings of why to use specific media forms (affordances) to communicate ideas in the long-term is a much-more valuable digital literacy skill and is integral to purposeful media making. Multimodal awareness is particularly important as we predict that programs, apps and devices will continue to evolve and change, as will technology, careers and the skills needed to enter the workforce. Nevertheless, the pedagogy and value of utilising different digital modes of communication is a transferrable skill that will lend itself to supporting learning in light of profound innovation and technological advancements.

Trend 6: Sharing and collaboration – Social media

Social media has completely revolutionised the means by which we interact, present and share science information. For students as creators of digital media, social media opens doors to gaining recognition of creativity and facilitates interaction at a global level with content and creators of content. Social media has become such a popular form of entertainment that, in many instances, websites such as Facebook and YouTube have been more widely accessed by the public than television and other popular mediums. Moreover, social media sites have more hits online than any other website, and while it is primarily used as a means of recreation, more and more individuals are turning to social media for educational purposes. Social media provides a unique platform for establishing relationships and building networks, and many educational institutions are exploring the value of using platforms like Facebook, YouTube and Twitter as portfolio and forum tools for the distribution of ideas and environments for sharing digital media and providing feedback regarding digital content.

As social networks expand to encompass online relationships with individuals across the world, the opportunity for sharing student-created digital media is profound. Digital media uploaded to social networking sites has the potential to reach such large audiences that it can be considered 'viral' and can lead to every day individuals gaining recognition, money, employment and fame for their media-making skills. Nevertheless, as social media platforms are continually being used as spaces for distributing and disseminating news, consideration needs to be given to the validity and credibility of information circulated especially in the sciences. Our use of digital media content on social media websites also brings to light the importance of content creators being aware of copyright and privacy laws concerning their use of digital media in public online spaces.

There is, therefore, more room for educational institutions to explore the value of utilising social networking as a means of encouraging students to create and share digital content for educational purposes. Further investigation is required into the value of how student-generated content shared on social media websites can be used to support students as creators of content, provide feedback and establish important networks that facilitate collaboration.

Trend 7: Where to with Web 3.0?

In summary, students' capacity to make and share media for science learning is increasing exponentially because of a confluence among students' disposition for media making driven by their own social media experiences, advances and accessibility to personal digital technologies and the affordances of the Internet to support sharing and uploading. It is hard to believe that the World Wide Web was only invented 25 years ago in 1990 when Tim Berners-Lee (a British computer scientist) and Robert Cailliau (a Belgium computer scientist) built and tested the first example of the web when linking computers with a common language, HTML. Since then there have been three generations of web designs with advancing capabilities. Web 1.0 was about read-only content using open standard languages such as HTML for viewers to access content. Web 2.0 was the second generation of web design with more user interaction involving user-generated content, leading to social networking sites, wikis and online collaboration. The third generation, Web 3.0 is still evolving, but it inevitably will be more intuitive based on the personal analytics of data that we input and so will become more responsive to our needs, or our supposed needs. Accordingly, Web 3.0 has been called the 'semantic web' or 'intelligent web' because it will be adaptable and intuitive more like a personal assistant. Hence, the world will become more connected and interactive with uploading and downloading of digital content that is increasingly fast and complex. However, there is a clear role for science educators amongst this plethora of digital content, especially in assessing the validity and accuracy of content.

We do not know what students' capacities for media making will be in 10 years' time, except that it will be greatly increased and diverse. Perhaps what is on at the cinema these days in terms of CGI (computer-generated imagery) and 3D will become possible on a hand-held mobile phone. One thing is for sure though; students will expect more engaging learning experiences than copying down notes in a lecture from PowerPoint slides. Importantly, the role of a science educator will not become redundant. Science educators at university and in schools have an essential role in helping students to navigate the endless sea of science information. Critically, the challenge for science educators is to guide and shape students' learning opportunities, especially using technology, so that they become engaged with content in creative ways to extend their educational opportunities. Science educators will always be content creators, but so will the students. The trick is to get the balance right so that expert-generated content and student-generated content inform each other.

Science educators also have a fundamental role in guiding students in becoming digital citizens of the twenty-first century. The pedagogical trick is to get the right balance as many of the ideas will come from the students themselves. Our role is to facilitate the creative space, capacity and educational directions necessary to scaffold and engage students in learning, explaining and communicating content.

References

Johnson, L., Adams Becker, S., Cummins, M. & Estrada, V. (2014). *2014 NMC technology outlook for Australian tertiary education: A Horizon Project regional report.* Austin, TX: Media Consortium/Open Universities Australia.

Johnson, L., Adams Becker, S., Estrada, V. & Freeman, A. (2014). *NMC Horizon Report: 2014 higher education edition.* Austin, TX: Media Consortium.

Keppell, M., Souter, K. & Riddle, M. (Eds.) (2012). *Physical and virtual learning spaces in higher education: Concepts for the modern learning environment.* Hershey, NY: IGI Global.

Lea, M. R. & Jones, S. (2011). Digital literacies in higher education: Exploring textual and technological practice. *Studies in Higher Education, 36*(4), 377–393.

O'Brien, T. (2010). Creating better digital citizens. *Australian Educational Leader, 32*(2). Retrieved from http://www.digitalcitizenship.net/Publications.html (accessed 26 March, 2015).

INDEX

CPSIA information can be obtained
at www.ICGtesting.com
Printed in the USA
FFOW01n1252301116
29930FF